Ralph Gregory

Sign Painting Techniques

Beginner to Professional

Illustrations by the author

ST Publications
Cincinnati, Ohio

Published by ST Publications
407 Gilbert Avenue
Cincinnati, Ohio 45202.

Dedicated to my wife, Hildegarde.

ISBN: 0-911380-29-9

Library of Congress Catalog Card
Number: 73-160520

Printed in the United States of America.

Preface

This book has been planned to teach you the basic fundamentals of signpainting. Every effort will be made to do this in a step by step manner. However, as you progress it occasionally will be necessary to page back and refer to preceding information.

My most earnest wish would be to tell you that the sign trade is a simple one to learn. Quite the opposite is true. As a source of encouragement, consider the following success factor. If the development of the skill and knowledge necessary to any intricate trade or profession could be acquired too easily, the compensation would accordingly be very small.

To write a book such as this is a difficult task. The author has no way of knowing whether you intend to open your own shop or plan to work as an employee. Therefore, to allow for the most complete coverage of the sign trade it will be assumed that you do intend to operate your own sign business. Those who plan otherwise can choose from this book the information that they so desire.

Also, in deference to the ever increasing number of ladies entering the field of signpainting, apologies are extended in advance. All reference to follow will be in masculine gender. This is in the interest of brevity and only to cut down a bit on the "he's and she's" that would otherwise be necessary. It is my thought that hundreds of other signmen join me in saying that we recognize and welcome your presence within the trade.

Left-handed signpainters will find certain procedures to be of little use, but these people usually have the innate ability to adapt. My oldest son is left-handed, yet is a most excellent signman and pictorial painter. He has developed his own techniques and is also a highly skilled commercial and technical artist.

With each passing year the sign trade is becoming more complex. Because of this there is a trend toward specialization. It would be ridiculous to expect any one signman to be an expert in every phase of the sign industry as it exists today.

However, for many years to come there will be a definite need for the smaller sign shops and men with a general all-around knowledge of the sign trade. Even if this were not the case and you should choose to specialize, it would be advisable to acquire as much general knowledge of the sign trade as possible.

For example, and only for emphasis of point, consider the medical profession. What would we do without the general practitioner? According to my limited knowledge, all specialists must first study the field of general medicine until such time as they receive the degree of M.D. Those who decide to specialize then continue studies into the specialty of their choice. Others begin general practice immediately, upon qualification, although their knowledge in some phases of medicine is sketchy. For example, should a complicated throat problem confront the family physician, he refers this patient to a throat specialist. So, what would we do without the specialist?

Similar situations often occur in the sign trade, so remember this example. Within the text of this book we shall discuss this type of cooperation as it applies especially to the small plant operator in the sign trade.

Years ago most signpainters learned this trade as apprentices. This is presently referred to as "on-the-job training" and is an excellent manner of learning.

Even this fine method carries with it a little "side-effect" frequently picked up by the novice. Usually in the apprenticeship method the beginner, for the most part, is taken under the wing of one man, usually an excellent tradesman. Without realizing it, the novice builds up a sort of hero-worship for this man's work. He develops the same basic technique, uses the same type of brushes, etc. and all too often thinks that this is the absolute—the one and only approach to correct signpainting. Seldom is this the fault of the teacher.

Later, this beginner becomes a signpainter and is employed elsewhere. At this point he finds other veteran signpainters using somewhat different tools and techniques. He is quite surprised to find other men doing the work faster and achieving better results than did his teacher.

It is then that the wise young workman should concede that signpainting is a flexible trade and open his mind to any change that may be of benefit. In so doing he must never cease to be grateful to his original teacher who perhaps did excel in other respects.

So it is when writing a book. My first sign was laboriously painted 42 years ago when I was 15 years of age. I am still learning. Frequently in my magazine articles, I mentioned that I have on occasion learned things from young fellows with but a few years experience. Any procedure or technique to be suggested within this book represents ONE method of doing a job with good result. This does not imply that is the only way or that better procedures do not exist.

Perhaps ten signpainters could each paint a sign with the same specifications with fairly equal skill and result. It is doubtful if any two of them would use identical techniques. The differences would be in the grasp of the brush, the style of brush, the manner of layout, the thickness of the paint, the brand of paint, plus other variances.

Few trades depend so much upon the workman alone. The signman has few mechanical helps. It is a personal thing between the signman, the brush and the surface. So signpainting remains unique. The printer has his press; the plumber has wrench and pipe; the electrician has wire, switch, and fusebox; the auto-mechanic has the engine, etc. These trades each demand a high degree of knowledge and skill. But the signman has no precise factory-made parts to fit together. He must create.

Even to the general public the signpainter seems to remain an enigma. People can identify with other trades and professions, but sign work for some strange reason appears to fascinate many.

How frequently is the professional signpainter approached with the following multiple question or fascimile? "I gotta' sorta' knack for painting—seems I was pretty good at it in high school. How do I go about learning the trade? Where do I learn? How do I support my wife and kids while I'm learning? How'd you learn it? How long's it take? I gotta' kid in high school who's real good at making posters; could you give him a job and sorta' teach him the trade?"

Because of the endless chain of letters to this effect, and the questions that I have put to me personally, week after week, and because at times my ears ring with this type of question—well, perhaps this is the reason for this book.

A final word to the absolute beginner. Signpainting with its related trades, is an excellent vocation. Good signmen are in demand, seldom out of work, and receive good pay. But, to become a really good signpainter requires hours and hours of practice, plus the utmost patience and perseverance. There is no easy way to master the trade—no big shortcut, and no substitute for conscientious effort. To some the skill develops quickly. To others progress is slow. There is sacrifice of time without pay. If you lack any of the above essentials, then my advice to you is to place this book aside and choose a less demanding profession.

If you do have a dedicated desire to be a professional signpainter, this book will help speed your progress and remove many of the obstacles encountered along the way.

Author's Note

During the process of writing this book it frequently will be necessary to refer to the tools of the trade. Among these will be items such as mahlsticks, pounce wheels, palettes, and brushes, including quills, fitches, cutters, flats, etc. References to equipment will include chalk lines, chamois skins, projectors, ladder jacks, to name but a few.

Paints and related items will be mentioned in terms such as, bulletin colors, japan colors, poster colors, tempera colors, gold sizings and fixatives, among others.

Therefore, to eliminate unnecessary reading and writing it seems advisable to clarify this point immediately. In this way, there will be no need to provide a repetitive explanation each time we encounter a specific tool or product within the following pages. However, a full explanation will be provided in regard to unique or uncommon tools or equipment whenever this need is apparent.

Nearly every item mentioned in this book can be purchased from any of the sign supply firms located throughout this country. The names and addresses of these supply houses can be found in abundance within "SIGNS of the Times" magazine. Send for these catalogs and consult the index for the item required. Usually, the product is plainly pictured with a full description pertinent to its proper use and the expected result.

The study of these supply catalogs, with pictures and descriptions can, in itself, be of great value to all beginners. This serves as an aid to quicker recognition of all tools used within the sign trade. This type of auxiliary study can speed up the process of learning to use the correct tools and materials for the job at hand. Much trial and error can be avoided by gaining a thorough knowledge of the many products that are available to you. In this way there is a better chance that the tools and materials will be used for the correct purpose.

Incidentally, SIGNS of the Times magazine should be the most important "tool" in any sign plant, for both beginner and veteran. This is a personal observation and is written without any "nudging" from the publisher. This magazine serves a vital function in keeping the signman abreast of all progress within the world of signs. The answer to many problems can be found within its pages.

If I were allowed to make but one statement within the pages of this entire book, especially to the beginner, it would be: Subscribe to, and study, SIGNS of the Times magazine. It will be the best "tool" ever to be purchased within your entire sign career.

Contents

Chapter 1

To Develop Salable Skill Quickly

After searching my mind for days in an effort to decide upon the ideal manner in which to present this book, I arrived at the following conclusion.

For best results our association should be very close and as informal as possible throughout these pages. Therefore, I would like to have you consider me to be your friend and teacher. In turn, I shall think of you as friend and student.

When any person first begins to learn a trade or profession he must bring with him some degree of dedication or he will never rise above a second rate level. As knowledge increases, the dedicated student will soon feel the sense of satisfaction that results from being able to accomplish those things so long desired.

A high degree of skill is developed only after a long period of time. It is then that all the months of training culminate in the fulfillment of the initial desire.

This sense of gratification and self-satisfaction is indeed partial payment for the long months of time and effort required to master any highly skilled trade or profession.

The foregoing might seem to be a bit poetic, but this state of mind is essential, if one ever hopes to be considered tops in any field of endeavor.

This sense of gratification, although most pleasant, must unfortunately give way to the urgency of earning a living.

So quite abruptly, we must face the material fact that we primarily enter a vocation with the ultimate goal of earning the highest income possible within the scope of our skill. This is cold hard fact.

Therefore, this book has been planned with this fact foremost in mind. It is frustrating for the beginner to practice day after day, making the various basic strokes. Also, it becomes tiresome to attempt to learn a dozen alphabets, numerous techniques and procedures, plus the proper use of countless tools and materials. Customarily, this is, in most cases, the manner in which a trade is taught.

Because this process can be so discouraging, it is my plan to depart from this time-worn method. My intention instead, is to develop your signpainting ability as quickly as possible up to a point whereby you can earn a few dollars. This will not be done haphazardly.

The amount of equipment, the number of alphabets, the variations in procedure will all be kept at a bare minimum. However, no attempt will be made to bypass or slight the sound fundamentals. Proper procedure will be covered thoroughly, even if it requires an entire chapter to explain one simple phase of the work.

Practice work cannot be avoided, of course, but even this will be presented in a manner designed to afford more freedom.

Within the preliminary practice work will be the basic advice in regard to the proper tools, equipment and procedure.

Then you will be taught, in completion, two of the most basic printed alphabets, plus one simple script. These three alphabets will be those most commonly used in the everyday practice of signpainting.

But you can be assured that as soon as you are able to skillfully execute the very first alphabet in completion, you will be able to do work good enough to be sold. This work naturally will be limited to the most elementary form of signpainting. In this category would be simple real estate signs, uncomplicated truck lettering, or any other type of sign that could be accomplished through the use of this single, most commonly used alphabet.

This is not as far-fetched as it might at first appear. Look about you and notice how very many signs, trucks, etc. are lettered completely with the use of this single, one-stroke Gothic alphabet. The letters may vary in size, but you will be surprised to note how much sign work is actually accomplished with this one simple style of lettering.

After you master the second alphabet to be discussed within this text, plus the script, you can broaden the scope of your signwork much further. In this way the old cliche, "Earn While You Learn", can become an actuality, instead of the farce it sometimes appears to be within certain get-rich-schemes.

The second part of this book will then continue on to completion providing more advanced information. Literally hundreds of more complicated procedures and techniques will be explained. Much of the professional "know-how" that might have been elusive to you up to that point will be described in detail within this second section.

My logic in preparing this material in this manner is based upon the following assumption. The sooner the novice signpainter develops skill sufficient enough to earn some money, the less chance there is of becoming discouraged. Each dollar earned should provide the extra impetus needed to "attack" the study of the advanced material to follow with renewed vigor.

Before getting to the heart of this instruction, please consider these words of advice. If you are now receiving instruction through an on-the-job training program, do not discard your present teacher's methods. It is quite certain that he is well qualified and that his methods are sound.

Secondly, other signpainters might at times criticize your methods, techniques, etc. Before letting such a person "bug" you, take a close, critical look at his work. Do this to determine if his work is of such excellence that it qualifies him to condemn another's methods.

In my experience it is the low-talent loud-mouth who generally has shown no improvement over a 20 to 30-year span that most frequently derides the work of others. The master signpainter will either offer kindly, constructive criticism and then only when his opinion is sought, or he will say nothing.

Most important, maintain an open mind. Be receptive to any new technique that might add to, or excel any that you are currently using.

Although I hesitate to admit this in cold print, it is the plain truth. It has happened to me upon several occasions. Just about the time that I think I'm pretty good at the trade, I might watch another man at work in a different city. His work will be so flawless and accomplished with such an apparent lack of effort, that by comparison, I feel like a "hack". So, somewhat chagrined, I make every effort to spruce up my own work and improve myself. Remember this throughout your entire career—no matter how expert you might be, somewhere there is somebody who is better still.

The manner in which this book is studied is a matter of personal choice. Best progress would result if you were to first read through the book in its entirety. During this reading no attempt should be made to study the contents. Rather, this should be done to provide an over-all picture of what it takes to become a signpainter.

This first reading is advisable because it should help you to better understand the reasons for the following: The detailed instructions contained within the preliminary work, the constant insistence that proper procedures be developed right from the start, the stress placed upon practice, correct tools and materials, personal attitude, etc.

A cursory reading should also help you to resist a temptation quite common to many beginners. This would be the refusal to master professional techniques because these might seem to be too complicated or unnecessary—to substitute instead, what might at first seem to be an easier method. The novice is indeed prone to this type of neglect, only to regret this later when he has need of the procedure so quickly discarded.

Perhaps the most important benefit to be gained through this complete preliminary reading is that you can more intelligently organize your initial approach to the sign trade. In this way you can gear preliminary planning to fall within your individual realm of possibility.

This involves the state of your finances, which determines whether you must begin with a bare minimum of equipment and the need to improvise, or whether your funds will permit the purchase of everything needed. Also to be considered is the space available to you in which to carry on the work, the location and the size of your city; whether you must order supplies by mail or are fortunate enough to have the availability of local sources of supply. To sum up, you will know what to expect and be able to plan accordingly.

If you must start on a "shoestring" do not be disheartened. This contingency has been taken into consideration. Whenever possible, throughout this book there will be described alternate methods and improvisations expressly planned to help you to surmount this handicap.

Chapter 2

Introduction To Equipment

We now begin to discuss the actual mechanics of the sign trade. There is no set sequence necessary to the order in which you assemble the tools and equipment. The primary concern is that you do realize the importance of using proper equipment beginning with the very first stroke of the brush.

The average young signpainter starting his own shop usually does so with a small investment. Therefore, he must not only settle for a smaller place to keep down the rent and overhead, but he must also get by with the bare essentials necessary to carry on the work. It is possible to operate a profitable shop by making wise use of the space and funds that you do have.

The following will be an attempt to show you several economical ways to provide some of your needs. Later, when you have more capital, better equipment can be acquired.

A very important part of your shop is the main work bench or drawing board, since a big share of the work will be done on this. It is next to impossible to do professional work without a proper working surface. Build your bench as long in length as possible in the space available, for it will be needed many times to produce long banners, as well as patterns. It definitely should be at least 4 feet wide.

Let us assume that you are to build a work bench 16 feet long. (See Figure 1 for a suggested idea of construction) First construct a framework of 1 by 4-inch lumber. It need not be top grade, but must be straight. Next, nail two sheets of ½-inch fir plywood, 4 x 8 feet end to end on this frame. Quarter-inch plywood is also satisfactory provided that more bracing is used in the supporting framework.

Determine the height at which you wish the top part of the board to rest on the wall and draw a level line at this point the length of the board. Fasten the top of the board to the wall along this line, push the bottom out from the wall to the angle you desire, and fasten the braces to the bottom of the board. The distance between the bottom of the board and the wall at floor level will determine the slant of the finished work bench. Therefore, these braces should be cut to whatever length is required to provide the desired slant.

After these braces are fastened to the board, then allow the board to drop down into position, arranging each brace to rest against the wall or mopboard at floor level. Fasten them securely at these points of contact. These braces can be of 1 by 4-inch lumber and placed about 42 inches apart. Detailed construction would be difficult to explain, because you must adapt the method of fastening all parts of this unit to the type of wall involved. You might be able to nail directly to the wall, or might find it necessary to first fasten an anchor strip of wood to the wall and nail the unit to this.

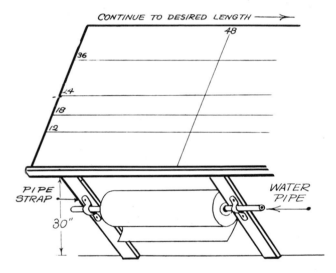

FIG. 1. "Build your work bench as long as possible. Construction details are illustrated here.

The angle or slant of the board must be determined by the individual. My preference is a sharp slant as shown in the illustration, because this enables me to do some of my commercial work on the board. Also if the slant is too horizontal or flat it is impossible to reach the top of the board without standing on a box. However, should you intend to use the board for showcard work also, then you will prefer a flatter surface, especially for pen and ink lettering. The sharp slant will not provide the pull of gravity necessary for normal ink flowage.

After the board is in place, the next step is to cover it with a softer material such as a light, compressed wallboard.

This material is usually available at building supply firms. It has a gray filler, much like the backing sheet of any tablet, and has a laminated, cream colored surface. This also comes in sheets 4 x 8 feet.

The plywood is used mainly to provide a straight, sturdy surface, but is not a good surface for general work. It is too hard for good pattern perforation, dulls the pounce wheel, and thumbtacks are difficult to insert and remove. The composition board should be $\frac{1}{4}$ inch thick. It can be removed and turned to the reverse side when it becomes rough from holes and cuts. There will be a great many thumbtack holes with burred edges on the reverse side, but these can be sanded to smooth condition quite easily. This material is economical and can be replaced frequently.

When the unit is installed the next step is to nail a long, smooth strip of wood along the entire bottom edge (See "A" in Fig. 2). It is important that this strip be very smooth for

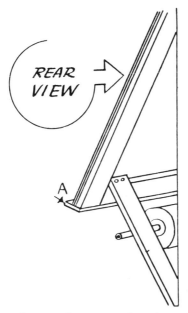

FIG. 2. (A) points out long, smooth strip to be nailed along entire bottom edge.

reasons soon to be explained. Also it should be fastened to the bottom of the board with extreme firmness. There must not be any waves or sags along its entire length, even if you find it necessary to insert nails at 4-inch intervals. This is important and absolutely essential to accuracy in layout work. Use a well finished clear pine strip $\frac{1}{2}$ to $1\frac{1}{2}$ inches.

The final step is to divide the board as shown in Figure 1. Draw permanent lines on the working surface at the most frequently used points of measurement. Use a sharp red or blue pencil for this, because this will avoid confusion with the normal hodge-podge of pencil lines that eventually result on a well-used drawing board. This step is optional, but these lines can occasionally save time in measurement.

The area beneath the board need not be wasted. It can be used for storage reasons such as rag boxes, empty tin can containers, small projectors, and other items that are used frequently and should be within easy reach. The space between the braces is ideal for installing a roll of paper as illustrated. The plumber can sell to you the pipe straps and pipe.

You might prefer to fix the entire unit so it can be folded against the wall when not in use. In this case, fasten the top of the board to the wall with hinges. Attach the legs or braces to the drawing board with hinges, leaving the opposite ends free. The legs can then be folded up against the rear of the board, allowing the unit to drop against the wall. To use, simply raise the board and prop the legs against the wall at floor level. There is little advantage in this method, however.

One little tip in erecting this unit is to avoid placing the left end against a wall. The right end can be flush against a wall, but leaving the left end open allows greater freedom for the work. Suppose you must paint a 20-foot banner on a 12-foot board. You can paint the first 10 or 11 feet, and then, with a little care, slide enough of this painted section off the end of the board to enable you to paint the remainder. If the left end is blocked you are at a standstill whenever you encounter a job longer than the board.

ADJUSTABLE DRAWING TABLE. In addition to this long work bench, you should have a small adjustable drawing table for smaller work, such as scale sketches and pen and ink work. These are available at most sign supply houses in all sizes and price ranges. Perhaps you cannot afford to buy one immediately. See Figure 3 for a simple method of constructing a unit such as this. The illustration should be plain enough to give you an idea of how to proceed. Use 1 x 3-inch lumber for the general framework.

The leg assemblies are held together with two carriage bolts on each side, and the unit can be folded up and set aside when not in use. The notches hold the unit together when it is set up and also provide three different working angles. The suggested measurements, also the tray, are optional. You might choose to eliminate the tray to provide sufficient area for a larger drawing board. If a standard

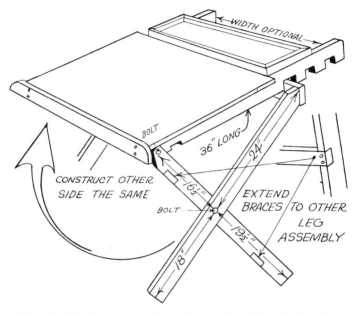

FIG. 3. *Simple construction of an adjustable drawing table.*

drawing board is not available, substitute a piece of well-sanded plywood. The board is not fastened to the framework but merely laid in place. To avoid thumbtack holes in the board, use small pieces of masking tape to hold the material in position. A sheet of cardboard can be placed on top of the plywood to insure a smoother surface.

SIGN STANDARDS.

The handiest items to have around the shop are sign standards, or "skids", such as shown in Fig. 4. It is advisable to have 3 or 4 pairs ranging in size from 6 to 12 feet long.

These are easily constructed of 2 x 4-inch lumber. Drill holes on a downward slant into the face side of each upright at about 6-inch intervals. Heavy spikes or pegs can be inserted into these holes to support sign panels. The holes can be drilled completely through the standard and capped on the rear side with either a thin slat or wood or a piece of sheet metal to prevent the pegs or spikes from slipping through. The bottom crosspiece is nailed to the upright as shown and should be 18 to 24 inches long. A small strip of wood can be nailed underneath the front edge of the cross-piece to compensate for the slant and to help prevent the standard from tipping forward. This entire bottom unit also keeps the standard from sliding off to either side.

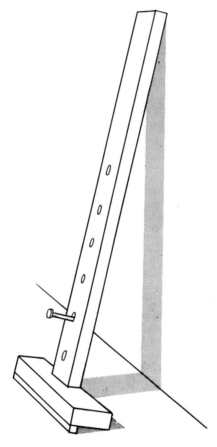

FIG. 4. Sign standards are handiest items to have around the shop. Four pairs, ranging from 6 to 12 feet in length are recommended.

The versatility of these wall-skids is limitless in regard to adaptability. One pair can be moved close together for small signs or can be spread apart to a distance sufficient to support a very long sign. The pegs or spikes can be alternately raised or lowered by one person without removing the sign. When resting a heavy panel on the skids, a wiping rag may be rolled lengthwise and draped over each supporting spike at contact points to cushion the weight and avoid bruising the bottom of the sign. A pair of these skids should be carried in your vehicle for possible use on jobs away from the shop. This will many times prevent the waste of time involved in searching for boxes or other objects upon which to rest a sign. Also, with the use of skids you can arrange to do certain work out on the job in such a way that it might be done in comparative comfort.

KITCHEN TABLE ALTERNATIVE. If you
cannot immediately construct a permanent workbench as described, there is an alternate measure that might at least serve to carry you through your practice work. A kitchen table, preferably one with a wooden top, can be converted into a suitable work bench. Purchase a piece of plywood sawed to the same size as the table top. This can be a bit longer than the table if desired. Place this plywood on top of the table and attach the front edge to the table top with several hinges. Leave the back edge free to be raised or lowered at will. The top can either be propped up or a slotted piece of strap-iron can be fastened to each side. A bolt may be permanently fastened to each side of the table. These bolts should be inserted from the inner side of the table so the threaded ends protrude outwards. Place a nut on each bolt and draw it up tight to hold the bolt in a fixed position. Countersink this bolt, if possible. The slotted ends are then arranged to run through the protruding ends of these bolts. Wing-nuts are then fastened to the bolt-ends to be turned loose or tight for adjustment of the work board to the angle desired.

Here then, we have discussed four items that are simply constructed, cost very little and yet can do much to provide you with working facilities in your shop.

JACK-OF-ALL-TRADES. In the descriptions of
these four items of equipment it has been assumed that you are able to do this most elementary carpenter work. If not, you must arrange to have this done for you. It would be advisable to at least try to do some of this yourself, if at all possible. The tools needed are few and very little carpentry skill is required.

A few observations fit in very well at this point. During

your career as a signman you will be faced with problems related to just about every vocational trade. Especially, as a shop operator, you will encounter side issues such as woodworking, sheet metal work, electrical wiring, sign construction, sign erection, masonry, boom operation, rigging swing-stages, etc. right on down to digging post holes. This is but a partial list.

Admittedly, no person could be expected to know all of these trades. Much of this work must be jobbed out. It is in your best interest, however, to develop at least a small knowledge of as many trades as possible. This of course applies only to those trades you must depend upon as a sign operator. If you must hire a tradesman every time it is necessary to drive in a nail, saw off a board, cut a piece of sheet metal, or accomplish a simple electrical hook-up, your profits will be a bit on the anemic side.

Also, a little know-how in regard to these various vocations can frequently prevent the unscrupulous tradesman from "putting the bite" on you should he be aware of your ignorance.

The big sign plants hire specialists in these fields, and as your business prospers, you too will be able to do this. But until such time as you reach this plateau, it is suggested that you try to pick up as much knowledge as possible about these related trades.

To repeat, the sign business is unique. There are few trades within which one man is expected to know at least a little bit about so much. My description of the successful sign shop operator is "a jack-of-all-trades and a master of signpainting".

THE FLAT WORKING SURFACE. During the discussion of work benches, etc. you perhaps noticed that no reference was made to working on a flat surface. For example: "Why not work directly on the top of the kitchen table? Why the adjustable board?"

First of all, to practice on a flat surface is difficult and is extremely uncomfortable. The physical strain and backache caused by long hours of work on a flat, horizontal surface would have you reaching for the liniment bottle more often than for the brush.

Secondly, there is seldom a need to do sign work on a flat surface, so why practice in this manner? The secret of developing good lettering speed is to practice in those positions that will later be most frequently used in doing the actual work.

LETTERING BRUSHES.

It is not practical to tell a novice signpainter which type of brush to use for each particular job. Each man must adapt himself to the tools that suit his individual technique. I can think of no other trade in which there are so many acceptable ways to do the same job with different tools and methods and still end up with good results. So, who can say, "This is the correct method. All others are wrong?"

As time passes, you will develop a preference for certain types of brushes and even particular brands. There are periods during which a particular type of brush might, for a time, be unavailable. For example, at the time of this writing, it is nearly impossible to buy gray-haired brushes. The brush manufacturers presently cannot secure the necessary hair due to a problem within the animal pelt market. The signpainter must, at times such as this, learn to adapt to the use of alternate brushes.

In regard to brushes, let us consider those most commonly used in commercial sign painting. These might be divided into two main categories, flats and rounds. In each category we have various hair types, each having a definite use. You must decide which you can handle most effectively, the flat or the round style.

There are no illustrations of brushes here because these are well pictured in all supply catalogs along with detailed descriptions.

During the early phases of practice and initial work you will need but a minimum supply of brushes. Additional sizes and styles can be purchased as the need arises. The descriptions to follow will help you to more intelligently make these additions.

RED SABLES.

Red sables are basically intended for use in tempera and water colors. For lettering, there are three popular styles, each having different hair lengths—long, regular and short. The latter is commonly referred to as the "rigger". The "highliner" is not a lettering brush, but is intended for outlining and underscoring. Another is referred to as the "script", which is a sharply pointed brush used principally for scrolling, etc.

Although most tradesmen confine the use of the red sable to water color, there are some who do extend this use to oil based paints. It is not advisable, however, to switch back and forth from oil to water color. Usually, once a red sable is used in oil based paints it will no longer work too well in water mediums. It apparently loses the desired snap to some degree.

My preference is to use red sables in water color only. I find them too stiff and snappy for truck lettering and other commercial work, especially glass. They are much too short and carry too little paint for general all around commercial signpainting. This, of course, is only my opinion. The red sable is a most excellent brush and a requisite in every shop. But, as is the case with all tools, it performs best when used for the purpose intended.

The important thing in buying red sables is to buy the very best quality. The time saved and the better results will quickly compensate for the difference in price. This applies to all brushes.

QUILLS. Next let us consider the quills. These come with the hair bound in either natural or patent quills. Some have handles and others do not. In the latter you can insert handles, which are available from the brush supplier. The same type of hair is also available in permanently bound metal ferrules, although the hair lengths may at times vary.

Gray quills will usually work to best advantage in the heavier synthetic bulletin colors and enamels because they have more snap than the brown quills. These are excellent for use on trucks and smooth finish signs of any kind and are considered by many to be the best all around brush.

Brown quills are softer and have less snap than do the grays. This factor makes this brush adaptable to lettering on glass and for use in lighter weight mediums such as japan colors.

Regarding size, the popular graduated lengths are about right for all uses. However in the smaller sizes, from a No. 4 on down, a shorter haired brush is a bit easier to manipulate on smaller lettering. This shorter style is available at most supply houses, but usually in brown only.

For larger lettering there are several choices, two of which are the jumbo round quills, or the gray "long-legs". Variations of the latter would be the "truck-letterer" or "greyhound". Here too, it is a matter of personal preference. I can make very fast time with the gray jumbo quills, and find them to be excellent for large one-stroke work on privilege or courtesy panels. These are also excellent for built up lettering. It takes considerable practice to learn how to use these large brushes with good speed. Once this skill is mastered, they can be the biggest time-saver in the lettering process.

OX-HAIR BRUSHES. There are also the various ox-hair brushes, some of which are blended with squirrel or camelshair. These are for the most part used in producing muslin and paper signs. This type of brush is economical, but it is difficult to do fine commercial sign painting with them.

BRUSH CARE. The service you get out of any of the brushes described, or for that matter from any brush, depends a great deal upon the care given to them.

Wash red sables thoroughly in water after use in tempera. Carefully shape the brush into a chisel shape while wet, and stand, handle down, in an empty can or jar with the hair straight up. Be certain that the brush does not touch adjoining brushes, or anything that might press against the wet brush and bend the hair to disrupt the chisel shape. Should the bristles dry while resting in bent position, they will retain this shape and it will be difficult to restore them to the desired condition. It is important that all paint be cleaned out of the heel of the brush at the point where hair meets ferrule.

All brushes used in paint other than water colors must be washed out in a solvent that will be certain to dissolve and remove any paint or material used in lettering. Generally, after using bulletin colors and enamels, turpentine or any good thinner will do for washing. If used in lacquer, clean with a mild lacquer thinner. If this type of thinner is too strong there is a possibility of "furring" the bristles and the brush will be ruined. If a brush is used in shellac it must be cleaned in an alcohol solvent.

After cleaning, dip the brush in either lard oil or olive-oil. Squeeze out the excess oil, but work the oil firmly into the "heel" of the brush. This is the part of the brush that is most apt to retain paint during the washing process. Vaseline also can be used in lieu of lard or olive oil, although some say that this is not good for the hair. I have found no basis to substantiate the latter.

A suitable receptacle in which to store brushes is a metal tray, preferably with a round bottom. (See Fig. 5) This tray can be of any size and if possible, should be made to fit into your sign kit. It is handy to keep several single trays such as this about the shop in which to store extra brushes. This type of tray is especially well designed for round brushes. The brushes seldom rest in odd shape for long. It seems that they sort of roll into shape even when the sign kit is being carried. The brushes never get pressed into an abrupt edge or against the side of a flat drawer or tray to assume an unwanted shape.

Before using the brushes again for lettering, wash out

the oil thoroughly in turp or solvent. All oil must be removed. This is important. After washing out lettering brushes at any time, this is a little procedure that works very well: Place your hands in front of you with the palms tightly together with the handle of the brush between them. The brush should be in vertical position. Next, move the palms of your hands back and forth very rapidly, much as

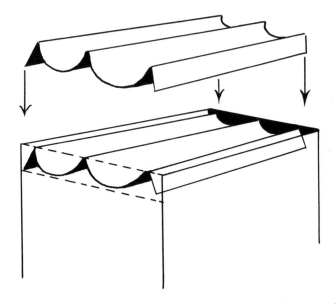

FIG. 5. *Brush tray can be made quite easily by any sheet metal shop for preserving brushes. Design it to fit in either the top compartment of your sign kit, as shown, or in a top drawer.*

though you were warming your hands by rubbing them back and forth, or modeling a cylindrical shape with modeling clay. Maintain tight pressure against the brush handle. (This works only when wearing a ring) In this rolling motion, as the handle hits against the ring it snaps the hair and shakes out all foreign matter. This process also dries out the brush completely in a matter of seconds.

SPLIT QUILLS. Sometimes upon purchasing quills without handles, the quill part of the brush will be pressed almost flat. It is then difficult to insert a round handle without splitting the quill. Following, is a suggestion that might be of help: Push the quill down into a raw potato with only the hair and wire binding protruding. After a time remove the quill and it will usually be soft and pliable enough to insert the handle, at the same time pushing the quill into the desired round shape. The length of time the quill is left in the potato can vary a great deal, so pull it out every now and then to check it or it might soften the quill too much.

If the quill still splits, put a coat of one of the new "sure-fire" glues on that portion of the handle that enters the quill and insert same. Press the split edges of the quill tightly in place and wrap rubber bands tightly around it to make firm contact with the handle. Set the brush aside for a day or two, and then remove the rubber bands. This should result in a usable brush.

Occasionally, a small split will occur in the edge of the quill at the point where it meets the hair. This is usually undetected until the brush is put to use. Then hairs of the brush will gradually work their way out of formation and into this split. In this condition the brush is useless.

In the past I have tried to repair these faults with many types of glue, shellac and other substances that normally are not solvent in sign paints or thinners. Eventually all of these repair substances have broken down or dissolved with continuous washings of the brush.

Quite recently, I think that I have discovered an effective method. First the errant hairs are gently eased out of the split in the quill and returned to original brush formation. Then a small dab of liquid solder is applied along the split and around the edge of the quill at the brush intersection. This solder is used sparingly and care must be taken to keep the solder off the hair of the brush itself. Liquid solder is sold in tubes, much like toothpaste, and the cap generally has a small flexible tip thereon to be used in spreading the material.

Since solder is for metal, this may seem rather unorthodox but many times in the sign field we must solve our varied problems in strange manner. I have repaired a number of such brushes in this way and purposely have washed these in all thinners and cleaners normally used. So far, this method seems to be effective.

CUTTERS. As we now discuss the fitches and cutters, it is best that we consider only the varieties most commonly used. For brick walls and cement block or other rough surfaces the pure white bristle fitches and cutters provide good results. My favorite method is to use a $1\frac{1}{2}''$ cutter for the biggest share of the work involving lettering, cutting-in, striping, etc. Then to use a fitch only in the trickier places such as the insert within the letter A or the peaks of the W or the letter N, etc. This method is especially suitable for cut-in work. One can develop great speed by holding the cutter sideways. Pull the brush down edgewise in a brisk manner. Then without turning the brush in the hand, immediately reverse the stroke pulling the brush upwards and back over the stroke just made.

There are signpainters who can make better time by using fitches for all cut-in work, especially if they have a competent helper, capable of filling in close up to detail work.

All wall work can be done most effectively by using proper pressure on the brush. Most beginners bear down too much on the brush. Remember that a hair being pressed flatly against a surface will not penetrate pits or mortar indents. Try painting with the tip of the brush. Apply just enough pressure to get down into crevices, varying the pressure according to the condition of the wall surface.

FITCHES. The white bristle fitches mentioned in the foregoing consist of the same type of bristle that is found in the cutters. There is also another fitch referred to as a "soft fitch". This is designed for use on smoother surfaces, such as siding or in such cases in which the common fitch is too stiff. Many phases of sign painting can be accomplished with soft fitches as skill develops.

COMMENTARY. Much more could be written about brushes. The brief descriptions just given are intended for "get acquainted" purposes. Through experimentation and experience, you will ultimately discover just which brushes can be used to best advantage. It is important to locate a dependable source of supply. Rather than order brushes by the dozen, just buy several of each until such time as you can decide upon the styles most suitable to your individual technique.

Although this has been a discussion of brushes in general, it will be some time before you will need all variations of the brushes described. For practice and initial work the brush requirements are few. As you progress with this instruction, the tools and their proper functions will be described in detail, and at such time as required. The purchase of these tools can also be delayed accordingly. This applies to all equipment described in the preceding chapter.

Chapter 3

Essentials of Practice

THE TRIAL PERIOD. It is a temptation at this point to describe in complete detail all the procedures that a professional signman would employ within the preliminary work.

Although these techniques are absolutely essential in order to reach the highest level of proficiency, it seems advisable to bypass these for the moment. This slightly unorthodox method of teaching is based upon the following logic. Some of these techniques, once mastered, are quite simple and are used almost automatically by the veteran in the trade.

However, at first it is a bit difficult to learn these professional methods. Based upon the individual's ability to adapt, these methods take time, patience and practice. The following fact must be considered. As a beginner, you might have great desire to learn the sign trade. But, as it is with all highly skilled trades, the possibility of disillusionment does exist. Early in the learning process you might discover that you simply cannot adapt to lettering, regardless of how conscientiously you practice. More simply still, you perhaps will find that you just do not like the trade.

These words are not written in the nature of discouragement, so do not adopt a negative approach. It is because of these possibilities that I feel it is my duty to get a brush into your hand and into the actual mechanics of practice just as quickly as possible. This approach might be compared to the man about to enjoy his first swim in early spring. He carefully dips one foot into the water to determine how cold it is. If it is warm enough, he then goes ahead and enjoys his swim. If not, he walks away, puts back on his clothing and discards the idea. It is a matter of trial and result, followed by acceptance or rejection.

Therefore, I can see no point in teaching to you the many involved professional methods at this point. It would be inconsiderate of me to cause this extra study on your part, without first making it possible for you to give the actual practice of lettering a fair trial.

All preliminary instruction will be offered with this consideration in mind. Take encouragement from the fact that, once involved, it is uncommon for a dedicated person to abandon the trade. This is said with thankfulness, because the sign industry at this time has a most urgent and ever increasing demand for well trained people.

Instruction will therefore begin in the manner described. Complete instruction will later be provided to surmount the more complicated procedures as the need arises.

There are several things to consider in your first practice sessions. Is it your goal to be a showcard writer, a sign painter, or both? The approach to each is different. For ease of explanation we shall discuss the practice work separately. Although showcard writing and sign painting are closely related, each is practically a trade in itself.

ACTUAL PRACTICE. Although the primary purpose of this book is to teach sign painting, the very first, and basic practice sessions will consist of showcard work. This is for the convenience of the beginner. The equipment and materials needed are comparatively few. The brushes can be quickly cleaned with water.

The equipment needed to provide a suitable working surface has been described in Chapter Two. You must either choose from those descriptions such equipment as you are able to provide, or must purchase similar furnishings from a sign supply firm.

Finally, we come to the actual practice. For years it has been traditional to practice brush strokes on newspapers. I heartily disagree. It would be difficult for an expert to letter decently on this material. The blotter-like surface of newsprint with an excess of capillary attraction, is a most unsuitable surface, especially for water colors.

Practice work is tedious at best for the beginner, without adding the frustration caused by a difficult surface such as newspaper. You will be more apt to enjoy practice, have better results and keep at it longer, by arranging practice work to be as easy as possible. Get yourself into the most comfortable working position possible, with good lighting. Secure reasonably good but economical surfaces upon which to letter and buy the best brushes available. It is better to have one good brush than a dozen "cruds".

For material you might try an economical bristol board— good on two sides and no heavier than two-ply. If this is too costly, try 24 lb. white poster paper. This can cause tedious practice also, since the capillary pull "drains" the brush of water color quite rapidly. You might find that stores have discarded posters to be had for the asking. Local print shops would perhaps be pleased to sell to you soiled cardboard at low cost.

Buy the highest quality, true red-sable lettering brushes possible. To begin, a No. 8, 10 and 12 is suggested. Choose the regular length, not the extra-long, nor the short style, commonly called a "rigger." Purchase a few jars of tempera showcard colors, since practicing with one color can become monotonous. Furthermore, by using various colors one becomes familiar with the working characteristics of each. (Request catalogs from suppliers).

Attach the material to the drawing board with small pieces of masking tape or thumbtacks. Draw cross guidelines with a pencil. A 2½-inch-high letter is a comfortable size for initial practice.

SINGLE-LINE LAYOUT. Fig. 6 shows the proper method for single-line, one-stroke layout. The beginner has a tendency to outline the entire letter with heavy pencil as shown. He then will fill in the letter with time wasting, laborious strokes. This would not be tolerated in any sign shop; so do not develop this kindergarten procedure. Bad working habits, once developed, are most difficult to break.

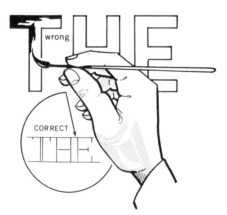

FIG. 6. The right way and the wrong way to letter showcard single-line layout.

It must be pointed out that the method pictured could be the proper method to letter other types of sign work. This would then be considered a "built-up" letter. However, the instruction now being discussed deals only with the one-stroke method of lettering. So, in this sense, the illustration does indeed show the incorrect method of producing any one-stroke lettering. Should a sign painter attempt to letter the cab doors of an average truck with this procedure, it would perhaps require two or three days instead of the customary two to three hours. Also, a scroll-type, pointed brush would never be used in the common one-stroke lettering process.

Layouts for one-stroke lettering should be prepared with quick, light, one-stroke lines, merely indicating the letter positions. For the letters T and I, a double-stroke helps gauge the space to be consumed. The size of the brush and the pressure placed upon it, in lettering will determine the uniformity of stroke.

SCRIBING LINES. Your potential as a sign painter depends to a great extent upon the work habits you develop as a beginner. To expertly handle a lettering brush is most important. It is also essential to learn the most basic auxiliary procedures if you are ever to achieve maximum efficiency.

At first these related abilities may seem to be of minor importance, but brush handling alone will never qualify you to refer to yourself as a sign painter. Therefore, it is advisable to use the professional approach and develop correct work habits starting with your very first practice session. At this point the instruction applied to these procedures will be kept at a minimum. However, certain fundamentals must be described because these are essential even to the efficiency of preliminary practice.

It is common for the beginner to place the material on the drawing board, painstakingly measure and mark dots on each end for the horizontal guidelines, and then place a yardstick from dot to dot; then to draw pencil lines from dot to dot to form the guidelines. A well trained workman would be well along with the entire layout before you will even have the cross lines marked in position. During the very early stages of the practice work it would be permissible to use this dot to dot method, at least until such time as you have practiced long enough to decide whether you will continue in the trade. Do not do this until you develop an ingrained sense of dependency on such procedure. This applies to all temporary, unprofessional methods that might be employed as alternatives during early practice. For best results, it is advisable to switch to the professional techniques as quickly as possible.

THE PROPER METHOD. Study the illustration, (Fig. 7). This is the proper method of scribing lines. The material to be lettered upon should be placed on the drawing board or working surface. If this is a panel of some weight, such as hardboard, it need not be fastened. Light materials,

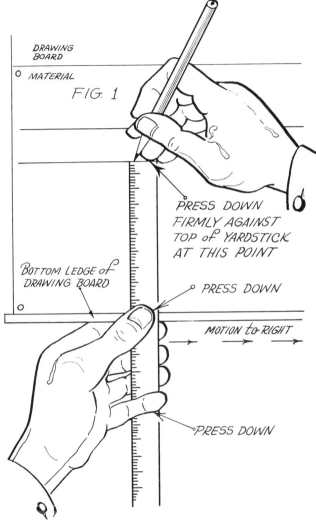

DRAWING BOARD

o MATERIAL

FIG. 1

PRESS DOWN FIRMLY AGAINST TOP of YARDSTICK AT THIS POINT

BOTTOM LEDGE of DRAWING BOARD

o PRESS DOWN

MOTION to RIGHT

PRESS DOWN

FIG. 7. *Suggested position of the hands for properly marking all cross guide-lines.*

such as cardboard or paper, must be fastened securely to the drawing board, either with thumbtacks or with pieces of tape. Otherwise, this light type of material might slide or tilt in the process of scribing lines in this fashion. Next, mark the dots for the guideline positions on the extreme left edge of the material. Grasp the yardstick as shown, placing the pencil point on the top mark. With the hands and pencil in firm position, move smoothly to the right, drawing the line as you move. Repeat this procedure at the indicated position of each guideline, until all lines are drawn. The yardstick must be held in a true vertical position at all times —a slant of any great degree will cause slight variations within the lines.

It is important that the bottom strip or edge of your drawing board be very straight and smooth for accurate results. Nails should not protrude. Slivers must be eliminated.

ADVANTAGES OF A FIRM GRIP. You may prefer a less complicated left hand grip, but I would strongly suggest using the grip as illustrated. This grip is one that I have developed after using and discarding several others through the years. The chance of the hand slipping is at a minimum, because you have complete control.

This particular grip and procedure may seem difficult for you and at first it might be wise for you to attach wrapping paper to the drawing board and scribe lines upon it, until such time when enough skill is developed to perform on more expensive material.

This method will take a little practice to master but will be well worth the effort. I will admit that at first I used this method only for pencil work. I did not extend its use to the pounce wheel or the blade until I perfected the use of the grip shown and the necessary skill.

There is a reason for all this stress about using this controlled grip. This factor will later enable you to extend the procedure to cutting pattern and poster paper. Consider the convenience of being able to cut paper into strips the entire length of the drawing board, perhaps 20 feet or longer in a matter of minutes. With this method, the pounce wheel can also be used to perforate patterns.

A controlled grip is highly essential, not only to insure accuracy, but also to prevent a slip which could result in a nasty cut from the blade. I have been cutting paper in this way for many years and have not once cut myself. The process in all respects is very fast and accurate if executed properly.

A FEW TIPS. Some of the following information will not be of use until later. It does seem advisable to include this instruction at this point.

On patterns with large letters, all the horizontal strokes on these, such as the bars on the letters E, F, T, etc. may also be made in this manner.

When laying out lines on banners in this fashion, a neater layout results by using a hard 6-H pencil. It is difficult to keep the lines light and even when using softer pencils, especially if the working surface is wavy in character.

Display cards are also laid out in the same way, using a good grade of white chalk sharpened or sanded to a flat chisel edge To prepare chalk for this purpose it is best to use a sharp, single-edged razor blade to roughly cut the chalk on each side until a fairly blunt marking edge. Then rub each side of the chalk upon a piece of sandpaper mounted on a sanding block to complete the sharpening process. This results in a piece of chalk with a neat sharp edge. It is my custom to keep a sanding block expressly for this purpose; to sharpen the chalk frequently during layout process, and also to sharpen about a dozen sticks at a time. The chalk layout is, of course, applicable to the darker colors of cardboards and other surfaces. Very little pressure is used on cards to insure lines that are as neat and light as possible. On light cards a hard pencil is used.

You will find many uses for this procedure of scribing. In addition to drawing board work, this method can be used on any sign panel or surface where you can successfully place your left hand in the proper position along a bottom edge. The method is especially handy at times to use on arced surfaces. A good example is along the front of a truck on the hood above the grill. It is frequently possible to do this layout work by running your left hand along the bottom edge of the hood-front.

The sides of the truck hood can be handled in the same way. Raise the hood and use the bottom edge, much in the manner applied at the drawing board. Because of space limits and obstacles, a very short section of yardstick must be employed when doing this type of layout. Also, in most of this type of work, a light, flexible yardstick is most practical, since it bends to conform to the various contoured surfaces. A rigid, heavy yardstick is not too adaptable in the process of most layout work.

When working around an arced surface, and especially around a sharp arc, you must carefully turn the wrist of your left hand gradually as you mark around the curve. The stick must always be at a perfect right angle to the bottom edge, and not on a slant, or the lines will neither be straight nor parallel. You will find much use for this method and will eventually become so adept at it that you will proceed almost automatically.

HAND POSITIONS.
Since you will begin your practice work in showcard style, you will at first use the hand-down method of lettering. Before you can intelligently begin actual practice there are things that must be discussed. Among these is the manipulation of the brush. So, although your initial work will be confined to the showcard medium, which involves only one hand position for the most part, we might as well consider all three of the hand positions at this time. Later, when you become involved in the instruction of sign painting in general, you can then refer back to this chapter.

In the practice of general signpainting you will perhaps discover that the most difficult skill to develop is mastery of the hand positions. Illustrated are the three most basic techniques. (See Fig. 8) These pictures show the hand-down method; the hand-over-hand method, and the mahlstick method. These positions are drawn "in general", of course, so you might alter them to suit your personal style and gain maximum flexibility.

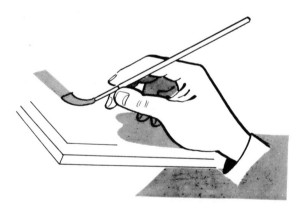

FIG. 8A. Hand-Down Method of lettering.

"Must I learn to use a mahlstick to be a good sign-painter?" This is a question frequently put to me.

Although I am always tempted to answer this question with a simple "yes", I do feel that this query cannot be answered this abruptly and must be qualified.

There are three basic ways to do lettering, as mentioned, and the best advice would be to learn all three methods and learn them well. This would seem to be the requisite for being a completely competent workman.

No part of the mechanics of lettering causes more controversy among signmen than does the use of these various methods.

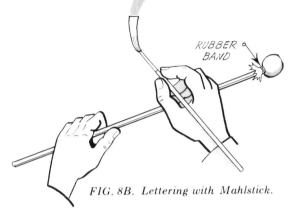

FIG. 8B. Lettering with Mahlstick.

The important thing to bear in mind is that you, and you alone, should be the judge of what method you prefer to use on the particular job you are doing. This statement refers, of course, to such time as you are a professional. In the beginning you must listen to constructive advice.

To better illustrate my point: Some years ago, as a new employee in a large sign plant, I was working on a volume order of cheap real estate signs. This was a fast, run-of-the-mill job, and I had developed good speed with my own adaptation of the "hand-down" method for this type of job. Actually, on larger letters I was fully capable of lettering free-hand with my hand up completely with no rest of any kind.

One of the older employees with a very superior attitude wandered over, watched for a while and said, "You'll never be a first class signpainter unless you use a mahlstick." Since he was an old-timer and I respected him, I hesitated to reply that I could work efficiently with the use of any method then known. Also that I was doing this job in this particular way because I could nearly double my speed. Later, I found that this man could only work one way, and although he did fine work, he was extremely slow. The foreman never put him on a volume or rush job where speed and price were a factor. After having the opportunity to watch him work, had he been working on this same order, I could very easily have completed two or more signs to his one with the same achievement of quality.

My thought in mentioning this episode is to emphasize the importance of your doing each job in the manner most suitable to your individual effort. In all fairness to the old-timer's comment, he was right in his statement, but wrong in the assumption that there is only one way in which to do a job. Flexibility and the sense to know when to use it can be a great asset.

FIG. 8C. Hand-Over-Hand Method.

There are excellent signpainters and pictorial men who use unorthodox procedures, but do fast, efficient work. It has always been my policy to refuse to work in a plant where a foreman dictates personal technique. When I was still working out, I made this very clear to the foreman before accepting the job.

It was in line with this that I heard some of the wisest words ever spoken by a foreman. He said, "I don't care if you stand on your head or paint with your feet. All I'm interested in is the end result, and whether you can do it fast enough to show a decent profit." This was one of the most pleasant sign plants I ever worked for and also remains today, very progressive and successful.

To reduce the confusion this entire question might be summed up in this way. The mahlstick is a very versatile tool and indeed there are certain types of work that practically demand its use. This would include such procedures as striping, underscoring, outlining, shading around wet lettering, etc. Also, the mahlstick keeps the hands off the surface when doing gold leaf work, dust-on aluminum jobs, or wherever hand smudges would be a hazard to the work. So in many cases the mahlstick has distinct advantages over other methods.

FLEX WITH THE OCCASION. This does not mean that the stick must be used constantly. The most versatile sign patterns learn to use all three methods and to flex with the occasion. Other writers for the sign trade, along with hundreds of signmen agree with this opinion. In these days of high-speed production the object is to competently do a given job in the quickest manner possible.

There was a time when a young signman was apt to be ridiculed should he be found working hand-down. The veteran would make the classic remark, "Showcard man, huh?" There are still those who cannot conceive of a job being done without using the hand-over-hand or the mahlstick method. In these days of change, with stress on production, it is ridiculous to cling to such hide-bound traditions. This attitude must give way to practicality.

These observations are not intended to belittle the mahlstick. It must be pointed out that when doing high-prestige work where very precise lettering and outlining and striping are required that the mahlstick has no equal. There is also a point where this tool must be laid aside in favor of faster methods.

The hand-over-hand method, too, is a great favorite with all top signmen. It enables you to work with good speed on precise work, without obliterating the pounce pattern marks. You can shade around wet lettering, do accurate outlining, and accomplish work in awkward places where the other two methods would be impractical.

Although the hand-down method was once considered taboo within the field of general sign painting, it is rapidly becoming acceptable to the trade as a means of fast production without waste of motion.

My advice is to consider each method equal in importance. My preference is to work by alternately using the hand-down method with the hand-over-hand method, using the mahlstick when practical. All three methods are often used on a single job.

Chapter 4

The Mechanics of Practice

Finally, we reach the point where you begin the actual practice of lettering.

For ease of explanation, let us assume that you have a sheet of white bristol board fastened to the drawing board and are ready to start. You can make the guidelines heavy for practice work. There is no need to strain your eyes unnecessarily during this phase of the training. Soon enough, it will be necessary to lighten these lines to near invisibility in order to present the ultimate neatness on salable sign work.

To repeat, an ideal height for practice strokes is about $2\frac{1}{2}$ inches. After the guidelines and the stroke positions are indicated, you are ready to begin. The tempera showcard color should be placed on a stand or table to your right, with a piece of scrap cardboard alongside to be used as a palette. A can or jar, half full of water should flank this so that you can occasionally rinse out the brush to eliminate the paint build-up in the heel of the brush. A No. 10 red-sable is suggested for strokes of this size. This number and size of the brush can vary, of course, since the size is determined by the amount of pressure applied to the brush by each individual. The showcard color should be mixed to workable consistency with water. This type of paint dries quickly and a thick residue of paint frequently builds up in the brush. So it is necessary to alternately dip the brush into the water and the paint and again palette the brush. This keeps the paint that is retained in the brush at workable consistency. This should be done between every stroke or two because it is in this manner that the brush is shaped for the stroke to follow.

THE PRACTICE STROKES. Preliminary practice work should be confined to plain, one-stroke Gothic letters. The illustration (Fig. 9) shows practically all of the strokes necessary to execute this alphabet. The term, "one-stroke" is sometimes confusing to the novice. This does not mean that the letters are made with one stroke of the brush.

Rather, the main part of the letter is formed by one stroke of the brush, instead of being built up to greater width with a series of strokes. The width of the stroke is determined by the size of the brush and the pressure applied.

Before beginning the practice strokes, study the strokes as shown on the illustration. It is suggested that you look ahead to the next several illustrations showing the entire alphabet. This will acquaint you with the characteristics of the finished letters. It will help you to better understand the goal you are striving to reach while practicing these preliminary strokes.

At first, it is best to confine your practice to strokes Nos. 1, 2, 3, 5, and 6. To get the feel of the brush, start out each practice session by making several lines of single, vertical strokes (No. 1), followed by a line each of the Nos. 2, 3, 5, and 6 strokes. As your skill increases, add the strokes numbered 8, 9, and 10.

You will note that No. 4 is a complete letter T. My contention is that certain strokes are easier to master by making the entire letter, which might also apply to the letters C and M, and others. If you feel that you can do better instead, by practicing the individual strokes singly, then do so.

FIG. 9. Strokes numbers 1, 2, 3, 5 and 6 are recommended for first practice. Numbers 11, 13, and 14 should be reserved until after some skill has been developed.

Do not "graduate" yourself to strokes Nos. 11, 13, and 14 until you have developed your skill somewhat, since these are a bit difficult for the beginner. No. 11 is the type of stroke necessary for the loops of the letters B and R. Nos. 13 and 14 are strokes used mainly in the formation of numerals, such as the numbers 8, 9, etc.

As the brush is pulled around a curve, it must be twirled in the fingers, smoothly and gradually, using the same amount of pressure. That part of the brush in contact with the surface should be at a right angle to the edge of the letter throughout the stroke. This results in a uniform width of stroke.

THOUGHTS ABOUT PRACTICE. Before proceeding with the actual alphabet, here are a few random thoughts that should help in practice: Twirling the brush is most important. When you are idly sitting about, perhaps watching television, keep a dry brush in your hand. Practice twisting it, flipping it about in your hand from one lettering position to another, until the brush seems like an extension of your body. Indeed, the real pro can flip a brush in less than a wink of an eye to come up with the brush-point in proper position for another stroke. This dexterity becomes automatic to the competent professional and he does not even realize that he is doing this. A parable to this would be a highly expert baton-twirler.

In practice, you will at first squeeze the brush very tightly and also bear down on it while stroking. As time passes you will find yourself holding the brush lightly and bearing down less and less. In fact you may have to use a larger brush to paint the strokes of the same width as you did as a beginner.

During the early years you will find yourself bearing down and practically painting with the heel of the brush. After a reasonable length of time you will learn to take advantage of using the natural spring of the brush. This is the manner in which the truly expert sign painter produces those graceful, sweeping letters and strokes that you so admire as a beginner. There are a few, unfortunately, who do continue to bear down on the brush year after year, much like they were trying to push a hole through the drawing board. This type of signman can usually do precise mechanical lettering, but never does get the knack of lettering with a flair . . . lettering that actually appears to have motion.

This lack of skill can usually be traced to the fact that he remained in a rut and refused to put forth the extra effort of practice that eventually separates the hack sign-painter from the real pro. How many years a man has been in the trade is not a true indication of skill. I know of sign-painters who have shown no improvement, nor have they changed their style, although they have been in the business steadily for 20 to 30 years.

On those days when your practice work does not seem to be going as fast as you might expect, remember this. After 40 years in the field of sign painting and commercial art work, I am still practicing new techniques, new alphabets, and ever searching for new and better ways to do my work. What I am trying to say is that experimentation and the practice that comes along with it never ends unless you want it to.

To break the monotony of hum-drum strokes, try your hand at lettering a few words occasionally. Practice on different surfaces, both matte and gloss finished cardboard, poster paper, etc. Change colors now and then. Set aside the No. 10 sable and drop down to a No. 8 or up to a No. 12, changing the letter heights accordingly. You can develop many personal ways in which to make practice work more enjoyable and less routine.

THE ONE-STROKE GOTHIC ALPHABET.

Oddly enough, the alphabet that we use for the biggest share of our work as sign painters is one of the most difficult to identify, or to "pinpoint" with a correct name. Among many signmen it is fondly referred to as "Egyptian". This is evidentally a nickname, because I have never noticed it described as such in an alphabet book or other instructional material. The lettering plates that do contain an Egyptian reference are vastly different in character.

The most correct name for this alphabet would appear to be "One-Stroke Gothic." The very fact that this is a Gothic alphabet may account for the confusion regarding its identity, since Gothic is quite flexible. If the letter forms are changed slightly, the results might be "Franklin" or "Grotesque." Should the letters G, O, and Q become perfectly round instead of oval, this alphabet could easily be confused with "Futura". If the strokes were thickened, it would then be "Futura-Bold."

Therefore, with slight modifications, this alphabet may have many names, but still remain within the Gothic family. An old-timer once said to me, "When in doubt use Egyptian." So, considering the wide acceptance of this alphabet by beginner and veteran alike, we could refer to it as our "Bread-and-Butter" alphabet.

Regardless of name, this alphabet is more frequently used than any other in the field of general sign painting.

There are many reasons for this. It is usually the first alphabet learned by the beginner. The letters are simply made, easy to read and are attractive. The formations are plain and uncluttered. Because of this the application of

34

shading and outlining requires a minimum of time and effort. This alphabet is so basically sound in formation that it becomes the foundation or springboard for other alphabet variations.

From a standpoint of the customer, it is a basis for economy. Many of your clients will come to you not by choice, but because the need for signwork is forced upon them. A good example would be in reference to truck lettering. In most states, the law requires that all trucks be lettered with full identification, such as, name, address, license number, etc.

The trucker usually has economy in mind. This is understandable, since he neither desires the lettering, nor does he need the advertising. Therefore, he might say, "Just use plain block-letters—nothing fancy." When any customer mentions "block-letters", he is generally referring to One-Stroke Gothic.

PRACTICE OF THE ALPHABET. Before beginning the study of the entire alphabet, you might wonder how long you must practice the preliminary stroke-formations. This decision depends on individual progress.

It has been suggested that you do include within the stroke practice occasional attempts to letter full words in completion. At such time as you feel that you can do this quite efficiently, it is then advisable for you to begin practice of the alphabet.

Fig. 10 illustrates a commonly used version of the One-Stroke Gothic alphabet. This consists of the capital letters only. Since most work does involve the use of capital letters, this is perhaps the most important lettering plate to consider.

Little need be said in reference to the manner in which you learn this alphabet. The primary method of procedure here is simple. Carefully study the characteristics of each letter. Pay close attention to stroke placement and letter formation in general. Then try to copy your practice lettering, forming the letters as closely as possible to those shown on the illustration. From that point on, it is practice, practice, practice! There is no alternative to practice. Lettering skill can be acquired in no other way.

Although this about sums up the basic method to use in learning any alphabet, the following comments might be of some help to you. As instruction advances much of this will be covered in more detail. This commentary is related directly to Fig. 10, but some of this applies to all sign work.

It is desirable in the production of the "One-Stroke

Gothic" alphabet to make all effort to maintain a uniform width of stroke. This can be done as nearly as possible by placing the same amount of pressure upon the brush throughout the process. Also, the brush must be twirled properly on curved strokes as previously described.

Avoid the following errors, most common to beginners. Do not make the upper loop of the letter B larger than the loop at the bottom. This also applies to the letter S. These two letters appear to be top-heavy even when the loops are equal. It is advisable in both cases to make the top loops a trifle smaller.

ABCDEF
GHIJKL
MNOPQ
RSTUV
WX&YZ

FIG. 10. The One-Stroke Gothic Alphabet (Capitals).

Do not skimp on width or congest either the letter M or the W. These two letters should be proportionately wider than normal letters, such as the letter H.

In all lettering, never cease to be honestly critical of your own work. It would be very easy for me, or any professional sign painter, to go through any of these lettering plates and point out my errors. Since the letters are well executed and of good formation, these slight errors would be noticeable only to another professional. But, I will mention one fault to demonstrate my point: The stroke on the right side of the letter U is thinner than that on the left. Other slight errors are present, but not sufficient enough to require the production of another lettering plate.

It is doubtful if any lettering artist has ever produced an alphabet in which he could not himself find something wrong. This would be considered "lint-picking" if done by another, and there is a difference between this and sincere, constructive criticism.

It is recommended that you subject your own work to "lint-picking" criticism as a means of improving your technique. However, confine this sort of thing to your own work. It is unethical to extend it to the work of others.

ONE-STROKE GOTHIC—LOWER CASE.

Those not familiar with lettering might refer to the lower-case letters pictured in Fig. 11, as the "smaller letters". Technically, an alphabet consists of upper and lower-case letters. The capitals in these terms would be referred to as upper-case-letters.

Although the lower-case letters of the Gothic alphabet are less frequently used than the capitals, they serve a definite purpose within the complete lettering process.

Lower-case lettering is mainly used in conjunction with the capital letters for lettering full sentences, or for blocks of descriptive copy. This type of copy is sometimes referred to in the sign trade as "paragraph copy" or "catalog copy." It is often used within one word on a truck door to break the monotony that would otherwise result from using capitals throughout. This would aptly apply to such a word as "Phone."

Practice procedure, for the most part, is the same as that described for the capitals on Figure 10. The manner of practice is essentially the same for all one-stroke alphabets that have a uniform width of stroke.

The lettering in Figure 11 is a bit more difficult to execute. The loops are sharper and require more dexterity with the brush. These lower-case letters require more room vertically, because some of them drop below the line. So you must plan the layout in advance to be certain that enough vertical space is available to provide the greater amount of room needed between each line of lettering. Note that a portion of the letters G, J, P, Q, and Y drops below the guideline that supports the capital letters.

If no capital letters are present within a line of letters, space consideration also must be given to the letters B, D, F, H, K, L, and T. These letters contain strokes that extend upwards. Because capital letters are generally used in connection with these letters, this is seldom a problem.

abcdefg hijklmno pqrstvy xzzɑɕ?

FIG. 11. One-Stroke Gothic Alphabet (Lower-Case).

When vertical space is limited, the space between each line of lettering can be cut to a minimum through careful layout. For example, the letter G might be positioned so the bottom loop falls into position above shorter letters in the line immediately below, such as the M or the N. This is not always possible. Should the letter G occupy a position directly above the letter T, then a maximum of space is needed between the lines of lettering. In all cases, the space between the lines must be uniform throughout the layout.

The space must not be changed from line to line to suit the letter positions.

These lower-case letters frequently can be used to gain space when width is limited. Much horizontal space can be saved through the use of the letters F, J, L, and T. These letters are narrow and require much less space than do their full formed counterparts within the capitals.

The letters shown on Figure 11 represent one basic version of the One-Stroke Gothic alphabet. Most signmen develop their own technique in regard to the entire Gothic family of alphabets. This is a matter of individual preference. Seldom do professional sign painters stray too far from the basics. This type of variation, within reason, is a plus factor. This flexibility allows each sign painter to best adapt the work to suit his physical manner of handling the brush. It also is the reason why the really good lettering artist is able to develop his own unique and attractive style or flair. These personal variations are so clever and slight that the lettering properly remains within the One-Stroke Gothic alphabet.

These facts are mentioned to you as a beginner to clear up any questions that might now be in your mind. In the study of other lettering plates you might have noticed variations of letter formations in every version. You are perplexed further still when you note that each presentation, regardless of these differences, is referred to as One-Stroke Gothic. Which is correct? Which is incorrect?

The answer is simple. If these are expertly done, all are correct. It is this acceptable flexibility that makes the sign trade so creative and unique.

Several examples of this are to be found within the two lettering plates just discussed. (See Figure 11) Note the first letter A. There is an alternate letter A on the bottom line. The letter is easier to do, and is used as a matter of preference. Also, when the letters must be squat in nature, the first letter A becomes "squeezed" as though under pressure from above. The less complicated letter A is then used instead.

The letter G is also a variation. The most correct letter G is rather complicated, so for ease of early practice, a simplified version was purposely used in the preparation of Figure 11.

Some sign writers use a capital letter Q to replace the one shown and also eliminate the small loop at the bottom of the letter T and bring it to a straight ending.

There are two versions of the letter Z. Either is correct and the one with the peaks can correctly be used within the capitals. The "and sign," or ampersand is also handled differently in Fig. 10. Both are acceptable.

Fig. 12 depicts the numbers suggested for use with the One-Stroke Gothic alphabet. Various signmen have their own ideas about numbers. This illustration shows a common version. Here, too, are variations and all are acceptable. There are two versions of the number 1, three of number 2, and two of number 7. Number 10 is seldom used in illustration since it is but a duplication of the letter O. The cent and dollar symbols have many versions, especially in showcard work. These can frequently be used in stunt-form for fill-in or decorative purposes and still be functional.

There are many acceptable variations possible within the alphabets, numbers and symbols. As a beginner it is suggested that you abide by those as shown for the present. Experience and a thorough knowledge of lettering is required to develop well formed variations. Do not attempt to do this until you are so qualified.

I1222345
67789 ¢ $

FIG. 12. One-Stroke Gothic Alphabet (Numerals).

MODIFICATIONS. A certain amount of modification is permissible during the process of reproducing any alphabet. This might be done for sound reasons, such as gaining or saving space. It may be a simple whim of the sign painter, or an effort to impart a touch of novelty to the sign.

Fig. 13 shows a group of the most common modifications. Since these are the variations most frequently used, it is advisable to include them within your regular practice work.

Either of the two letters G are acceptable, and in many cases, preferable to some signmen, instead of the G used in Fig. 10. The same applies to the letter M. The first letter M is a handy modification to use for gaining space when necessary. The acceptable width of this letter is quite flexible, as is the letter W. (Not shown)

The letter O and the two letters Q are round, compass-type letters. The letter Q is also flexible and there many variations of the manner in which the stroke is attached to distinguish it from the letter O. The two methods shown are neat and quite attractive. This stroke is sometimes limited to the space between the lines of lettering. The modification of the letters O and Q also provides an excellent means of gaining or saving space. In no case should either be too congested.

The letter Z has previously been discussed and is not a true modification. It properly belongs to the original alphabet. Because of its peaked ends it is more difficult to make than the square-ended Z in Figure 10.

G G M M
O Q Q Z

FIG. 13. Correct Modifications.

Most letters in the alphabet can be modified, within limits, to gain or save space. Once a letter is modified, the change must remain constant as it occurs within any one sentence or copy-grouping. You should not produce a letter in normal form at the beginning of a sentence and then modify the same letter at the end of the sentence to accommodate the remaining space.

STUNT LETTERS. To become an expert at lettering, the art of modification is a necessary factor. However, there is a sharp line between a good modification and a stunt-letter. It is easy to cross this line unless all variations are wisely developed. Stunt-lettering should be avoided within any of the true Gothic alphabets. Most of the letters in Fig. 14 are Stunt-Letters. The first letter A would appear to be a symbol on a mummy's tomb. However, several of the other letters belong and look well when used in other alphabets. The second letter A, when correctly used in a display-type alphabet is neat, but only when other letters are also rounded. Another exception is the first letter R. This would be acceptable in the Gothic alphabet, providing that the right-hand down-stroke of the letter K would also be brought down in the same curved manner. All "companion-strokes" within an alphabet should be executed in the same fashion.

ΛABEO
RRRSU

FIG. 14. Stunt Letters.

The other letters in Figure 14 may all be used within complete "stunt-alphabets" or on display cards, but must be used in proper context.

BAD LETTERING HABITS. Illustrated in Fig. 15 are some of the bad lettering habits apt to be developed by the newcomer to the sign trade. Fortunately most beginners remedy these faults as they gain experience or during instruction. Others cling to these habits until retirement.

The first letter A is not a bad letter, but the extended cross-bar changes it into a stunt-letter. If this extension is used on the letter A, it must then, for the sake of conformity, be used on other cross-strokes to follow such as the letters E, F, H, etc. Some beginners tend to feel that this letter A is cute, but fail to follow through with it on all successive cross-bars.

The cross-bar of the second letter A is much too low, causing a squat, unattractive letter. This error is very common.

AABEE
GJSYZ

FIG. 15. Examples of bad lettering habits.

Consider the first letter E. Note the unpleasant formation caused by this short center stroke. There are many who do use this snub-nosed stroke. This stroke should be a bit shorter than the top and bottom strokes, or of the same length, should you prefer. Never should it be longer. The second letter E has two errors. The cross-stroke is too high. (Too low is just as bad). Also, note the slanted ends on the top and bottom strokes. These oblique stroke-endings are favored by some, but a much neater letter results if you keep all of these stroke-endings as perfectly vertical as possible.

The long cross-bar on the letter G is ridiculous. There is no need to over-extend this stroke. It would be better to use this paint and surplus of energy to lengthen the stubby little stroke at the center of that letter E as suggested.

All too often we see the letter J turned into the monstrosity shown. Untrained beginners just cannot abide the blank space at the top of the letter J, so they feel obliged to fill this area with an ugly, overlong serif. To further fill this space, they bring the bottom stroke up too far. This is unnecessary. The letter J looks fine in proper context.

The top loop of the letter S is much too large in proportion to the bottom loop. This sweeping stroke should be farther up with the greatest space at the bottom, rather than at the top. This accounts for the clumsy appearance and lack of grace.

The letter Y is out of proportion. The down-stroke is too low and too short. Occasionally this error can be so pronounced that the letter Y might well be mistaken for the letter V from a distance.

The letter Z appears to be falling over to the left. This letter should stand erect. When laying out the letter Z, make two vertical marks, such as you would for the letter H. Keep the letter within the confines of this box-like area with the top and bottom strokes of the letter Z ending flush with the two vertical lines.

COMMENTARY. The foregoing should demonstrate to you the various reasons why it is advisable to avoid self-developed modifications until such time as you can do so with intelligence. The ability to modify is gradually developed through experience.

On specific occasions there is a definite need for the use of well designed stunt letters. You must first learn how to properly develop this type of lettering, and then to use it wisely.

This brings to an end the introduction to the basics of the One-Stroke Gothic alphabet. More detailed instruction will follow in reference to this letter within the specifics of proper layout, spacing, etc.

Chapter 5

Introduction of Proper Spacing

General layout instruction will not be included at this point. However, it is impractical to continue practice procedure without first considering the basic fundamentals of spacing.

To sit at a work-bench, practicing strokes and lettering without giving any thought to proper spacing can only retard development of skill.

Professional lettering is nearly as dependent upon correct spacing as it is upon expert strokes. Therefore, it is advisable to learn proper spacing methods at the same time that lettering skill is being developed. This will speed progress and prevent formation of bad spacing habits which, once acquired, are most difficult to correct.

Too frequently we see signs that are quite competently lettered but immediately stamped as the work of an amateur because of improper spacing.

MECHANICAL vs. OPTICAL SPACING.

Study the illustration (Fig. 16) to see the result of mechanical spacing as compared with optical spacing. The first example shows the result of mechanical spacing and the negative effect caused by providing an equal amount of spacing between each letter. This is sometimes referred to as "Stick-Spacing", and is, in most cases, incorrect. This method can be used in rare cases when a word is completely composed of straight, full letters such as the H, N, V, etc. It might also be used with the condensed Gothic alphabet, especially the modern round-top style.

Note on the example of mechanical spacing how the word, "Schultz" nearly appears to be two words due to excessive space between the L and T. Study this line of lettering and the unpleasant, irregularity of layout will be apparent. Yet, the space between each letter is equal.

Then compare that word with the optically spaced example and you will see why it is so essential to learn to do visual spacing.

Letter by letter, let us discuss the logic involved in

optical spacing. The dividing space between the letters S and C is not a full space because the irregular edge of the letter S and the circular letter C both contribute blank space by nature of their shape. So the dividing space is diminished accordingly.

The space between the C and H is greater because the letter is a full letter and provides no optical space. A full dividing space is still not used here because the letter C is irregular and open-faced and provides a small degree of optical space.

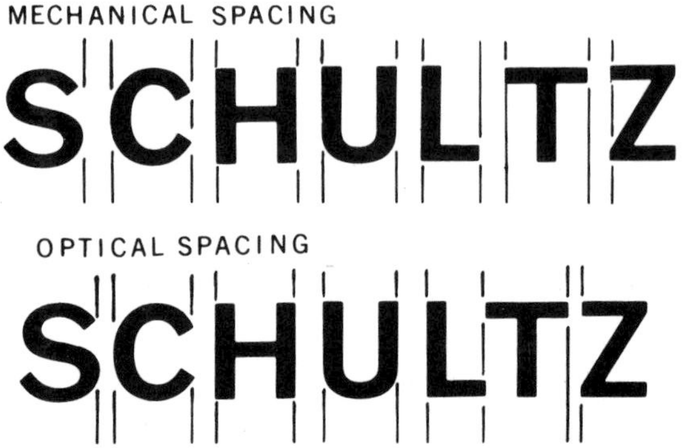

MECHANICAL SPACING

OPTICAL SPACING

FIG. 16. Comparison of mechanical and optical spacing.

Full dividing spaces are used between the H, U and L because all adjoining edges are straight and full. Note that there is no space at all between the L and T, since the open nature of these two letters provides all the optical space required. The dividing space between the T and Z is also a minimum for the same reason.

LEARNING OPTICAL SPACING. Optical spacing is learned much the same as lettering, through trial and error and experience. The basic principle is to study the characteristics of the adjoining letters. Use a full space between two full letters such as H and U. Allow less space whenever irregular letters are involved such as the letters F and K and X, etc. The dividing space between round letters such as an O followed by a C should be quite small. Open letters such as A, J, L, T, etc., should be placed comparatively close to the adjoining letters. Be careful with the letter I. Except for several of the newer, exotic alphabets, the letter I should never be crowded. In most standard alphabets, the novice is inclined to allow too little space between it and the adjacent letters.

The letters in very few alphabets are of the same width. Still it is not uncommon for the beginner to measure off an equal space for each letter, regardless of whether the letter is wide or narrow in character. When using the plain Gothic alphabet, the approximate widths might be determined by use of the point system. In this procedure, it is assumed that a regular unit such as the letter H equals one point. With this "rule of thumb", you can classify the letters M and W as $1\frac{1}{2}$ points; the letters A, C, G, O, Q, $1\frac{1}{4}$ points; others 1 point.

If space is limited the letters E, F, J, L and T can be diminished. The letters L and T can stand the most reduction, when necessary, but in all cases, if you must diminish a certain letter, then confine that letter to the same width throughout the sentence or copy-grouping. For example, do not use the letter T at its full width at the start of a message and continue to diminish it as you proceed, to come out right on the end. Letter size changes should be uniformly made throughout a message.

Once you have developed a thorough understanding of these elementary rules of optical spacing, you have taken a long step toward good layout.

Chapter 6

Practice For General Sign Painting

Up to this point practice work has been confined to the use of red sables and tempera colors. This method was suggested because the least amount of effort is required for cleaning of equipment after each practice session.

If it is your plan to specialize in showcard writing and to go no further into general sign painting, then practice work should continue in this medium.

Since this book is primarily intended to teach sign painting, any reference to showcard writing will be slight and only as occasion demands.

Although sign painting and showcard work are closely related, it has long been my opinion that each is almost a trade in itself. During my early years in the trade I spent much of my time doing free-lance display card painting for high class department stores.

About this same period I worked for five consecutive years as a steady employee for a national chain-store firm, where I did, in fact, do nothing but display card and banner painting. My duties involved doing the biggest share of this work for over 30 stores. Therefore, I have great respect for good showcard designers, but do feel that this is somewhat of a separate phase of the sign trade. The complexities of this specialized field could best be taught in a separate book or a series of magazine articles.

THE CHANGE OVER TO SIGN PAINTING MEDIUMS. Assuming that you have reached that point in practice where you can letter with reasonable ease and space the lettering properly, it is time to change over to the tools of general sign painting. This is necessary to intelligently cope with the instructions to follow. Also, you were assured earlier that your knowledge would be developed in such a way that you could reach the "dollar-earning" stage as rapidly as possible. This stage cannot properly be reached until you learn to use at least the most basic tools necessary to do general sign painting.

As we move on to signpainting in general, you will be

pleased to find that preliminary practice is quite similar to that which you have been doing up to this point.

The prime variance will be in the use of different brushes and materials.

Since initial practice will again be done on cardboard, the first need for brushes should be small. It is suggested that you buy the following: Two each of No. 6 and No. 8 gray quills, and two each of ¼ inch and ½ inch flat, camel-oxhair flats or "strokes". (See Fig. 17) The best chance of getting good brushes is to buy the highest priced brushes available in the above-mentioned styles.

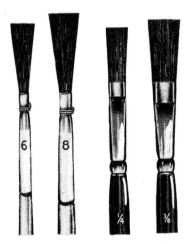

FIG. 17. For initial practice, two each of these brushes are recommended: No. 6 and No. 8 gray quills and ¼-inch flat, camel-oxide flats or "strokes."

You will not know until you experiment in actual practice which style of brush you can use to best advantage—the flats or the rounds. It will soon be evident which style suits you best, and then you can order more brushes at a time and also a wider variety of sizes.

Should you have a problem with the use of a certain brush do not be discouraged or too quickly blame this on lack of ability. In many cases the brush is at fault and even the most expert signman could not use it effectively.

When you order a dozen lettering brushes, do not expect all twelve to be usable. Experience has taught me that in the purchase of a dozen brushes of an identical series, size and price that the average efficiency breakdown might be as follows: Four brushes will be excellent. Two will work passably well. Two may be usable, but cause a little cussin', and the remaining four are apt to be useless.

Reasons for this could be the presence within the brush of crooked or curled hairs, broken down corners at the tips, steady loss of hair due to improper binding. The hair might be trimmed crookedly at the brush ending, or the quill is sometimes split or crooked, etc. Sometimes the ends are blunt and cannot be shaped to a chisel-edge.

These are just some of the faults commonly found even in the highest priced brushes. This is especially true in regard to the pencil-type quills. Seldom is this the fault of the supplier. One cannot always tell by merely looking at a brush whether it is a good tool. Some faults are immediately visible, such as split quills, etc. But in regard to the hair, the faults seldom show up until the brushes are put to use. Personally, I would rather pay six dollars for one brush that I knew to be excellent than to buy a half dozen for two dollars a piece and take my chances.

Although one cannot always spot faults when buying brushes in person at the point-of-sale, there is a better chance of securing better brushes. Some faults can be discovered and the best appearing brushes can be purchased. This fact poses a problem for the small town signmen who have no local source of supply, but must order by mail. This is especially true of supply firms that maintain a retail store on the premises. The local signmen pick out what are apparently the best brushes, so it is natural that those brushes remaining are sent out to fill the mail orders. Therefore, whenever possible, it is best to buy brushes in person.

So be prepared for much disappointment in regard to the purchase of lettering brushes. Never buy a large quantity of a new or unfamiliar series of brushes. Merely buy several and first put these to a test to determine their possible value.

In all fairness it must be emphasized that the suppliers, wholesalers and retailers are merchants. These people could not be expected to recognize most of the faults in lettering brushes. To them one brush looks pretty much like another. It is to their advantage to send out top quality supplies, especially when the buyer is willing to pay for high quality. Therefore, no reliable supply firm would knowingly send out faulty brushes. (For more detailed information on brushes in regard to selection, proper use and care, refer back to Chapter Two.)

PAINTS AND THINNERS NEEDED FOR PRACTICE.

There are a great number of paints, thinners and mixes used in the practice of signpainting. These will be discussed at the proper time. By far, the paint that is used to the greatest extent is referred to as "Bulletin Colors." So during this early phase of your practice work it is suggested that you use bulletin colors. Buy the quantity that you need in all of the most commonly used colors and alternate the use of each color in your efforts. In this way you will gradually become familiar with the working qualities of each color. There is a difference.

The actual practice work is performed in the same manner employed previously during the tempera or water-color phase of your training.

Thin down the bulletin color to a workable consistency. For work on cardboard or paper, the paint is thinned more than it normally would be for lettering painted surfaces, such as truck doors, etc. Use the thinner recommended on the label, which is usually turpentine or mineral spirits. Do not develop the habit of placing a can of thinner next to the paint and thinning as you proceed, by dipping the brush into the thinner sporadically, and paletting. Even though this is common practice even by veterans in the sign trade, it is not advisable to do this. It is easier to letter in this way, but it is a poor procedure.

Later, on permanent signs, certain letters where the paint was excessively thinned will fade out or chalk off sooner than those letters applied with full-bodied paint. Mix the paint to proper consistency and should the brush pull or cake-up in the "heel," wash the brush out completely. If the paint becomes too thick, thin the entire mixture. Avoid the erratic deterioration caused by the "thin-as-you-go" method.

Chapter 7

Practice Surfaces

At this stage of progress it is assumed that you have spent considerable time practicing on cardboard with red sables and tempera colors. Therefore, the time that you now spend working on cardboard, paper, etc. can be comparatively short. This practice should continue only until such time as you develop a "feel" for the different types of brushes and paint to be used.

Very soon you should begin practice on surfaces similar to those you will be required to work upon as a signpainter.

One suggested surface might be a smooth panel such as overlaid plywood or a similar material. Any smooth, non-absorbent surface is satisfactory. The surface chosen must be such that it can withstand the constant use of the various solvents that will be employed to remove the practice lettering.

Should overlaid plywood be chosen, this must first be painted a light color, preferably white. This can be done with bulletin color paints and in doing so follow the directions printed on the label of the paint can. The panel should be of a size that can be comfortably handled, perhaps 2 feet by 3 feet. This type of panel, when properly painted, quite closely approximates the surfaces that will confront you in the early months of doing actual sign work. This would include such surfaces as truck doors, real estate signs, and other small commercial sign panels.

The practice procedures are quite the same as those previously used on cardboard, with several exceptions.

In initial practice work, to avoid unnecessary eyestrain, you were allowed to make heavy layout lines. It is now advisable to become accustomed to professional methods. Poor procedure habits, if used for a long period, can become deeply implanted and difficult to discard.

Therefore, the first exception here would be to draw the horizontal guidelines very lightly with pencil. The lettering should then be indicated by using soft, round charcoal sticks. These tentative layout marks should be applied lightly. If layout changes are needed, these marks can easily be wiped off with a soft rag.

Once the layout is in correct position, many signpainters will lightly pencil the preliminary charcoal marks and wipe off the original charcoal. This is done because the charcoal will sometimes discolor bright colors such as red, etc. This is especially true should the charcoal layout be too heavy.

The second exception is that the same panel must be used over and over. For obvious reasons it would be impractical to use a new panel for each practice session.

When the practice panel is filled with strokes or lettering, the manner in which you prepare it for further use is optional. The panel can be washed off with rags and solvents such as gasoline, mineral-spirits or any paint thinner and is immediately ready for further use. This should be done in a well ventilated area with ever present concern for the fire hazard involved.

The alternative is to allow the practice work to dry and then to repaint the panel with bulletin color. The time lapse necessary for drying all but rules out this procedure as a practical method for concentrated continuation of practice.

DARK COLORED SURFACES. In line with this type of practice, it is advisable to prepare a second panel with a dark colored background such as red, black or blue. This will afford the opportunity to practice with the various high-cover lettering enamels. You will find that it requires much more time and patience to letter with light colors upon a darker surface.

For any acceptable degree of one-stroke coverage the paint must be mixed to the correct consistency. The strokes must be applied with a high degree of efficiency and the lettering must be "nursed" along a bit to achieve good coverage. This requires a feather-touch at times that can only be acquired through dedicated practice and experience.

The strokes must be executed quickly and confidently. Any clumsiness of stroke or slow, painstaking procedure will result in poor coverage, paint pile-up and mottled areas on the letter-strokes.

To obtain perfect coverage it is sometimes necessary to allow the lettering to dry and apply a second coat. This is referred to as "double-coating." It is especially difficult to achieve one-coat coverage with the true, bright yellow lettering colors. Pastel lettering colors such as the pale blues, greens, grays, etc. seldom present a problem. Usually, these provide excellent coverage. Also, it is difficult, if not impossible to get perfect one-coat coverage on large or built-up letters.

The layout work on dark panels can be done with soft white blackboard chalk. With a single-edged razor blade or similar sharp cutting tool, shave the end of the chalk stick roughly on each side to a blunt, chisel-shaped tip. Then rub each flat side of the chalk alternately back and forth across a piece of sandpaper, preferably a sanding-block or device, to "hone" the marking end to a finely chiseled, knife-line edge. Repeat this sanding process as necessary whenever the edge of the chalk becomes blunt and no longer draws a fine line.

These are several of the reasons why it is advisable to extend the practice work to a dark colored panel. Incidentally, the background color of any sign is referred to in the trade as the "field-color".

CONSISTENCY OF LETTERING PAINTS.

As practice work graduates to the permanent sign mediums, such as these panels, the proper consistency of the lettering color becomes an important factor.

Bulletin colors of the highest quality, for example, cannot provide maximum durability if thinning is excessive. All paints must retain as much of the original body as possible in order to withstand the attack of the elements.

In early practice you were advised to thin the paint to a greater degree when working on surfaces such as cardboard, paper, etc. This was suggested only as a method to facilitate practice, and also, even in actual use the finished product can never be any more durable than the cardboard itself. Generally, even the thinnest of workable permanent paints will outlast the cardboard.

Excessive thinning cannot be tolerated in any phase related to the production of permanent signs. This applies to all paints used throughout the entire process of preparing all signs where durability is a requisite. Included, are primers, finish coats, etc.

For the moment, this concern will be confined to lettering colors. These colors should be thinned only to the extent necessary to allow for lettering efficiency. The paint should retain enough body to assure durability and still flow freely from the lettering brush. If there is too much drag, or the brush does not release the paint with sufficient ease to form sharp letter-edges, it is then too thick. This especially applies to curved strokes where free paint release is necessary.

It seems advisable to mention that the reverse of excessive thinning can be a problem. The novice will frequently attempt to work with lettering colors that are much too thick. This is quite common when working with light colored paints upon a dark surface. In the attempt to achieve perfect one-stroke coverage, the beginner will try to "load" the color upon the surface. This logic will be based on the thought that a thick, heavily pigmented mixture is bound to cover. The results will prove otherwise.

Actually, a thick, heavy mixture of paint will result in very poor coverage. Smooth, well covered letters depend upon good paint distribution. This particularly applies to the lighter shades of the high cover lettering enamels. Better coverage can be expected when the paint is thinned to proper consistency. In fact in this particular procedure you might find that the most effective consistency will be thinner than you would normally expect. Also, if the work is prolonged the paint will thicken somewhat as the work progresses. You must then add a bit of thinner occasionally and again stir the mixture. You will learn through experience when this is necessary. The paint will become sticky in substance and cause a greater pull on the lettering brush. Things such as this will also vary with different brands and colors.

A CLASSIC EXAMPLE.
It is always a temptation, even among veterans, to thin the paint excessively in the interest of speed. Maximum lettering speed can be attained in this way.

For example, several years ago I watched a younger sign painter lettering one of several cement-block walls. The design involved a pictorial of a comic baker, a very large, sweeping script, plus the average lettering. Working with both fitches and cutters, his speed was far above average. The layout was rather haphazard, yet attractive and professional.

This set of circumstances and the involvements are immediately apparent to the veteran sign painter.

In this case, from a 50-foot viewpoint, my deductions were as follows: Although I could match his speed, I could do so only with the use of excessively thinned bulletin colors. Because of this young man's apparent professionalism, I realized that he was aware of the layout faults. In the interest of speed, he did not bother to adjust the layout but compensated instead.

To put it bluntly, this was a "dynamite job." Since he was from out-of-town, he couldn't care less about durability. When premature paint break-down occurred he would be miles away. His color set-up was flamboyant enough to divert the attention of the layman from the faults within the layout. These would immediately be noticeable to another professional. In fact this young man knew and was using every short cut known to the sign trade in regard to speed, quick completion, and the "fast buck".

Upon closer contact, all of these earlier deductions proved to be correct.

These signs soon began to lose brilliance of color; the gloss was lost in a matter of weeks. Now, a little over 2 years later the present condition of these signs proves the point. The colors have reached a high degree of transparency and color breakdown.

Chances are that in his permanent locality, this young signman would have used full-bodied colors and corrected the layout. Because in his own vicinity he would most likely be held accountable for this lack of durability. Also, other professionals would very soon point out the obvious layout faults to the customer.

This sort of thing is not uncommon. Certain signmen do excellent work in their own vicinity, but do nothing but "knock-out" jobs in the hinterlands.

Fortunately, reliable sign firms do not resort to this practice. This is why they remain in business year after year and become a credit to the sign industry.

This example was related mainly to prove that to build up a good reputation in your territory you must use good procedure.

Most paints are composed of two basic elements—the pigment and the bonding agent. Break these down and the remaining chemical content cannot possibly provide its original durability. Although some speed must be sacrificed in order to use a full-bodied mixture, this is necessary if you hope to build up a reputation for reliability.

Therefore, at the very start of practice work it is to your advantage to use all materials conscientiously and in keeping with reliable procedures. Effective shortcuts are fine, but poor working methods serve only to abuse your personal reputation and discredit the entire sign trade.

THE GLASS PRACTICE SURFACE. In the field of general sign painting you will eventually be required to work upon dozens of various surfaces.

During early development, however, the work should be confined to the least complicated and commonly used surfaces. The initial signwork that you do for pay will be done upon surfaces similar to the panels previously discussed and upon glass.

Therefore, within the period during which you do practice upon these painted panels it is advisable to alternately extend this practice to glass panels. The methods used in this effort depend upon the number of glass panels available to you.

The glass necessary for practice can be secured in many ways. New glass can be purchased, but there are other possible sources. It is possible to contact glass installation firms and to buy sections of glass that are stained or flawed, with no salvage value. Old storm windows are often available at rummage sales, etc. You might use your own storm windows, or practice upon the windows of your work-room or shop. The availability of glass should not be a great problem.

The actual mechanics of working on glass can vary. Let us assume that you have a plain, movable glass panel. This panel can be placed on the work-bench with a piece of white poster paper beneath it to provide for excellent visibility. A piece of paper can be taped directly to the reverse side of the glass instead. In both cases, the guidelines and layout can be placed either upon the paper or applied directly to the face of the glass.

Another method would be to paint the reverse side of the glass with a light color and to practice upon the clear glass on the opposite side.

Should the windows of the work-room or shop be used during daylight hours, the light from without will provide a natural background. This method of practice also approximates conditions that will commonly be encountered during your career as a sign painter. The only difference here would be that, under such conditions, on an actual job, the lettering would be done in reverse or backwards in order to be readable from the exterior.

However, no attempt should be made to accomplish reverse lettering this early in the training period.

The removal of the practice work to permit further use of the panel is always a factor. This is optional. Should you have but one glass panel available, the lettering must then be washed off to free the area for continued practice. But the very nature of glass makes it more convenient to have a number of panels. The lettering can then be allowed to dry. Later, the paint can easily be shaved off with a single-edged razor blade within a holder. This is the most practical method and less messy.

Otherwise, the procedure for practice work on glass is quite similar to the other methods.

For marking directly upon the glass it is not advisable to use the heavy grease pencils. These are much too heavy for utmost accuracy. Also, grease and paint are not compatible. In actual signwork, the letter-edges will break down wherever the paint overlaps the grease pencil underlay.

There are a number of excellent "mark-on-anything" pencils available for layout purposes. Most of these can be sharpened to a precise point in a pencil sharpener. You need only read the descriptive copy of the pencils in the supply catalogs to determine their adaptability. The graphite, graduated, pencil is excellent for marking on glass when a dark line is adaptable.

Also, do not confine the practice lettering to the thinner types of glass. Extend the work to include heavy plate-glass.

When the layout lines are directly on the surface, there is no difference. But, suppose that you prepare the layout on a piece of white paper and place it beneath the glass. Since plate-glass is quite thick, you must look directly at the layout as the lettering proceeds. Should you follow the layout from an oblique position, the letters will not correspond with the layout when viewed head-on. The thickness of the glass will cause considerable variance and distortion.

Each stroke must be executed with the vision directed absolutely straight ahead at the layout lines.

When working on glass, most sign painters prefer to use soft, rather than snappy brushes. With the use of pencil-quills, for example, some signmen use brown quills in preference to gray. Others use gray quills almost exclusively for commercial sign painting.

During the practice work described in the preceding pages, it is advisable to consider the three basic hand-positions as discussed in Chapter Three. Try to incorporate these methods within your practice. In this way you can gradually become familiar with all of these techniques.

Chapter 8

The Basics of Elementary Layout

Without personal contact, it is difficult to say when a novice is ready to accept sign painting for pay.

No definite time period could be suggested in terms of weeks or months. This would depend upon individual development of skill, adaptability to the work, and upon the ability to absorb general knowledge.

At such time as you can correctly execute the complete one-stroke Gothic alphabet and have a genuine understanding of everything that has been written up to this point, you can begin to accept sign work on a very limited basis.

The reference here, would be to signs of minimum complication. Included, would be small, plain panels such as, "For Sale" signs and very simple truck lettering. For example, trucks that are to be identified only with no desire on the owners part for advertising impact.

This initial acceptance of work might extend to simple identification lettered upon the glass of office doors, etc.

If your practice work still demands "tongue-biting" effort you are not yet ready to accept sign work for pay.

However, if you do feel capable, follow these additional words of advice in regard to spacing and elementary layout.

Do not crowd the lettering into the available space. Allow for comfortable margins on both sides of the copy and at top and bottom. At first it is best to center each line of copy. The important parts of the message should predominate and therefore be larger. The incidental copy can be smaller, proportionate to its importance.

Study the sample layout No. 1 as shown in Fig. 18. The words "For Sale" are most important, so the letters are bold and large.

How do we determine the importance of the copy? Unless the customer specifies otherwise, the emphasis of the copy is determined by logical reasoning.

Let us suppose that this sign is mounted in front of a home which is to be sold. The primary concern is to advise the driver passing by that the property is for sale. If the reader of the sign is not interested in the property the layout is immaterial.

But should the viewer be interested in the property, he will then read the entire message. He will perhaps stop immediately and converse with the owner. If he is pressed for time, he might merely stop long enough to jot down the phone number and when convenient call the owner.

If the name of the owner was listed on the sign, the passerby would most likely commit the name to memory and later consult the phone book for the number. In such case the phone number would not be of great importance. But since this sign does not identify the owner, the phone number does become a vital part of the message and the numbers are quite large.

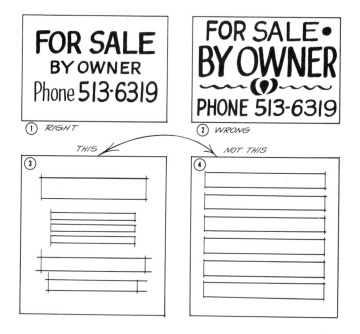

FIG. 18. Layout should aim for expression and eye-appeal.

In regard to phone numbers, many sign painters feel, as I do, that phone numbers on most signs are a waste of space. This especially applies to trucks. It is doubtful if anybody will remember a phone number listed upon a vehicle. But truck owners feel that this is of some consequence and generally insist upon its application.

THE MECHANICS OF ELEMENTARY

LAYOUT. At this point of progress you should strive for neat, sharp simplicity. Shading and outlining should be avoided. Do only those things that you can do well.

Study both the right and wrong layouts on Figure 18. The layout No. 1 shows the value of generous margins and the ample amount of space between each line. It also shows the dignity provided by simplicity.

Compare the first layout with that of No. 2. There are numerous faults in the second layout. The margins are much too skimpy and the lettering is crowded. The emphasis is placed on the wrong parts of the message. The word "Phone" is too close to the numbers. This space would be sufficient if lower case letters had been used in the word "phone" as it appears in the first layout.

The layout of the words "For Sale" contains a fault most common to the novice. The letters in the word "For" were applied and it then became evident that the word "Sale" would not fill the remaining space. The final four letters were progressively expanded in an effort to further compensate for the excessive space. Faults such as this should be corrected in the layout process and not during the actual lettering.

There is also no need for the rippled cross-lines or the clumsy attempt to place a decorative symbol below the letter W. This sort of thing is referred to as "gingerbread" in the sign trade. Do not confuse this example with the well designed decorative effects that are intelligently used by professional sign painters.

At all times there should be a planned and definite reason for decorations. A plain, well executed sign is better by far than an unskilled attempt to embellish the work with meaningless scrolls, dots and flourishes.

Early in your career, develop the habit of being your "own worst critic." To back up this statement, let me point out a careless error of my own. On the layout No. 1, notice the words "For Sale". The letters L and E in the word "Sale" are too wide to correctly correspond to the width of the preceding letters.

When any person can no longer find fault with his own work, he has lost the ability to learn.

The two layout forms No. 3 and No. 4 show the correct and incorrect methods to be used for distribution of copy.

The six copy areas shown on layout No. 4 result in a monotonous sign. This layout would of course find its place on building directories and on other listings where uniformity was specified. However, in general sign work, extreme similarity of line such as this, does not allow for the "punch" necessary to emphasize the key words or copy-lines. Nor, does it afford the opportunity to subdue the secondary copy according to its importance.

Compare this layout to that of No. 3. Notice how the copy areas vary in size to allow for variations of copy predominance. Also study the procedure used to break down the copy into isolated areas. This technique of copy-grouping is a most basic factor in regard to good layout and extends beyond sign painting to include magazine and newspaper advertising and most forms of graphic arts.

When planning this type of layout, the copy must be carefully edited before it is broken down into separate copy blocks. You would not divide a sentence or a connected thought and place part of it into another grouping. All the words within these groupings should be closely related.

The exception to this would be a group of rather abstractly connected words. For example, in connection with a lounge, the three smaller lines near center could be successively used for such words as, "Excellent Food," "Cocktail Bar," and "Air Conditioned." So, actually this simple layout alone can form the basis for many signs, whether they be for a boiler factory or a beauty salon.

COMMENTARY. To sum up, do not at any time crowd the lettering too close to the edges of the sign or the available lettering area. It is better procedure to reduce the size of the lettering than to hug the edges.

For example, on a panel measuring 18 by 24 inches there should be at least a 2-inch margin on all four edges. More space should be allowed if possible, especially at top and bottom.

In regard to predominance of copy, the intelligent use of color can be effective. Use bold, bright colors for emphasis and subdued colors for secondary purposes.

Do not attempt to do fancy layouts beyond your capability. In no case should you accept sign work for pay until such time as you can do the lettering with a minimum of effort and with full knowledge of the materials and instruction covered up to this point.

Chapter 9

The Thick-and-Thin Alphabet

Early in this book it was pointed out that you would be taught two of the most basic printed alphabets, plus a simplified utility script.

At such time as you have learned and mastered the execution of these three alphabets you will be sufficiently equipped to cope with much of the sign work that comes your way.

We will now consider the second alphabet in this preliminary group. Much as it is with Gothic lettering, this alphabet too is difficult to pinpoint with a single correct name. (See Fig. 19)

This letter-style and versions of it are referred to by many names. At various times these versions are referred to as Gothic Bold, Franklin Gothic, Grotesque, Modified Roman, Sans-Serif Roman, etc.

In sign painter's parlance it is commonly nick-named "thick-and-thin." Since I was taught that all letters with strokes of uniform width are basically Gothic and, that letters with thick and thin components are classified as Roman, I must abide by this teaching.

For the benefit of the beginner, the word "serif" applies to the flanges or spurs that branch off from the stroke-endings of the letter. These serifs are present on the type face you are now reading.

The word "sans" is an archaic term for the word "without." Therefore, when an alphabet is referred to as "sans-serif" it means, in effect, "without spurs." Consequently, the name "Sans-Serif Roman" would imply that the letters are basically Roman without the customary spurs.

Although the serif is usually a common characteristic of the true Roman alphabet, logic tells me that with the advent of diversified lettering instruments and brushes these spurs were in some cases eliminated. This resulted in a more simplified letter, but retained the stroke variances common to Roman lettering.

Therefore, my preference would be to call this alphabet "Sans-Serif Roman." But, because most sign painters, including myself, quite simply refer to this as "thick-and-thin" it seems advisable to do so here. Perhaps the early day lettering artists adopted this very name in an attempt to avoid the constant arguments surrounding the true name of this alphabet.

**ABCDEF
GHIJKL
MNOPQ
RSTUVW
XYZ234
56789 &**

FIG. 19. Sign Painters' Thick and Thin Alphabet.

A VERSATILE ALPHABET. The name of a letter-style is really not too important. The manner in which the alphabet is put to use should be the primary concern.

Regardless of name, the thick-and-thin alphabet provides the lettering artist with a style of lettering that allows for practical, interesting, and diversified layout. This spurless letter requires less horizontal space and furnishes the necessary flexibility for condensation when this is required.

The plain simplicity of this alphabet is of great advantage when very bold letters are desired. The space normally occupied by the serifs can instead be used to expand the width of the downstrokes, or thick elements of the letters. Because of this, the utmost boldness is possible.

The versatility of this alphabet is almost limitless. Equal to its adaptability in regard to condensation and boldness is the flexibility it provides for maximum expansion. It is especially suitable when you are required to letter a very short word on a long horizontal panel with little height. With a few exceptions, these letters can be expanded to a great degree and still retain good form.

Upon larger signs, where letters 6 inches in height or larger are required, this alphabet is almost as common in usage as one-stroke Gothic. This thick-and-thin alphabet is an old standby in the sign trade. It was popular many years before my time, is still used extensively, and will no doubt be a favorite alphabet as long as there is a need for signs.

This alphabet has also been the springboard for many modifications and you need only to page through any catalog of alphabets to see that it has been used as a nucleus for numerous other alphabets.

STUDY OF THE ALPHABET. The long and continued acceptance of the thick-and-thin alphabet is due to its adaptable characteristics.

The lettering plate as shown in Fig. 19 is but one version of this alphabet. There seems to be no one, single, absolutely correct version of this lettering-style. For example, let us assume that you were to ask five topnotch sign painters to enter separate rooms and prepare a lettering plate for the thick-and-thin alphabet, plus numerals, etc. Upon completion, it is doubtful if any two of the five resultant plates would be the same. Similar perhaps, but not identical.

Although all five plates would be fundamentally correct, each lettering artist would impart to the lettering an individual technique developed through the years. You would most likely notice a slight variance on every letter and numeral on each of the five plates. Still you could not point to any one character and say, "This is incorrect," because each sample would be skillfully done and acceptable as a good version of the alphabet. The results of such an experiment would be quite the same with most alphabets.

So it is in this sense that we now study the mechanics of this version of the thick-and-thin alphabet. As a beginner, it is suggested that you practice these preliminary alphabets as illustrated. Additional instruction is being offered occasionally only to provide you with a better understanding of the alphabets. The various modifications, etc. should not be attempted until later, after a period of experience.

Previously, we discussed the flexibility of this alphabet in regard to expanded letters and condensed letters. There are limits to this and these limits are often determined by the letters to be used upon the particular job that you are doing.

So, before beginning a layout you must consider the letters in the copy to be lettered. If extreme expansion is desired, you will find that the thickness of the bold, or center stroke, of the letter S will determine the maximum width of the thick elements of all the letters within this part of the layout. Especially on a long, expanded letter with very little height, the bold strokes of the letter S must be thin enough to allow room for the thinner, curved strokes at top and bottom and for the space in between.

Therefore, to maintain uniformity, the thick strokes of the adjacent letters are limited in width to the maximum width of the wide stroke of the letter S.

If the lettering is extremely squat, you may find it wise to abandon the thick-and-thin alphabet in favor of one that has letters of uniform stroke, such as Gothic.

The width of the thinner strokes are generally determined by the letter E. The three horizontal cross-strokes of this letter must be thin enough to allow a comfortable amount of space in between each stroke. For convenience, let us assume you are considering a letter $7\frac{1}{2}$ inches in height. If you decided on a stroke width of $1\frac{1}{2}$ inches, these three strokes would consume $4\frac{1}{2}$ inches of the space. This would leave 3 inches to be divided for the two spaces between the strokes, or $1\frac{1}{2}$ inches. So, the strokes and spaces, which are five in number would each be $1\frac{1}{2}$ inches.

Regarding both the thick and thin strokes, the letter B poses the biggest problem, especially on a squat, extended letter. If the letter B does exist within the copy to be lettered, it is advisable to first experiment with this letter. This must be done to determine the width of the strokes possible. The available height should allow you to design a presentable letter B. The requirements for this would be two graceful curves, or loops, a sufficient amount of blank space for the centers of the loops, with the thin strokes still generous enough to be attractive and easy to read.

The letter B is most difficult to design in this squat, extended form. It might be necessary to decrease the width and to leave more space between each letter. If the vertical space is not sufficient enough to accommodate a well-designed letter B, it will again be necessary to switch to a thin-stroke alphabet. In all cases, when the letter B is present, the stroke widths of all adjacent letters depend upon what it is possible to do with the letter B.

If none of the "problem-letters" are present in a line of copy, then extreme expansion is simple. This would apply to letters such as H, L, and T, among others. It is also possible to use very wide strokes on the thick elements in such cases.

The letters M and W can often be expanded to gain a considerable amount of space, but not to the point of gross distortion.

This is about as far as we shall proceed for the present with the characteristics of this alphabet. Much more could be written about the possibilities and restrictions pertinent to this letter style. More advanced information will be provided as you progress in this study and at such time as is necessary.

PRACTICE OF THE ALPHABET. The actual mechanics of practice in regard to this alphabet are basically the same as those used for Gothic. The big difference lies in the fact that this is a "built-up" type of letter. Therefore, you must now extend your knowledge to include proper use of double-line, or full-outline layouts. Up to this point all the work has been confined to single-line layouts.

No specific practice height is suggested. By now you should have enough experience to choose the height that is most adaptable to your personal method of procedure.

At first, you might find a 5-inch practice height to be ideal. After you do become familiar with the alphabet it is advisable to lower this practice height to 3 or even to 2 inches. In actual sign work this letter style is used in both very small and in extremely large form.

Fig. 20 illustrates several layout procedures. Throughout this discussion, for convenience, the instruction will pertain to a white painted panel.

After determining the available horizontal width, draw the main cross guidelines at top and bottom. Use a stick of soft charcoal and with very light strokes, begin to indicate the letter-positions. You will perhaps find it necessary to remove and to reapply this tentative layout several times, adjusting the letters with each application.

At such time as the charcoal layout places the letters in proper position, you can then lightly draw over the charcoal

lines with a pencil for a precise outline. The original charcoal lines are then removed.

In this layout process, many sign painters use two strips
of cardboard. One strip is of the same width as the wide
strokes and the other corresponds to the narrow strokes.
You would alternately place the strips over the charcoal
layout and draw pencil lines on each side of the strip. This
method avoids much measurement and results in uniform
strokes. Do not discard these strips. Mark the width directly
upon each strip, punch a hole in each end and hang these
on a nail. Gradually, you will accumulate strips of every
size, to be available for further use.

You will observe on the word "WORK" in Fig. 20 that
the straight lines are solid and the curved lines are broken.
In all layout preparation, you will find that it is easier to
indicate all curved lines with the broken-line technique than
with the continuous line.

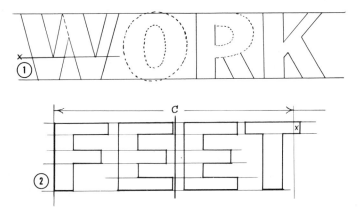

*FIG. 20. In (1) note that it is easier to use dots, rather than
lines, on curves, how the O extends above and below guide-lines
and the W is two Vs. In (2) extending the cross-stroke of the T
beyond layout area gives visual balance; there is less space between the E and T than the other letters; where there are
numerous cross-strokes, guide-lines can continue across several
letters.*

Also note on the sample layout No. 1, that the letter W
is actually two letters V joined together. It is a general
rule of thumb that two Vs joined together result in a presentable letter W. This rule cannot always apply as would
be the case should the letters be condensed to a great degree.

The letter O should slightly extend both above and below

the guidelines as shown. This is an optical rule of layout that applies to all round letters such as the letters, C,G,O,Q,S, etc. If the letter O were to be placed precisely between each guideline it would optically appear to be smaller than the adjacent straight letters. The slight extension of round letters compensates for this illusion.

It is quite common for beginners and even some veterans to overdo this trick of layout. All professional layout gimmicks, such as this, should be conservative and must never be distorted beyond the limits of good design.

The extra line across the letter W, marked with an X, is merely to show that the companion peaks should be symmetrical. A line such as this within the layout assures this desired conformity.

The No. 2 illustration of the word "FEET" depicts several layout helps. Frequently, a word or line of copy will contain letters with a profuse number of cross strokes. It is then advisable to draw light, continuous lines across the entire face of the copy, sufficiently long to indicate these strokes as they occur.

Note also, that a small section of the letter T, marked X, extends beyond the right side of the copy area.

If this were not done, the entire word would appear to be off center. The excess of white space on the right side of the letter T demands this extension. This same technique would apply to the word, "FEEL," in which case the letter L would likewise be extended.

If the word "FEED" had been used here, it would then have been proper to keep the word within the confines of the copy area. Such extensions are used only when a copy line begins or ends with an open letter such as L and T. To a lesser degree, this applies to certain slanted letters, such as the letters A, W, and Y. The letter J is only affected when it occurs as the first letter of a word-grouping. If four full letters had been used in this illustration, the center line would then have appeared at an exact halfway point between the two center letters.

There is also less space between the letters E and T, compared to the space allowed between the preceding letters. This, too, is to compensate for the open nature of the letter T. When necessary, the space between the letter T and adjacent letters can be minimized more than is shown here and still be acceptable.

The opposite would be true, if the word "FEEL" had been used in Fig. 20. The space between the letters E and L would have been greater than that between the other letters. If not, the letter L would appear to be squeezed against the letter E.

The foregoing comments have been written in an effort to impress upon you the extreme importance of optical spacing and layout. With a few exceptions, mechanical spacing is of small value in either the field of sign painting or in commercial art.

THE SEQUENCE OF BRUSH STROKES.

Many instructors and authors place much stress on the sequence of strokes and efficiently depict each brush maneuver with well conceived clarity. My admiration for these people and their talent is profound.

At the risk of much criticism, and only after much thought, I choose to bypass this effort.

In my opinion, it is no more possible to dictate each and every stroke to a new sign painter than it is to control another person's handwriting. If you are now in the midst of a type of instruction that does involve a prescribed stroke sequence, please do not abandon this effort. It is not my intent here to disrupt any course of study that you might be receiving from a most competent instructor. This is my opinion only, and it is my hope that you take it as such.

The fact that a series of stroke sequences can work well for a highly skilled craftsman does not mean that another can successfully duplicate this technique.

Regardless of how conscientiously the novice sign painter attempts to copy the strokes, finger positions, etc. of his teacher, the physical and mental characteristics of each individual will invariably nullify the effort.

Each new sign painter eventually develops his personal methods of working. The structure of the fingers, the wrist, the arm, etc. might prohibit the execution of the brush strokes as illustrated in books or even as demonstrated in personal instruction.

Also, the lettering brushes, etc. must be a factor. The instructor might be highly skilled in the use of a certain series of quills, while the student adapts more quickly to flat-type lettering brushes. It would be impractical to list the countless pros and cons of this subject.

Some young people might make great progress by following a set sequence of stroke developed by another. However, the diversity of human nature and the natural tendency to improvise in order to bring the impossible into the realm of possibility would eventually prevail.

Therefore, it would seem that the beginner alone should be the best judge of what constitutes his most effective manner of lettering. After prolonged practice and experimentation he should be able to determine which sequences of strokes are most comfortable for him to accomplish. He will also know which hand positions allow for the most facile use of his fingers. All of this effort must, in every case, adhere to the other basic fundamentals of sound procedure. Because of this, the actual manipulation of the brush will here be confined only to the bare essentials.

A well defined layout is a primary factor. You were previously advised to pencil the corrected charcoal layout. This is mainly for ease of early practice. Most professionals would letter directly over the charcoal. Few would pencil the layout unless absolute preciseness was required. There are also other reasons why the charcoal layout must be removed.

In regard to brushes, use the highest quality brushes you can possibly buy. Use the style of brush that you can handle most effectively. Try to develop a sequence that requires the least number of strokes. Load the brush with lettering paint of free-flowing consistency and try to accomplish the longest possible strokes in single, confident, sweeping movements.

Clumsy, unprofessional letters are generally the result of choppy, painstaking strokes. Smooth graceful letters are the result of the least number of expert strokes. The paint should be clean, free of grit, lumps, etc. It should be strained if necessary.

The beginner has a tendency to use brushes too small for the letters involved. When practicing the thick-and-thin lettering, try to use a brush at least as wide as the thin stroke. You can then do such strokes with one motion to form the body of the stroke. If the letters are under 6 or 7 inches, you can usually do the entire letter without using a larger brush for fill-in purposes.

For example, on a 6-inch letter, I would use a No. 20 gray jumbo quill for the entire letter. If you use flats, then choose a brush of similar size. The larger quills and flats are difficult to master. It is well worth the effort, because once you do learn to use these proficiently, the time that you save will more than compensate for any extra hours spent in practice.

Early in practice you were advised to use bulletin colors. As a secondary measure, you can use any of the high-quality permanent poster colors, especially if you are practicing upon paper or cardboard. Do not confuse this type of paint with tempera or showcard colors.

Bulletin colors were suggested because the biggest portion

of your work in general sign painting will be done with these colors.

Study the lettering plate, Fig. 19, thoroughly. Copy the letters over and over until you can do so from memory.

This thick-and-thin alphabet is nearly as essential as your tool-kit. You will find much use for this good old standby throughout your entire career as a sign painter.

Chapter 10

Introduction To Script

For both the beginner and the veteran, the subject of script seems to hold more fascination than any other style of lettering.

One of the most frequently asked questions by the beginner is, "How long does it take to learn how to do a decent script?" Another familiar comment might be, "Boy, no matter how hard I try, I can't seem to come up with a good script."

Any attempt to explain the many varieties of script would result in a very large book. Even if a group of skilled lettering artists were to pool their efforts and transcribe their combined knowledge into book form, the result could not completely cover the subject of script.

Through such an endeavor, it would be possible to cover the traditional and standard scripts. Also, many of the existent casual scripts could be presented. This would indeed be a most excellent book.

But, it will never, at any time, be possible to include all of the existent scripts within the course of any instruction. Every professional sign painter in the country has developed several scripts of his own. Since there is no limit to variety in regard to script, new styles are constantly being developed. This is the result of individual effort, widespread in nature, and therefore, the subject of script can never be confined within the pages of any single book.

Experienced lettering artists realize this fact. They do not expect to find such a book, nor will the lack of it cause any concern. Even the most expert signpainters are not expected to be familiar with an unlimited variety of scripts. This variety need only be sufficient enough to provide a pleasant versatility.

As a novice sign painter you will discover that it is possible to do a substantial amount of sign painting with a workable knowledge of one simple utility script. Added to the two alphabets you have already learned, the ability to letter in script style will equip you with enough variety to do simple, but attractive sign work.

It is essential to extend your talents to include at least one script. This provides the necessary flexibility needed to put professional "snap" into the work. The use of printed letters alone, will often result in a monotony of layout that can effectively be eliminated with a well-placed word or two of script.

There is a strange quirk present in the process of learning to letter in script style. At first, it is more difficult to learn how to gracefully letter the script forms, as compared to the printed letters. As skill increases, quite the opposite is true.

At such time as you can letter script with effortless freedom of movement, you will gradually find yourself using script more frequently. Once mastered, script is actually faster to do and more easily accomplished than most printed letters. In fact, it is often used to save time and to speed up the work.

Upon personal contact and through correspondence, a small amount of disagreement has been encountered in regard to the difficulties of learning to letter in script style.

In rare cases, certain signmen have informed me that, for them, it was the easiest form of lettering to learn right from the start. Personally, I cannot recall having any undue problem with script. My first efforts with it were about equal to those with the printed letter. As it is with many sign painters, my favorite style of lettering is definitely script. The ability to adapt to any skill varies with each individual.

SIMPLIFIED SCRIPT FOR THE BEGINNER.
My first inclination when preparing this material was to use a "pencil-stroke" script for illustration. The strokes of this script are of uniform width throughout and similar to those of a ball-point pen. Although the pencil-stroke script would be easier for you to learn, it would merely be a continuation of the same brush technique previously used in the practice of one-stroke Gothic, extended to script form. This would not provide the opportunity for you to expand your versatility or to develop further skill with the brush.

Therefore, it seemed advisable to present a script that would provide a wider range of possibility.

The script as shown in Figs. 21 and 22 was developed expressly for use in this book. Actually, it could correctly be referred to as, "Orphan Script." It has purposely been simplified to the greatest degree possible without sacrificing too much professionalism.

The absolute purpose of this modified version is to provide a means for the beginner to approach the practice of script with the least amount of difficulty.

The script, as shown, would not be used by a professional. It is not necessarily a well designed script, but it will adequately serve the purpose of the beginner.

Difficult strokes have been kept at a minimum. The more complicated and graceful curves can be added as skill develops. Certain letters can later be abandoned and supplanted with the traditionally correct letter formations. Many of the letters are basically correct. These can be retained.

FIG. 21. "Orphan" Script.

The most pronounced deviation from the standard forms of script occurs within the capital letters, as shown in Fig. 21. Most of these letters have been severely modified for simplicity. In fact, quite a few are nothing more than printed letters in italic form. This is the major difference between this beginner's script and the traditional script.

Generally, these capital letters are more complicated, and consist of graceful curves to correspond in context to the lower-case letters. On this plate, the letters E, L, Z, and the second of the two letters J would be among the letters that might find a proper place within a standard script.

Professional sign painters would seldom use capital letters such as this within a rendition of script. The exception would be to save space. For example, the capital letter I is sometimes used in straight printed form to save room. Normally, the correct letter I contains graceful loops that do consume a considerable amount of space.

In regard to Fig. 21, about all you can do is study the letters carefully and copy them constantly, until such time as you can letter them from memory.

There are two examples of the letter J. The second is more complicated than the first. The letter L also has a simple alternate. The small letter S was inserted at bottom-right mainly to demonstrate the grace of curve that should gradually be developed as you progress. This small letter L shows the sweep of stroke so common to more advanced forms of script.

LOWER-CASE SCRIPT.
Most alphabet books illustrate script lettering in the ABC or complete alphabet form. As we now discuss the lettering on Fig. 22, you will notice that every letter of the alphabet is represented.

My logic in presenting this alphabet in this manner is based on the following fact: Seldom do we find certain letters connected, in actual use, as they occur in a sample of the alphabet from A to Z.

For instance, it would be difficult to find within any word, combinations such as, fgh, klm, or xyz. Because of this, the beginner often finds it difficult to properly connect the letters as they occur in an actual word or sentence. Fortunately, some instructors include sample words and sentences adjacent to the full alphabet. Others do not.

Therefore, it seemed advisable to present the entire alphabet, but to do so in word-form. In this way it is possible to show the letter connections as they are most apt to occur in everyday use.

The professional can modify any letter for satisfactory connection, or use a "broken line" technique to avoid awkward connections. A good example of the "broken-line" is evident on Fig. 22 in the word, "dozen."

Let us now consider the lettering as shown in Fig. 22. The letter C in the word "Special" can be replaced with No. 5. The letter B, No. 2 can be used as an alternate to the letter B in the word "Table." However, the connecting flange on the left side of No. 2 would then be eliminated. The adjoinment would depend on the preceding letter as it does in No. 5. Alternate letter Gs are shown in No. 3 and No. 4. The choice is yours.

Special | Phone
dozen | ajax b
Age ag | Table
few five | chh
Perfume | kno
isquik | Equity

FIG. 22. Every letter of the alphabet is represented here.

Three versions of the letter F are depicted. No. 6 is a simplified letter. No. 7 is a bit difficult for the beginner, but is more acceptable. An optional loop is indicated on No. 8. This loop can be adapted to replace the loop of the B, as in No. 5.

Two adaptions of the letter H are illustrated in No. 10 and No. 11. The use of these is optional. These are shown mainly to demonstrate how the connecting strokes to the left of each letter can be adapted to accommodate the preceding letter. This flexibility can be used on most letters to form proper connections.

No. 12 shows a more complicated form of the letter K than that shown at the end of No. 13. Both versions are interchangeable and could be used in either position.

No. 13 is a complicated version of the letter Q. The second letter Q, No. 14 is actually a diminished capital letter, but can, in this way, frequently be used to good advantage.

COMMENTARY. Again it must be pointed out that this "orphan-script" was developed for utility purposes. Beauty of design, although important, became secondary.

The lettering could have been simplified to a still greater extent, but to do this, one would too closely skirt the edges of good design.

This letter style was chosen because it is quite commonly used. The thickness of stroke, ranging from narrow to thin, provides great flexibility. With experience, you can maintain the basic form, but increase or decrease the stroke width to design either bold or light-line scripts.

Also, the practice of this graduated type of stroke improves the dexterity with which you manipulate the lettering brushes. This teaches you how to use the "whole" brush, not the heel. It is doubtful if anybody could execute an attractive script or any graduated letter by bearing down on the brush and using the heel.

The most vital factor in all lettering is to take advantage of the natural spring of the brush. The ability to use both the very tip and the fullness of the brush and to increase and decrease pressure will enable you to do much lettering without switching brushes. For example, all of the lettering on Figures 21 and 22 was originally done with one No. 4 gray lettering quill, using permanent-type poster color.

Some sign painters, especially on larger lettering, alternately use two brushes of different sizes for graduated script. This is common procedure and you might find it convenient to proceed this way.

The "heel-painter" usually switches brushes for each stroke-width.

The brush should be held with a light, confident grip or the flexibility of the fingers is hampered. Shaping of the brush on the palette is also important, as is the consistency of the lettering colors. Especially when working with script, free paint flow is necessary. Single-stroke execution results in the graceful sweep inherent to script. To go over the same line repeatedly can only result in a clumsy, belabored script. All neat, professional lettering depends on quick, capable strokes.

As it is in all lettering the strokes should be uniform and the slants should be of the same degree throughout the sequence.

It is advisable to include the practice of script, to a minor extent, within your early practice sessions. Gradually, increase this effort. Beginners have a tendency to try script too soon on salable work. Confine all script to practice, until such time as you can handle this type of lettering with confidence.

As we end this discussion of script, remember that this particular version was developed to be used only during the early period of your sign painting career.

It is intended to be a "stepping-stone" to better procedure. As practice progresses, you can gradually change over to the more acceptable forms that lead to a degree of perfection.

Chapter 11

Instruction On Lettering Pens

No preliminary study of sign painting would be complete without some reference to the reservoir-type lettering pens. The use of these pens is mainly confined to showcard work.

Even though you might plan to specialize in sign painting, and gradually eliminate showcard work, it is still advisable to learn how to use lettering pens. Especially, in a one-man shop, or even in a medium sized plant in a small city, it is almost impossible to bypass showcard work.

Suppose that you performed the general sign painting on a steady basis, for a large company. Occasions would arise that demanded showcard work. The refusal or the inability to do this work might result in the loss of all the work available from this firm. This is but one example, among many, that shows how vital it is to round out your knowledge.

Regardless of how you slant your career, it is recommended that you become familiar with at least the basics of pen and ink lettering.

The highly skilled sign painter becomes so adept at using brushes that he is capable of making very small letters by properly charging the brush with color, by shaping the brush on the palette and by expertly reducing or increasing pressure on the brush. Because of this skill, he will eventually use pens to a lesser degree. But in the interest of uniformity and speed he will indeed make use of pens when the nature of the work demands such use.

Since you, as a beginner, cannot expect to develop such skill in a short period of time, it will become essential to supplement this brush work by learning how to properly use the various pens necessary to handle all types of showcard work.

As training progresses it is advisable to develop this skill with pens during the same period of time that you develop skill with the brushes. Both techniques are necessary to become an efficient, all-around sign painter.

TYPES AND SIZES OF PENS. Most reservoir pens are available in eight different sizes in each style.

Each style has a pen point or nib shaped to form a certain type of stroke or letter. The most commonly used styles are, the round-nib, the oval, the flat and square.

The round-nib point is used mainly for the common single-stroke Gothic alphabets, consisting of uniform strokes with round endings.

The oval-nib is an excellent point to use for bold, single-stroke alphabets, either vertical or in Italic. The result is a thick and thin type of letter with the thin element being quite bold.

The flat-nib is extremely versatile, since it is adapted for thick and very thin Roman alphabets and text styles such as Old English. This style is also used for a variety of scripts, scrolls, cartooning, illustrating, etc.

The square-nib is for square-end single-stroke letters.

The illustration, Fig. 23, shows the use of three different pen styles. The first alphabet was done with a round-nibbed pen and is composed of simple, one-stroke Gothic letters. The final letter M is an alternate.

The second grouping was lettered with an oval-nib using a very fast one-stroke casual, Italic style. The word "Practice" was lettered with a flat-nib point.

ABCDEFGHIJKLMNO
ROUND NIB
PRSTUVWXYZ&?M
23456789 *ABCDEF
OVAL NIB
GHIJKLMNOPQRSTU
VWXYZ * Practice!
FLAT NIB

FIG. 23. Demonstration of lettering with three different styles of pens.

The need for pen and ink work in showcard writing comes about in this manner: You might have a card with a large, brush-lettered heading. Below this will be a block of descriptive copy consisting of 30 or 40 words. The available space might allow for half-inch letters. It is then practical to switch to pen and ink to letter this block of copy. This is good procedure whenever one is confronted with an abundance of small sized copy.

For practice work in pen and ink, the materials needed are few and inexpensive. You might start with the two most basic style pens at first, which are the round type and the oval type. The sizes No. 2, 3, 4, and 5 in each style will be sufficient, with pen holders for each. The flat-style and additional sizes can be added as your skill increases.

Also purchase a small bottle of standard India drawing ink. Do not use a poor grade of transparent, watery ink.

The working surface should not be as sharply slanted as that used for brush work. The pens must be free-flowing and depend on gravity for this factor. With this in mind, adjust the slant of the surface to the degree most suitable to your personal comfort.

A smooth, economical bristol board is satisfactory for practice, but it should be of a grade good enough to eliminate any "blotter-like" spreading of ink. (The correct term for this reaction is "capillary attraction.")

PRACTICE LETTERING WITH PENS.

The guidelines are drawn in the same manner used for brush practice. A T-square can be used for small work. The practice height of about ¾ in. is suggested and a round-nib B-4 or oval-nib D-4 might be used to begin with. It is a good idea to become familiar with both styles. You might find that a B-3 or D-3 is easier for you to manipulate.

At first you might prefer to concentrate on the various practice strokes. There is nothing wrong with immediately practicing the entire alphabets as illustrated. This is a matter of personal preference.

Try to master a freedom of arm movement. Do not bear down on the pen, but let it ride the surface smoothly.

Shake the ink bottle thoroughly before each use. Place a piece of scrap cardboard on work table next to the ink bottle. After dipping the pen into the ink, draw the pen across this cardboard several times to remove excessive ink and insure free-flow. Then make the strokes. Do this each time the pen is dipped. This eliminates the chance of a thicker letter from an overloaded pen and results in more uniformity of stroke.

Place a can or jar next to the ink bottle with just enough water within to cover the pen-portion. A pen will cake-up in a few minutes, so if you cease using a pen and switch to another, place the one just used, point down, in water.

Do this with each pen as soon as you finish using it. All of these can be cleaned out later by holding the pen under a running water faucet and gently brushing it with a toothbrush.

If you intend to again use the same pen in a short time, then wash it out immediately so the water dries out of it meanwhile. Shake or blow the excess water out of the pen after washing. If you wipe it with a cloth, check to be sure that no lint is caught between the flanges.

Around the tip of each pen holder, I wrap a small piece of masking tape with the number of the pen-point thereon. This is much easier to identify than the marking on the pen-flange.

Do not use old, dirty ink. Even the best inks, if not used frequently, become caked in the bottom of the bottle. Ink might chalk off if it becomes old or has been frozen, and certainly will not withstand erasing. If there is any doubt about the ink, throw it out! It is cheaper to buy a fresh bottle than to ruin a piece of work.

Pens may become damaged. If you are having undue difficulty with a pen, try another of the same size. If progress "bogs-down" it might be the tool, not you. This applies to both pen and brush.

For example, I have about five C-5 pens on hand, all in holders. Still, only one is my favorite, especially for illustration work. The others work, but I usually fall back on the old "trusty" which I have had for about 20 years. It is flexible from much use and good care. Every tool has a personality of its own. This type of pen, especially, seems to "mellow" with age. If these nibs are kept clean and well cared for they develop a flexibility that can only come from continued use. Recently I accidentally dropped my most favorite pen and damaged the point. When I tossed it into the garbage container, it was much like parting with an old friend.

Chapter 12

Earn While You Learn

At this stage of instruction you have reached the first plateau in your development as a sign painter.

The material offered so far, although elementary, provides all the essentials needed to begin to do a considerable amount of sign work for pay.

This is based on the assumption that you have followed the method of study suggested in the early part of this book.

The extent to which you can now produce salable sign work must therefore be based on the following assumptions:

(1) That you have read through the entire book in a cursory manner to give you an idea of what sign painting is all about. (Actual study was not to be attempted in this first reading. This preliminary reading was to be done in story book fashion).

(2) That you faithfully studied all procedures and adhered to them, except for minor adjustments to suit your individual manner of working.

(3) That you thoroughly studied the characteristics of each alphabet.

(4) That you have learned the fundamentals of proper spacing and layout.

(5) That you maintained a constant and concentrated routine of actual practice with both brush and pen.

(6) That you can now execute every letter of each alphabet with a reasonable degree of skill and in a professional manner.

(7) That you have committed much of the foregoing instruction to memory, and need only consult the book to occasionally refresh the memory.

It is hoped that you can place all of these assumptions into question form and answer each with a confident "yes!" If so, you can begin to sell your talents, and during the broad-form instructions to follow, you can indeed put some truth into the old cliche, "Earn while you learn."

Chapter 13
The Proper Approach

We now approach the broad and complex field of sign painting.

It would be impossible to gear this instruction to correspond to the planned efforts of each individual. Therefore, instruction will continue with the assumption adopted early in this book, that you plan to operate your own sign business.

The logic of this is based on the fact that knowledge needed to operate your own business must be broadest in scope. This affords the opportunity to provide the most complete and varied form of instruction.

Fortified with this type of instruction, those readers who plan to seek employment can quite easily adapt to most situations. The established sign plant offers many advantages. As a new employee, you need only learn to flex according to the requirements of your employer.

Generally, you will have access to materials and equipment, and the plus-factor of working with skilled veterans.

As a new operator, starting from scratch, you quite possibly will have few of these benefits. Therefore, you must not only have full knowledge of the most common traditional procedures, but also the ability to improvise.

Because of limited equipment and material, the small operator must be equipped with a good degree of diversified knowledge. This is essential in order to cope with the problems that normally would not confront the employee in an established sign plant.

The instructions to follow depart from the time-worn method of teaching each and every subject in theoretical context. Instead, this will be an effort to show you how to deal with the problems as they actually will occur in the process of your everyday work as a sign painter.

THE DEMANDS OF THE TIME. We are living in an age of progress. To keep pace, we cannot adhere to the hide-bound traditions of bygone days. This would require complete instruction in regard to every minor detail, even though such knowledge might seldom be required.

Consider the constant change in teaching as applied to our public school systems. This new form of progressive teaching is a demand of the times. A splendid example would be the small significance now placed upon handwriting. Years ago a continued study of penmanship was required and equal in importance to English, Mathematics, etc.

The demands of progress forced the need for faster academic development. Certain subjects were abandoned. Stress was placed upon others. The need for new study-courses became constant.

Personally, I cannot say why the study of handwriting was practically discontinued. However, few people among the masses can trace their earning power to the excellence or non-excellence of writing ability. Nor, are any great things achieved because of it.

Perhaps educators feel that once the student learns the very basic fundamentals of handwriting, he can develop this ability to the desired extent without further instruction.

This would not, of course, apply to those students who choose careers such as bookkeeping, accounting, etc. where skill of penmanship is essential. Also, should the student be highly talented, he may extend his study to calligraphy. He would then be a specialist.

This logic might very well be applied to the less important factors of sign painting. The stress in initial training should be placed upon the most commonly required forms of knowledge.

There is no intent here to downgrade the long range benefits of traditional knowledge. This is necessary to ultimately become a highly skilled technician in any field. As a sign painter, it would be ideal if you could learn all the facets of the trade right from the start. This would require prolonged and concentrated study.

Therefore, it is suggested that you as a novice sign painter, acquire the most commonly required knowledge. If you are mentally alert, you will automatically learn the finer points of the trade. This comes about as you progress, through observance, association and participation. Supplementary study can also speed your progress.

Should you choose to specialize, then all study can later be concentrated upon this effort. Even then, you will often have reason to be thankful that you first studied this broad form of sign painting.

Chapter 14

Skill Plus Common Sense

The first thing that enters the mind of the novice about to embark on a career as a sign painter is to learn how to use a lettering brush. You might assume that once you acquire a certain amount of skill with a brush, that you have it "made," and everything thereafter will be a breeze.

Fortunately for all of us, this is not so. If skillful brush-handling were all that one required to be a master sign painter, this would not be the exclusive type of trade that it is.

The importance of learning how to handle lettering brushes must not be minimized. Indeed, this is without question one of the most important qualifications you must have to be an expert craftsman. In fact, you should develop your lettering skill to a point where the brush seems to be almost a part of you. Develop your skill with a brush until you can twist it, twirl it, and toss it about in your fingers almost instinctively. This dexterity or "feel" for the brush might be compared to the skill of the master violinist in the handling of the bow.

It is difficult to say just what percentage brush handling contributes toward becoming a master sign painter. I'll go out on a limb and assume that this is about 50 per cent. The remaining 50 per cent might consist of other highly necessary components such as good design and layout and also a complete understanding of the characteristics of paints, materials and all the mediums with which you must work. To round out this percentage, let us not forget plain common-sense and integrity.

You, as a beginner, may have already discovered the importance of this second 50 per cent. If not, you soon will. For your benefit, let us briefly qualify the remarks of the preceding paragraph.

GOOD DESIGN AND LAYOUT, for instance, must be considered the "mother" of any really good sign. The best lettering artist in the world can not pull a poorly designed sign out of the "doldrums". If you begin with a poor layout, you have failed before you pick up the brush to make the first stroke.

UNDERSTANDING THE MATERIALS AND ME-
DIUMS is truly important, because with the wrong brush,
in the wrong paint, on the wrong surface, you will find it
impossible to do competent lettering, regardless of highly
developed lettering skill. Furthermore, the use of any combination of improper materials usually results in unsatis-
factory appearance, in addition to limited durability.

Each of us must understand the media we have used in
the past and are now using. Also, we must continue to stay
abreast and become familiar with the new materials being
placed on the market, including procedures for their proper
use.

COMMON SENSE must be considered a factor in all
trades and is something that you alone must develop. Quite
simply, it means that you should profit by trial and error.
The man who never made a mistake never did anything, but
one thing a man can do is to try to avoid making the same
error repeatedly.

Many times, 5 or 10 minutes of extra thought and
planning before beginning a sign job might later save hours.
It is ridiculous to begin any job until you know in your own
mind how to follow it through, step by step, to successful
completion.

Finally, we come to the word, "INTEGRITY." If you
look deeply enough, you will discover that integrity is the
tap-root of every successful business, large or small, in any
field of endeavor. You will not have to look very far to find
how frequently this applies to the sign business.

Let us consider a hypothetical case, such as might be
found in any average city. This would involve two sign
plant operators of equal ability in regard to talent and skill.
One operator always has an abundance of work, scarcely has
to advertise and perhaps never finds it necessary to solicit
work. The other fellow, with the same potential of business
available to him, is always "hungry" for work, short of jobs,
and spends a big share of his time soliciting work, many
times resorting to "hard-sell" methods, such as price cutting, etc.

A case such as this does not come about by accident. If
you check, you will find that the successful operator never
makes promises that he cannot keep. He uses the very best
materials available, plans his jobs carefully and is willing to
put forth a little extra effort to do a topnotch job—some
thing that raises the quality of his work above the commonplace. The value of the "word-of-mouth" advertising he
receives because of this high quality work repays him many
times over. The extra effort and consideration he extends to

his customers is not lost time, but a wise investment with a good return.

SLIGHTING THE WORK. The other fellow, who constantly complains about his business being "lousy," usually lacks integrity. Perhaps he does not even realize this, because shiftlessness shows up in many variations. He might, for instance, definitely promise to have a sign ready for his customer within a week, when he knows full well that he cannot possibly finish this sign within two or three weeks. This might cause great inconvenience to the customer, especially if such sign is intended for a "Grand Opening" or for any other timed event.

Another habit might be that of quoting a price of $40 for a job, and upon delivery attempting to jack the price up to $52.50, using a lame excuse for doing so. This same fellow may also present an impressive sketch to a customer and sell the job on this basis. Later, when doing the actual sign job, he might not abide by the sketch and cut so many corners that the finished sign has only a slight resemblance to the original sketch.

These are several of the less serious breaches of integrity and are not as flagrant as those of the completely unscrupulous operator. On quite a few occasions, I have heard men such as this say, in essence: "Don't make 'em so they last too long, or we won't get enough repeat business." In accordance with this philosophy, they do not etch sheet metal, skip the use of primers, use inferior materials, and purposely avoid the procedures that would normally result in maximum durability.

This is foolish thinking. Poorly painted signs deteriorate rapidly, and instead of the executed "repeat business," this signman loses a customer. No businessman is apt to again patronize a sign company whose signs chip, peel, or fade in a few months.

That type of sign operator soon develops a habit of "chiseling" at every opportunity. On exterior jobs that specify the use of overlaid plywood, he will attempt to get by with the use of a much cheaper grade of material or put in four posts to support a highway bulletin that in reality requires six posts. He will shop around for the cheapest paints and materials. Seldom will he try to diversify his work by preparing an extra neat layout, or use a new and attractive alphabet. He remains in a rut, using the same old layouts and lettering style year after year.

What is the end result? He gets "word-of-mouth" advertising just as frequently as the good operator, but not the right kind. Soon his business falls off more and more, and where, in the beginning he may have cut a few corners on purpose to turn a "fast-buck," he now must start to cut the price and chisel through necessity. Soon he will be out of business.

Fortunately for the sign trade, this type of operator is in distinct minority. Most signmen have realized the value of integrity, and are therefore successful. They have long since discovered that the best way to develop a healthy business is to do the best work possible, use top quality materials and to keep their customer's best interests in mind. If a sign goes to pieces too quickly (and this does happen in the best shops) they will repaint it and work out a satisfactory rebate or discount with their client.

There is no better advertisement than a satisfied customer. If he has complete confidence in both your ability and integrity, he is certain to recommend your services to others.

Chapter 15

Advancement Requires Practice

The fact that you can letter several basic alphabets and earn a few dollars is commendable and should be a source of gratification. It is a partial reward for all the tedious practice session. However, do not assume that your practice days are over. They are just beginning.

You need only to check the attitudes of the top men in the field. Invariably these men are constantly developing new techniques, learning new alphabets, and keeping pace with progress. This is why they are, and will remain, top men. Should you inquire, most of these professionals, will state a simple fact: Practice never ends.

As you now approach the more advanced phases of sign painting, it actually becomes essential to broaden your field of practice. Concentration on practice should be intensified, rather than be diminished.

For example, you must become accustomed to working on surfaces placed at diverse heights and angles. A pair of skids, as previously described, can provide an excellent means of assimilating these various positions. Fig. 24 shows such standards in actual use and as you might use them for practice work. Place the practice panel across the skids and by manipulation of this set-up you can approximate a generous variety of required working positions.

During the advanced phases of practice it is also advisable to train yourself to work in awkward positions. In the years ahead as a working sign painter, you will be required to do lettering in areas that, at first, might seem impossible. Yet, because you have seen the same type of work in completed form elsewhere, you know that somehow, in some way, another sign painter managed to accomplish these feats. You would be cheating yourself if you did not at least try to accomplish the same thing.

There will be situations where the copy must be placed in positions so inaccessible that it would be impossible to letter these areas by hand. In such cases, substitute applications must be devised. You can use the spray-mask method as described in the plastic section of this book. Or, you can cut a screen and use the screen printing process.

But, when you are out on a job and there are signs in identical positions nearby, that have obviously been hand-lettered by another sign painter you have no choice but to do likewise.

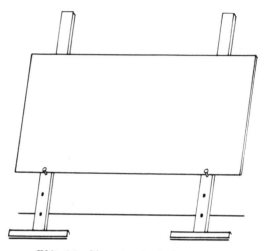

FIG. 24. Sign standards in use.

For instance, let's assume that you are asked to letter a sign on a wall with the top of the sign about 18 inches above the sidewalk. The sign is to read, "Barber Shop Downstairs," with an arrow pointing to the stairwell. The bottom of the letters is but a couple of inches from the sidewalk. You can't tell the man it is impossible, because right next door "Joe's Pawn Shop" has a sign in the same position. So, what do you do? Get down there on the sidewalk and paint the sign! Period.

Second example: A round tanker truck, with a horizontal catwalk extending out 30 inches from the lettering area. A close-packed list of 2 inch license numbers must be lettered on the side of the tank with the bottom of the letters only an inch or two above the flat walking surface. Again, you cannot tell the man, "Impossible," because right next to it is an entire fleet of trucks already lettered freehand, and in the desired positions. There is no way to move your lettering arm down any farther than the catwalk. What do you do? Get busy and letter the numbers. How? By clever, tedious manipulation of the fingers, a slight chance of some hand-movement, and with your soon-to-be-aching arm resting across the flat surface of the catwalk.

So it is not an attempt at humor when I advise you to fasten a painted board against the mopboard of your shop at floor level and practice lettering upon that. I am also serious when I suggest that you place a table, 28 to 30 inches wide, against the wall. Fasten a board flat against the wall on the far side of the table. Remain on your side of the table, reach across; prepare the guidelines for 2 inch lettering and practice lettering on this board. This is still better than the catwalk, because at least your feet are on the floor. On the tank truck you would probably be standing on a box and stretching way out, or laying on the catwalk upon your chest, with your feet dangling off the ground. Thankfully, there are times when conditions do permit the use of a box or a stepladder during this process.

The lettering on the practice boards may be washed off with solvents, and the boards can be used over and over. This type of practice may seem a bit ridiculous now, but any veteran sign painter will tell you that at times he has wished he were a contortionist, an acrobat, a midget, or 7 ft. tall. It is all in a day's work.

Chapter 16

Basics of Layout

A common fault of the novice sign painter is to concentrate too much on the handling of the brush and not enough on layout. Quite frequently, he considers the knowledge of layout to be of relatively small importance.

As a beginner, you could not possibly make a more unfortunate mistake in judgement. Mastering the use of lettering brushes is indeed essential. But good lettering and layout are inseparable. Even the most skilled lettering artist can be certain of a poor result if he starts with a bad layout. The success or failure of any sign begins with the layout.

Quite often we see a sign upon which the lettering is not too precise, but because of a well-balanced layout the sign as a whole is attractive.

Figure 25 shows the most basic fundamentals of layout. The first layout incorporates many of the faults common to the novice. In some cases these same layout faults are made by veteran "sign painters" who have no desire to improve. This layout has absolutely no coordination. The copy is too crowded and is jumbled to an obnoxious extent. The inept scrolls and clumsy decorations add to the confusion. Every possible area of white space has been violated with these meaningless decorations. The complete lack of margins surrounding the copy is the true mark of the amateur.

Pay special attention to the bottom line, "The Reader." Note the adjoinment of the top stroke of the letter T to the letter R. This is a poor attempt at "stunt-lettering." Combinations such as this can be used to good advantage by the skilled designer. As a beginner, you should avoid freak lettering such as this until you develop the skill to do so in a graceful manner and for reasons of good design.

Study this layout well. It contains many of the characteristics that you should know in regard to "how NOT to prepare a sign." The copy thereon is self explanatory. The most precise lettering could do little to improve this extremely poor layout.

The second example demonstrates the benefits of a well planned layout. Practically the same copy has been used. It is true that the letter sizes have been diminished to provide adequate margins. The attractive quality provided by these margins more than compensates for the sacrifice of letter size.

Also study the pleasant contrast that results from the variance of letter sizes. The principal words have been increased in size to accentuate their importance within the message.

Note how the copy has been divided into groupings to allow for the vertical decorative stripes. When using stripes in this context or for other decorative effects, it is advisable to use subdued colors. For example, if the letters on this panel were to be brown on a white field, then a pale tan or pastel yellow could appropriately be used for the vertical stripes. In no case should decorative effects predominate the message. Trim work should enhance the lettering, not detract from it.

The lettering on the No. 2 example is not too precise. This proves the statement, previously mentioned, that a well balanced layout can bring about an attractive result.

COMMON FAULTS OF LAYOUT. Fig. 25 illustrates many of the bad and the good points of layout. However, there now follows a brief summary of the most common errors that contribute to a bad layout!

(1) FAILURE TO CENTER THE LETTERING: On some layouts, portions of the lettering may be placed off-center purposely. But when a line of lettering is supposed to be centered, it should be just that with no compromise. If one line is off-center as much as 1 inch on a truck door, for example, it can ruin the symmetry of the entire lettering job.

If a pattern is being used and a line of lettering is placed off-center a distance of 1 inch, this automatically causes a variance of 2 inches. This equation stems from the fact you add an inch to one side of center, and simultaneously subtract this inch from the other.

This does not apply to direct layout. If you are doing a free hand layout and you begin a line of lettering 6 inches from the left edge and end the same line 5 inches from the right edge, it is then only 1 inch off center.

(2) NOT ENOUGH "WHITE SPACE": The novice as a rule feels that he must fill every bit of available space with some sort of "dingbat." These silly little designs merely confuse the reader. Do not hesitate to leave open space as it occurs within the layout, because it is neater. Furthermore, leave generous margins on all edges. Do not start the lettering too close to the top, or bring it too close

to the edges. It is better to use smaller lettering, than it is to crowd large letters within the copy space.

For example, on a 14 by 22 inch display card, try to allow a margin of 4 to 6 inches at top and bottom rather than 2 inches. On a 6 by 12-foot panel start the lettering at least 8 inches from the top and leave a 12-inch margin on each end. Stay within such boundaries and note the pleasant result.

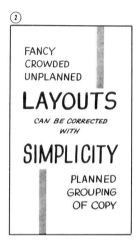

FIG. 25   Bad layout.   Good layout.

(3) CROWDING OF LETTERS: The spacing of letters should be governed by the visibility desired. Upon a sign that is to be primarily viewed close up, such as a display card, the lettering can be condensed and still be readable. There must be a generous space between letters on any sign that is to be viewed at a distance. It is wiser to reduce the size of the letters enough to allow for more space between, than it is to squeeze larger letters so closely together that they become unreadable at a distance. This applies especially to highway bulletins.

(4) TOO MUCH "GINGERBREAD": This is a term used by old-timers for a sign that has a profuse amount of elaborate trimming. For example, when shading the lettering on a truck, confine this trim work to the prominent copy such as the title, etc. The incidental lettering can remain plain, or can merely be underscored with a fine-line stripe. Avoid the practice of painting dots and curlicues

all over the sign for no reason. All decoration should be a planned part of the layout and serve a purpose. There is beauty in simplicity, so save the "gingerbread" for circus wagons.

(5) Nothing can cause a more amateurish appearance than a large number of letters, mechanically spaced, in the same size and style as they might appear on the page of a book. You have developed several styles of lettering and know at least one script. Study the copy and group it according to its importance. The vital copy should be larger, with a lot of punch, and the subordinate copy should be played down accordingly. Break the monotony of the printed words with a line of script. Sometimes just the addition of the word "Phone" in script will spruce up a humdrum layout. The signman who can lay out his copy in good optical balance, so it is pleasing to read with just the right emphasis on each line according to its importance, has taken the first big step toward being a first class tradesman.

The foregoing merely covers the most common errors that must be overcome. Sometimes in the process of learning, we all tend to follow certain little tricks to the extreme. Caution must be used not to overdo a good thing. A good example of this would be the previously suggested professional trick of extending the round letters over and above the guidelines. From an optical standpoint this is a good procedure. If the letter O for instance is placed exactly on the guidelines it will appear to be smaller than the adjacent letters. (See Fig. 26). So it is customary to extend the round-type letters.

On several recent trips, I paid particular attention to this custom on signs, trucks, etc. along the way and was surprised to see how many otherwise efficient lettering artists have done this to the extreme. On certain gasoline tanker trucks that regularly come to our city, I have noticed this trick of layout exaggerated to a ridiculous degree. The letters O on a 12-inch letter will often overlap the guidelines at top and bottom as much as an INCH! Of course, in this case, the rest of the lettering is also done in a most slipshod manner.

When using this layout procedure, one steadfast rule applies. The round letters should be extended just a fraction, and optically should appear to be of the same size as the rest of the letters. If the extended letters appear to be larger, then you are extending them too much and have defeated your purpose. Habits like this can become so routine that even the person doing the work does not realize that it is becoming grotesque.

LION

FIG. 26A. Incorrect—The letter O has been over-extended and sloppy, unsightly peaks prevail on other letters due to excessive speed or carelessness.

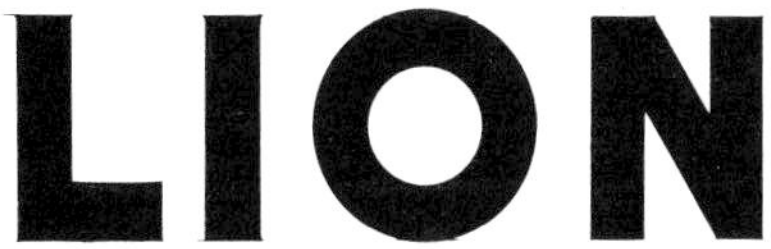

LION

FIG. 26B. Correct—The O has been enlarged just enough to make it appear equal in size to the adjacent straight type letters.

Another habit that can develop into a handicap rather than an advantage is the peaking of the letter strokes. In several alphabets, this does add to the gracefulness of the letters to bring each corner to a neat, sharp peak. This is common practice among lettering artists. But as time goes by, the peaks, through force of habit, become longer and longer until instead of peaks, you have obnoxious serifs.

I have been guilty of both of the last mentioned extremes. It was only by standing back and severely picking my own work to pieces that I managed to overcome these extremes.

ADAPT THE LAYOUT TO THE PURPOSE.

Layout in general is not completely a matter of arrangement of copy or variety of lettering. There are other things to consider. All layouts should be adapted as much as possible to the customer's type of business. A sign for a flower shop should be done in a graceful manner, showing good taste and refined beauty. On heavy duty trucks and equipment, power and massiveness should be the keynote. Designs for banks, funeral homes, professional men, etc. should reflect quiet dignity.

Color is also a vital factor. You would no more think of painting a cement truck in lavenders and purples than you would of lettering a sign for a mortuary in bright red trimmed with yellow. Poor color choice can kill the effect of a sign no matter how excellent the layout and lettering may be.

Good layout, like lettering, comes with experience and a sincere determination to improve your talent. Observe the work of other good signmen, especially when in a larger city. If you see a unique layout, try to make a fast "thumbnail" sketch of that layout, or commit it to memory and then use the idea at the first opportunity.

In my filing cabinet, there is a well-used folder labeled, "Sign Ideas." Into this, I place rough sketches picked up here and there, as well as ads from magazines that might suggest a good layout. Interesting treatments of both script and printed letters can be found in abundance in magazines and newspaper ads, on matchbooks, packaging, etc. When you seem to be in a rut and groping for a new approach, a collection of ideas such as this can be a convenient crutch. Just to browse through this material will usually spark an entirely new chain of creativeness through suggestion. Try not to copy the ideas directly, but instead use them to stimulate your own imagination.

COMMENTARY. As a newcomer to the trade you might be inclined to question the stress placed upon the significance of layout. Perhaps the following incident will help you to understand:

When I was just out of the apprentice stage, and working in my first big shop, I was a bit peeved when the foreman asked an older hand to lay out several signs that I was scheduled to letter. Later, after I had lettered these signs, I realized the wisdom of this foreman's maneuver. Working on these professional layouts showed me, upon completion, where I had been making many mistakes in my own layout work.

But, when I first began to letter these signs, and with the smart-aleck attitude of youth, I was tempted as I proceeded to change the layouts that were prepared by this veteran. I considered his margins to be a waste of space. For my benefit, he had prepared a full-outline layout for each thick and thin letter. To me, his letters seemed to be too full and round. Vividly, I recall that I very nearly decided to chop off the two right-hand loops of the letter C when it first occurred in the lettering sequence. My thought was that these loops were too long and swung around much too far in their curved sweep to the right.

However, I resisted temptation and grudgingly followed

his layouts in precise manner. All through the process, I mentally condemned the foreman. Silently, I cussed the entire procedure, thinking such things as, "Why should I follow this crummy layout made by an old buck who should be put out to pasture"?

Upon completion of the work, I carefully studied the finished signs. Looking about the shop, I compared the results with other signs nearby that had been completed by other professionals. Although the techniques varied, these signs were quite similar in regard to margins, spacing, letter-shapes, etc.

Fortunately, there were also several signs standing about that I had done completely by myself. These signs seemed to stand out among all the others. Because they were good? Hardly.

Once again, I honestly appraised the work that I had just completed. The professionalism was indeed apparent. Not because of the brush work, but because of the layout! It was at this point that I dropped the role of the smart aleck. The comparison made at this moment showed me that although my work was neat, it still bore the unmistakable mark of the novice.

This happened many years ago, but I recall it now as though it were yesterday. I can still see those charcoal marks, and every time I lay out the letter C to this day, I remember the urge that I had at that time to rub them off.

No incident stands out more clearly in my memory. Perhaps this is because in a flash I realized that I did not know as much as I thought I did, that I had much to learn, and never again did I underrate an old pro.

It is likely that each of us goes through a smart-aleck phase. To some this period might be short, to others prolonged, and to the less fortunate it might endure and become a lifetime handicap.

The most important part of the incident just related is that it changed my attitude and I have always considered this to be my most valued lesson.

I never knew the last name of this veteran layout man. The age factor tells me that he has passed on. But this little tale is dedicated to a nice guy named, "Chet."

Chapter 17
Preparation of Patterns

It is quite natural for authors of instructive material to receive letters from newcomers to the trade. Most of these letters are in the form of inquiry. If the reader asks but one question, this can usually be answered with a short explanation.

Unfortunately, most of these queries consist of a long list of questions, or contain one very technical question. In either case, an intelligent answer would require a long and involved explanation. These letters are appreciated, but seldom does time permit a complete answer.

Whenever possible, and if a brief reply will suffice, I try to answer these queries. There are times when I do not know the answer, so the reader is then referred to a source where this information might be available. Occasionally, it becomes necessary for me to write to an expert in a certain field in search of an answer to a problem of my own.

Among these inquiries, the following question is quite common: "Would you advise the preparation of a pattern for just one job?"

This can be answered pro or con. If the layout is quite simple with small chance of a repeat order, it would seem advisable to bypass a pattern and use a direct layout.

As a beginner, you might have no knowledge of the mechanics involved in the preparation of a pattern. Except for the perforations, the procedure for making a pattern is quite the same as that used for direct layout. The additional tool needed is referred to as a "pounce-wheel." This instrument is illustrated in all sign-supply catalogs. It is advisable to purchase one fine-tooth wheel for small, precise patterns and a coarser toothed wheel to be used on larger work.

If white paper is used, round charcoal sticks should be used for preliminary markings. Generally, brown kraft wrapping paper is used for patterns. Cross guidelines are drawn with an ordinary lead pencil. The tentative layout lines are indicated with either white school chalk or charcoal sticks. These marks can be removed and progressively adjusted until the layout is in precise position.

At this point, most professionals proceed no further with the layout but perforate the paper directly over these layout lines. Any additional preciseness automatically results from the straight-edge used in the perforating process. A thin yardstick is generally used for this purpose.

If a high degree of accuracy is required, or the layout is very technical, then the chalk or charcoal lines are first gone over with a pencil. Triangles, T-squares, etc. are employed in this process to assure the necessary preciseness of layout.

When this pencil work is completed, you perforate all of the lines with the pounce-wheel. This tool is held in the hand in the same way as a brush or pencil and you simply run the wheel over each line, using sufficient pressure to complete penetration of the paper.

Some sign painters reverse the completed pattern and lightly rub over the perforations with fine sandpaper to remove the burrs.

Most pounce wheels are adjustable. By tightening the handle, the shank can be locked into a fixed position. A reverse turn of the handle will free the shank to work on a loose, swivel principle. How you use the wheel is a matter of preference.

Lightweight paper can be used for small or intricate patterns. Heavy paper is suggested for patterns intended for exterior use where even a light wind can be a factor. A slight gust of wind can quite frequently tear a pattern into shreds. This also applies to patterns that must endure frequent use over a prolonged period. Use heavy paper on all patterns that might be subject to abuse.

When perforating the cross guidelines, avoid running these lines off the edges of the paper. Otherwise during the rolling process, the paper will rip at these points and require patching with tape.

THE ADVANTAGES OF PATTERNS.

In most cases, there are distinct advantages in the use of patterns. Following are some of the good points to be considered:

POINT ONE: If you use a perforated pattern, without supplementary direct marking, you eliminate the possibility of scratching the surface with chalk, charcoal or pencil. Regardless of how carefully you might apply a chalk layout to an automotive finish, or similar surface, it is apt to leave slight scratches. Shadow-type scratches still remain even after chalk lines have been removed with a damp chamois skin.

This also applies to charcoal layouts. In the case of pencil marks on a light-colored surface, it is difficult to apply these lightly enough to avoid an unsightly appearance.

POINT TWO: Actually, it does not take much longer to prepare a pattern, because you must only lay out the design but once. Certainly, it takes less time to perforate a prepared pattern than would be required to apply a direct layout to the second side of any sign. You also have the comfort and flexibility of working on the drawing board.

In all cases it is easier to execute a more precise and detailed layout on pattern paper. If it is a prestige job, you can make change after change, experimenting with several tentative layouts as you proceed. This would be poor procedure to use directly upon the surface, since this would involve the hazard of marring the finish with latent scratches and smudges.

POINT THREE: Paper patterns also afford the advantage of preparing the various fold-patterns, scrolls, fancy panels, etc. Fig. 27 illustrates the procedure to use for the preparation of such patterns. This method can be used for any design that is symmetrical on both sides. The paper should be folded at center. Reopen and lay flat on the drawing board. Draw the left side of the design roughly with charcoal, and refold the paper with the face sides together. Firmly rub over the back of the marked side of the paper with your fingers. The left hand design will transfer to the right side of the fold. Again reopen the fold and lay flat. Consider the complete design. If it is well balanced and satisfactory, you can then accurately pencil the lines of the design on the left side of the fold.

Finally, fold the pattern with the back sides together, and the pencilled side facing you. Tape to the drawing board. Next run the pounce wheel over the pencil lines with enough pressure to go through both left and right sides of the paper.

On patterns where four corners are symmetrical, use the same procedure, except to fold the paper twice to provide four corners. Indicate the design on the upper left hand quarter only. When perforating this design you must use maximum pressure on the pounce wheel since it must completely penetrate through four layers of paper. This method cannot be used if the vertical edges are slanted. Designs with oblique edges as shown in Fig. 27 must be confined to a single fold.

POINT FOUR: The use of patterns also provides your

customer with the ultimate in uniformity. All of his work will be identical and will result in better identification with the public. This is especially important in the case of company trademarks.

Preparation of patterns in the shop is recommended for duplication of trademarks and other intricate designs. You can then use a projector to speed up the work and to provide authentic reproduction of design.

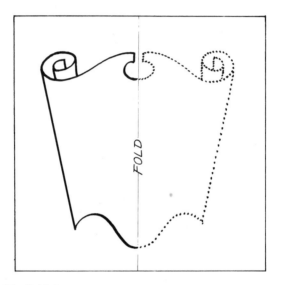

FIG. 27. Fold Pattern: Use for any design that is symmetrical on both sides. Fold paper in center. Reopen and lay flat. Draw left side of design roughly with charcoal and refold with face sides together. Rub over back with fingers. Left hand design will transfer to right side of fold. If design is to your liking after consideration, draw in the left side accurately with pencil. Finally, fold the pattern with the back sides together and run the pounce wheel over the pencil lines with enough pressure to go through both left and right sides of the paper. On patterns where four corners are symmetrical, use the same procedure, except to fold the paper four times and draw the upper left hand quarter of the design only.

It is quite common for a driver to bring a truck to the shop saying: "The boss wants this one painted the same as his other one." What a relief it is to have patterns on occasions such as this.

A little tip: Mark the colors used directly on the pattern, such as: color of truck, color of letter, shade or outline, etc. In general a brief synopsis of the procedure followed. This avoids the nuisance of chasing about to look at one of his other trucks. Or, to locate the boss to ask him what colors, etc. were used—he probably would not remember anyhow. That would be an unnecessary waste of time and runs up the cost of the job.

If you have an order blank system with all the pertinent information on record from past orders then the marking of the pattern is not required. Your customers appreciate efficiency such as this. (Order blank systems will be discussed later in this book.)

POINT FIVE: Patterns are big time savers on repeat orders. A system of filing or storing these patterns must be established so you can locate them without a tedious search. This system will depend on the space available for this purpose and on the number of patterns involved. You might prefer to group them in bins in alphabetical order, such as, A-B-C-D patterns in one bin, E-F-G-H in another, and so on through the alphabet. Each pattern should be plainly marked with the name of the customer and the date showing when the pattern was last used.

Another method is to stand the patterns on end in boxes with each pattern rolled and marked, with this identification uppermost when placed in the box. For example, you might label one box, "Trucks—current" and another just plain "Trucks" for patterns seldom used. Follow this same procedure of having two boxes each for, "pictorials, trademarks, commercial signs," using as many category breakdowns as you deem necessary.

It is true that a pattern might not completely fit on a repeat job. However, in many cases the pattern can be shifted about on the surface and adapted for use with slight adjustments. You might only be able to use the title part of the pattern at the top, but even this can be of great help since it usually involves the trademark or the most complicated part of the design. Then by laying out the incidental copy directly to the surface and adjusting it to the remaining space you will still have saved time through the use of the most complicated part of that pattern.

There will be times when it is not practical to prepare a pattern such as when you are called out of town to do a job, and you have no idea of what is to be required. It is then best to proceed according to your own logic. After considering the job, if you decide that a pattern is advisable, the following make-shift procedure might be used: It is wise to carry a roll of pattern paper in your vehicle for emergency use. First, try to find a good sized corrugated box. These can generally be found in discard behind local stores.

A mattress or bicycle carton provides an excellent surface upon which to place the paper for the layout procedure and this material is especially adaptable to the use of a pounce wheel.

TIPS ON DIRECT LAYOUT. If a pattern is not used, the following information will be of some help to you in regard to layout directly upon the surface. These principles can also apply to other surfaces such as windows, panels, etc. For ease of explanation let us assume that you are required to letter the cab doors of a dark-colored truck. First, clean the doors thoroughly being especially certain that road-tar, finger marks, etc. are removed.

The tools needed for simple layout are a piece of white chalk, sharpened as previously described, a thin yardstick, and possibly a length of string. A heavy rigid yardstick is not recommended, because it will not bend to make proper contact with the curved contours of most trucks.

Determine the center of the horizontal area and place a small chalk-mark at this point. Next, use the yardstick for a straight-edge and draw a vertical center line from top to bottom. If the first line of lettering is to be an arc, use a piece of string with a loop in one end and through which to slip the tip of the chalk. With your right hand, hold the chalk within this loop at the very top of the proposed arc. Then grasp the string with the left thumb and forefinger and bring it down to the very bottom of the vertical line, holding it at center. With the string held taut, swing the chalk over to the extreme left, place the chalk in marking position, and with a firm, sweeping motion bring the string up and around to the extreme right, marking as you go. Then shorten up on the string, and make the bottom guideline of the arc in the same manner.

If an arc of sharper degree is desired then do not use the bottom of the door as the center point for the string. Place a check mark on the vertical center line and as far up from the bottom of the door as is necessary to provide the roundness of the arc. Use this check mark as center for all guidelines concerning the arc.

Next, place very small chalk marks along the vertical center line to indicate the desired positions for the horizontal guidelines to contain the rest of the copy beneath the arc. Hold the yardstick in vertical position immediately to the left of the vertical center line, and flat against the surface. Now place small, accurate chalk marks directly upon the right edge of the yardstick to correspond with the marks you just made on the truck, including the two marks that indicate the position of the arc.

These chalk marks on the yardstick now constitute the basic guide for the complete layout process. Therefore, take care not to obliterate these marks before their purpose is served. Hold the stick flat against the extreme right edge of the door in the same position and place small chalk marks on the truck to correspond with the marks on the stick. Move the stick to the left edge of the door and repeat this process.

You now have marks on each side of the door to position the guidelines below the arc. Move to the other side of the truck and draw the vertical line at center. Lay the yardstick in vertical marking position along this line, and mark the two points for the arc only, at top center, again matching the marks to the yardstick. Follow this same procedure to transfer the marks to each edge of the door. You should now have identical marks to indicate the guideline positions on both sides of the truck. All that remains is either to draw or to snap these guidelines connecting all the marks just made and continue with the rest of the layout. This method is fast and results in uniformity.

If the door of the truck has a curved bottom edge, draw one level horizontal chalk line near the bottom of the door and use this line as you would normally use the bottom edge of a straight door as a basic guide for the work.

Should the vertical measurement of the door be too shallow to allow for a satisfactory arc by holding the string at the bottom center, then bring the string on down to the running board. Place a mark at this point on the running board. Use this mark as a center mark for the lines of the arc.

In the case of no running board, lay a block of wood on the ground or floor directly below center. Bring the string straightly down across the vertical center line on the truck directly down to the block and mark this point. This block must not be moved until the arc lines are completed. Fasten the loop of the string to the block at the check point. Bring the string up to the top of the arc, wrap it several times around the chalk near to the tip, and mark the guidelines in this way. It is advisable to hold one foot firmly on the block during this process to prevent it from raising up when you put tension on the string. Wooden boxes of various heights can be used in the same manner as the block to provide the degree of arc desired.

COMMENTARY. As a sign painter you will frequently have no choice but to work in awkward, back-breaking positions. So take advantage of comfort whenever you can.

A very essential factor in the art of expert lettering is to be comfortable. You cannot apply the graceful sweep to script or to any lettering from a cramped position. Try not to squat, kneel, etc. If possible sit on a box. When placed on end, sideways or flat, the right type of box provides three convenient heights. Some of the new pick-up trucks, vanettes, etc. are built so low that a person practically has to dig a fox hole in order to letter the bottom lines. If possible try to jack up the truck or run it onto a hoist.

Years ago I would letter trucks squatting, kneeling, laying on the floor or in any way possible. Eventually I learned that better, faster work can be done if one is relaxed, comfortable and in a position that allows for freedom of movement.

Several little tips to end this chapter: When perforating patterns on the drawing board, try stretching a piece of thin cloth blanket material to the board. Lay the pattern paper over the blanket and note the ease with which the pounce wheel will perforate the paper. This is especially helpful when perforating intricate patterns, or when perforating through several thicknesses of paper at a time.

Avoid using the pounce wheel over brittle, hardboard surfaces. Also place a drop of oil on the wheel axle periodically. Metal revolving on metal requires frequent lubrication.

Chapter 18

Truck Door Layout

Much of our work as a sign painter will involve the lettering of trucks. Although this work will include a wide variety of vehicles, ranging in size from the smallest of pick-up trucks to the mammoth vans and semi-trailers, the biggest demand will generally be for the lettering of the two cab doors only.

Perhaps a bit of history in regard to the evolution of truck door design will be of interest.

Fifteen to 20 years ago it would have been a simple matter to present the basic instructions for this phase of the work. Perhaps eight to ten illustrations, in different dimensions, would have been sufficient to show the most common body styles manufactured up to that time.

Recalling those days, I frequently find myself wondering how many other veteran signmen wistfully remember those many years during which the lettering of truck doors was a pleasure, instead of a challenge. The doors were plain and uncluttered. Body styles changed and became more stream-lined every three or four years, but for the most part, the cab doors remained flat and plain. The major changes in door design were confined only to the variation of dimensions.

This stability of design, whether planned or coincidental, was of great advantage to both the sign painter and the truck owner. This permitted the signman to develop striking lay-outs. Beautiful designs and lettering were possible. The signman could prepare a single pattern for a fleet of trucks and use this same pattern year after year with little, if any, adjustment. Company trademarks and decals could be ap-plied without complications. All of this was beneficial to the truck owners. Their identification was uniform and well designed. The adaptability of these plain truck doors kept the cost at a minimum.

All good things come to an end. The changes in body design began to trespass upon the cab doors. My initial ex-perience with this major change was one of consternation, not only for myself, but for my customer.

A steady client asked me to go down to a local garage

and to letter a new pick up truck, just purchased. Upon first glance at the truck, I was aware of the complications to follow. The body design of this new model was such that the downward sweep of the front fender wells extended nearly across the width of the cab doors. This caused a large, rounded hump to occur in oblique position across the center of each door. Naturally, the contour swept upwards on one door and downwards on the other.

Obstructed surfaces, such as this, are not too complicated if the identification only requires run-of-the-mill lettering. This applies to most modern day trucks. With careful consideration the layout can be adjusted accordingly.

But on this particular job the complications were as follows: This truck was owned by the dealer for a very large nationally advertised product. Specifications demanded that the well known trademark of this firm, in decal form, be placed at center on all truck doors. This decal was circular and about 18 inches in diameter.

Normally, the name of the dealer was lettered above the trademark and the address below. The space limitations of the door scarcely allowed room enough for this copy set-up. Therefore, the decal could not be adjusted to bridge the "fender-bulge" in the most strategic place. Our state laws require that the name and address of the truck owner be placed on the cab-door. Otherwise this copy could have been lettered elsewhere upon the truck.

The doors were finally lettered using the best layout possible. The decals were painstakingly applied over the prominent bulges. Unfortunately, these were no longer round, but distorted on each truck door into the shape of a kidney bean.

Upon completion I called the company field man. This was also his first experience with this new body design. Since the job was done in the best manner possible, he did not blame me, but he was less than happy with the distorted trademark. I also pointed out to him the fact that rain water, etc. would eventually run down the trough provided by the fender-wells, and that his company could expect premature breakdown of the decals from the constant attack of this water drainage. He had mentioned that his company customarily used this same brand of truck, and purchased them in volume on a nationwide basis.

To avoid later misunderstanding, I mentioned that my bill for the work would be about twice as much as previously charged to cover the extra time involved.

For some time thereafter I wondered whether this firm discarded thousands of expensive decals, changed their established emblem, switched to a more adaptable brand of truck or continued to present their attractive, circular trademark in the shape of a Mexican jumping-bean.

Soon, I received letters from other signmen condemning this new trend in truck design. Other customers complained because I either had to distort their decals or was unable to use them at all. They inquired about the increased charge for doing the work.

The end result was that I wrote a friendly letter to the motor company that produced these trucks and advised them of these facts. I doubt if this letter ever got beyond the first wastebasket.

MODERN DAY TRUCKS. Without question, the body designs of present day pick-up trucks are excellent. Outside of the stripped down economy models, they no longer have the "work-horse" appearance of yesteryear. The deluxe models, especially, are beautifully designed.

Each motor company presents a variety of models. The different sizes and shapes all seem to vary in design. Although it is doubtful if any one manufacturer changes body styles on a yearly basis, major changes do occur at planned intervals. The result is that by today's standards the sign painter must contend with hundreds of truck body styles.

Therefore it would be impossible within this instruction to even scratch the surface in an attempt to illustrate a set group of standard layouts adaptable to the lettering of truck doors. Any such effort would soon be obsolete due to the ever increasing changes of truck design.

Because of this constant change, it is advisable for you to approach each new design with an open mind. As all sign painters do, you must accept this part of the work for what it is—a challenge. Develop the ability to improvise on the spot. The required lettering must be adapted to take advantage of whatever space is available on each particular truck door. This requires careful consideration of the existing obstacles and a thorough knowledge of layout.

The presence of the mirror supports, as shown in Fig. 28, can cause a problem. It is my understanding that this mirror arrangement is optional equipment. Yet, many people request this form of mounting, in addition to others, at the time of purchase. They do this even though their customary identification includes the use of company emblems, ready for application, in either decal or film form.

Seldom does the truck buyer realize at the time of

purchase that the infringement of such equipment upon the truck door will complicate, or possibly negate the application of the company trademark. Neither does he realize the difficulty this causes for the sign painter.

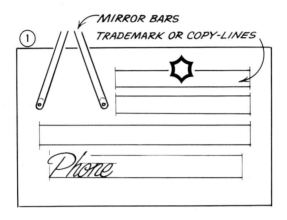

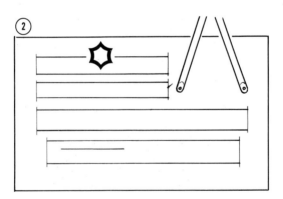

FIG. 28. Supports of mirrors can complicate truck lettering layouts. On the driver's side (1) where layout is forced to the right, there is more of a problem than (2) where the lettering reads toward the obstacle.

The fact remains that once such equipment is installed, it becomes your task to overcome the problem.

The illustration, Fig. 28, was particularly prepared because the mirror supports do consume a large portion of the most valuable advertising area available on the doors of a truck. This reduces the flexibility of layout to near zero.

The company title generally occupies top position on all truck doors.

On the driver's side, No. 2, the position of these supports forces the title to the right. In modern day advertising it is common within exotic layout to purposely arrange all copy to be flush or straight on the right vertical margin. The "ragged" copy-endings are then on the left.

However, the lettering on most trucks is for reasons of utility and identification. Instinctively, we read from left to right.

Forcing the principal copy to the right can sometimes be obnoxious. This is especially true if this part of the copy consists of plain lettering and is in direct continuity with the copy below the mirror bars. There is small problem if the company trademarks will fit within these top areas. A design such as this is a separate entity and seldom will this change of position have an adverse effect on the copy below.

The passenger side, No. 2, is less of a problem, since the mirror supports are to the right. The lettering automatically reads from left to right.

The illustration shows one acceptable layout procedure to use when confronted with this or a similar type of obstacle. It is rarely possible to adhere to the customer's usual form of truck identification. A fleet of trucks might be involved with all of the units uniformly lettered according to company policy. It is then advisable to explain to the owner the reasons that forced you to deviate from this policy on this one "orphan" vehicle.

Although well designed, some truck doors are plain and layout is simple. Fig. 29 is a photograph of such a truck.

The single obstruction is the horizontal ridge. This would only be a major nuisance if specifications forced you to apply an emblem over this ridge. In the course of normal lettering, all you need to do is to arrange the layout to entirely avoid the ridge. This is self evident on the photograph. Note that the word "Carpenter" was raised above the ridge to allow space at the bottom for shading.

The vertical space between the ridge and the door handle is limited. Yet, all space has been wisely used to provide the customer with the large sized lettering desired. The keyhole is usually of small significance. You will notice, however, that in this case, it had to be considered. On the side of the truck, as pictured, the letter R is just below the keyhole. The word, "Roger" automatically occupies this position on the opposite side of the truck. This was planned beforehand.

If the word, "Koehler" had been composed of a word of script ending with a tall letter, this layout could not have been used exactly as shown. A tall letter, such as a D, L or T would have surmounted the keyhole. So even an item as small as a keyhole can become a factor in layout.

FIG. 29. *Where truck doors are relatively plain, layout can be simple.*

Normally, a number of alternate layouts would be possible on a door of this type. For example, the script could be smaller or could be changed to printed letters. However, on this job both script and large letters were desired.

COMMENTARY. Although the trend toward more fanciful truck-body design constantly seems to increase, there are still a number of models that are quite plain. In fact one major manufacturer maintains a reasonable amount of progress in body design to keep pace with the trend, but does not extend this change of design to include the cab doors. These doors remain plain and contain only those obstructions that must be installed for functional reasons.

When working on plain-type truck doors you can approach the layout work and the lettering in the same manner used on any other panel of a similar size.

The plainer type doors provide a distinct advantage for both signman and truck owner. At the moment I have a situation to demonstrate this logic. For many years a large firm has used the same design on their truck advertising. This consists of a sweeping scroll at the top for the long firm name. The abbreviation, "Inc." nestles underneath the righthand loop of the scroll.

Recently, this firm purchased a different brand of truck. This truck has two pronounced, prismatic ridges spanning the width of the door at top and near the bottom. These ridges are wide and greatly reduce the available lettering area.

The main lettering space between these ridges is about 12 inches. There is no possibility of using the graceful scroll design so familiar to the public.

Instead, it will be necessary to use the entire 12 inch area to contain the firm name and to place this on two lines. The address must be squeezed beneath the bottom ridge. The license numbers will be jammed into the area above the top ridges. Our state laws do not permit placement of this copy elsewhere on the truck. This much of the copy must be lettered upon the doors to comply with legal requirements. The phone number and other incidental copy can be positioned upon any available area.

When I explained this to the owner, he was disappointed, and said that he was sorry he had purchased the truck. Although the lettering will be simple, my dislike for the job is that compared to his other trucks this layout will be no more attractive in design than a six-line want-ad in a newspaper. Since I cannot use any of the various sized patterns on hand, a free-hand layout will be necessary. This will again raise the cost of this job.

This is but one example, among hundreds, in my personal experience. Salesmen for the firms that load these cab doors with ridges, etc., claim that this adds strength to the metal. With this, I agree, providing the metal itself retains the same gauge used on the plain doors of years past. But, if these ridges are designed to compensate for the use of thinner and cheaper metal, the claim of greater strength becomes a travesty.

This is not an accusation but an observation. It is an observation, because through the years I have relettered the same trucks two or three times upon changes of ownership, etc. Many of these units have been logging or construction trucks, which are subject to abnormal abuse. At no time have I noticed any greater deterioration on the flat-doored trucks than that to be found on those trucks with the "reinforced" ridges.

Actually, the visible wear and tear has been more apparent on these prismatic ridges. These protrude from the surface and are more susceptible to gouges and scratches. Any body-repair man can justify the statement that it costs much less to repair a banged-up flat door than it does to restore a door of irregular contour.

Since design is an integral part in the life of any signman, he would be the first to recognize the beauty of truck design. Also he would admire the skill required to develop such design.

Most states require by law that trucks be identified. A vast majority of truck owners do have their vehicles lettered for the value of advertising. It would seem that the producers of these trucks would consider these facts.

This has long been a source of irritation to many signmen. Since most trucks ultimately are lettered, we wonder why these intelligent designers appear to use every effort to convert the average lettering surface into an obstacle course.

The best advice to the beginner in regard to truck-door lettering is to be prepared. Learn all that you possibly can about on-the-spot layout. Each new truck-model demands the need for improvisation. The tricks that professionals instinctively use in the process of truck lettering will gradually be developed through experience.

It's the little things that count. Each little time-saver might individually appear to be of small consequence. But when a number of these minor procedures are consecutively used during the progress of a job, the benefits will soon be apparent.

One example of this would be the single-rod mirror support. Quite commonly, this rod will suspend downward from the mirror and the bottom of this support will be attached to the face of the truck door. Generally, it is easier to loosen this rod than it is to leave it in place and work around it. Do not loosen the end that is attached to the door, because this could be fastened with a bolt instead of a metal-screw. Should you remove a bolt, the nut will fall off within the interior of the door. It might then be a major problem to dismantle the inner side of the door in order to replace the bolt.

It is best to remove the top of the rod from the bottom of the mirror. You can then swing the rod off to one side while working. Be certain to securely replace the rod upon completion.

Since you can expect frequent mechanical adjustments such as this, it is advisable to have the necessary tools. At all times carry in your vehicle several adjustable wrenches, pliers, screw drivers, etc. To chase about in an effort to borrow tools is not only a waste of time, but also an annoyance to the lender. It certainly presents a poor picture of your personal efficiency.

This is just one of the small procedures, among many, that you will automatically learn through actual experience.

In your approach to truck lettering, carefully study the techniques of other good professional signmen. Note how they have handled the layout work on complicated truck bodies. Keep a camera handy and whenever possible snap pictures.

The actual study of professionally lettered trucks can provide you with more practical knowledge about layout and lettering than one could possibly describe within a book. Pay close attention to the layout, the letter formations, the quality of paint coverage, the color combinations, etc.

Especially study the manner in which the professional has distributed the copy and used the available space. The phone numbers might be lettered along the sides of the hood or moved back upon the sides of the pick-up box. If the front of the hood is lettered, discover for yourself how the signman arranged the copy. Frequently the truck manufacturer has a plaque-type emblem attached at center, or the entire lettering area might present a difficult contour.

In this type of on-the-spot study it is important that you study the work of the expert professional. Be certain that the work is well designed, expertly lettered and attractive. To study the sloppy work of a "hack" sign painter can do more harm than good.

When you personally begin to letter trucks, be prepared to cope with ridges, beads, bulges, hinges, handles, road-tar, wax, etc. Also, local dealers have a nasty habit of slapping their own identification emblems right across normal lettering areas.

The important requirement is to learn how to arrange an attractive layout in nearly every shape and position. Develop your personal knack for the effective distribution of copy.

Once you learn how to properly letter all of the truck-designs now on the market and those still to come, you should be able to letter just about anything.

Chapter 19

Working Knowledge of Layout

The mental knowledge of a process is necessary. The physical dexterity required to make use of such knowledge is of equal importance. Each is dependent upon the other. Therefore, before proceeding further with the general instruction of layout, we should now concentrate upon several of the more important physical manipulations that aid in laying out signs for lettering.

In previous discussions of procedure it was pointed out that the methods described would not always be practical and more advanced procedures would be considered. We discussed methods of marking lines in the layout process. It is now essential to describe additional methods.

The young tradesman, upon observance, will find that the highly skilled signman can successfully adapt his procedure to execute any job he is required to do, regardless of conditions. This is no accident but is the result of thoroughly learning his trade. The true expert will try to master every method that can possibly help him to be a better tradesman, no matter how difficult this might be. He will do this even when he knows that he could get by without doing so, although not as efficiently.

As a beginner, you might kid yourself by thinking, "Why bother learning this method, when I can get by without it?"

A good case in point would be the snapping of lines, without assistance, by means of the two-handed method. I have been somewhat dismayed in past years at the large number of sign painters who have not yet learned this method. Several younger workmen have told me that they never had anybody show them and that previous written instruction was too vague and not detailed enough to make it clear to them.

Before explaining the procedures, let us consider some of the advantages. It is the neatest and most professional method of making layout lines. On a light colored truck, for example, the only other way you could make the lines, outside of using a pattern, would be with a yardstick and either charcoal or pencil. These lines are not always easy to remove, even with a damp chamois skin. Stubborn pencil marks can be removed with a rag dampened with turpentine, but the shine on the lettering might be dulled in the process. If these marks are not removed they present an unsightly appearance. Certainly, they are not desirable on a prestige job. Furthermore, when they are removed, you might find that the pencil, charcoal or chalk might have left permanent scratches on the surface.

Once the procedure is mastered, snapped lines are more accurate, in many cases are more convenient to apply and will cut down on layout time.

Illustrated in Fig. 30 are two commonly used hand positions for the snapping of lines. No snapping can begin, of course, until you have placed a series of small check marks or dots on each side of the layout to indicate the position of the guidelines.

You will note that the left hand does the tricky work. The right hand is merely used to hold the string in proper position across the opposite check marks while the left hand completes the snapping process. You might find it more personally adaptable to reverse the hand positions, and use your right hand for the snapping procedure.

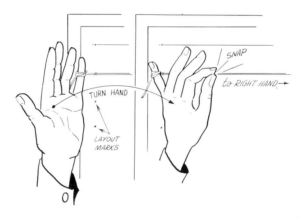

FIG. 30. With all fingers extended, it is easier to snap a line, but unless you turn your hand as shown on the left, the extended middle finger will obscure view of little finger and interfere with accuracy of position.

To begin this maneuver, wrap the left end of the chalk line around your little finger as shown, so the string comes out on the underneath or palm side of the hand. Next, chalk the line by rubbing it with a half-round piece of either blue or white carpenter's chalk. Stick charcoal might be used for this, depending on the color of the surface. Then, place the hand in position as shown in Fig. 30-A, with the little finger resting firmly against the surface so the string runs directly across the layout mark. Grasp the other end of the string with the right hand and pull it tightly across the surface so it intersects the corresponding layout mark on the opposite side.

Now, keeping the little finger firmly in place, turn the left hand over to the position shown in Fig. 30-B. Your little finger should be a bit to the left of the mark. This check mark should be visible at all times in order to check for accuracy. In this way, should the finger slip a bit, you can readjust the position so the string is again accurately across the check mark. You are now ready to snap the line. To make this easier, raise the string away from the surface with the right hand, enough so that the left hand might easily grasp the string. Take hold of the string as shown, with the finger and thumb of the left hand, place the right hand back in its previously gauged position, pull the string taut, and snap.

Practice will soon help you determine the degree of tension to place upon the string. It is important when using this process to keep the little finger in exact position at all times, especially when turning the hand.

It would not be necessary to turn the hand, but it seems that the two middle fingers, extended as they are in this position, tend to block the view of the little finger, so it cannot accurately be placed on the mark unless the hand is turned to provide clear vision for this placement.

There is an alternate hand position shown in Fig. 31. This maneuver is a bit more difficult to learn, but with this technique, the hand need not be turned, but can be kept palm down throughout the entire snapping process. The middle fingers are tucked under as shown and therefore do not obstruct a clear view of the little finger at point of contact. This method has an advantage over that described in Fig. 30. The hand need not be turned and can be progressively moved down to each check point without change of position. Unfortunately, some find that their hand is not flexible enough to execute the snap in this way. Otherwise the snapping process is accomplished in the same manner as described in connection with Fig. 30.

To obtain maximum results from this technique, you might try to learn to use either hand for the snapping process. This can be a great advantage. When snapping lines across long spans, the lines do tend to become faintly indicated at the right or stationary end. With both hands in the snap-position the lines can be consecutively snapped on each end. This double snap provides very clear lines, but requires considerable dexterity.

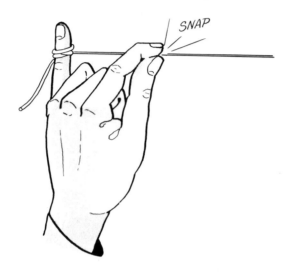

FIG. 31. *With middle fingers tucked underneath, the snapping is more difficult, but the hand can be positioned without being turned.*

The hand positions as illustrated are suggestive. Each of us may have a varying degree of flexibility in our fingers. The illustrations can be used as guides, and beginning with these, you can work out the method that is most comfortable and efficient for personal use. The essential factor is to try to master this technique. This effort will seem clumsy and slow at first. But as it is with all things that require a high degree of skill, you will gradually become adept at it. Later you will discover that you are snapping these lines instinctively and with scarcely a thought.

SNAPPING LONG LINES WITHOUT ASSISTANCE.
Although snapping lines with the aid of a helper presents no problems, it is possible in most cases to do this without assistance. Upon long spans, the free end of the chalk line can be secured by looping it around a small nail driven slightly into the surface when this is

practical. A small suction cup of the type that has a bolt-end protruding from the center with a small nut attached can be used. The nut should be loosened to allow enough space between the nut and the suction cup for the string. The loop on the end of the chalk line is placed within this space and the nut prevents the cord from sliding off the end of the bolt. This suction cup can be moved to any position on the face of the sign to serve as an anchor for the snap-line on the opposite end. The line can also be fastened at each check point with several strips of masking tape. A large knot arranged at the string end will prevent it from pulling through when you place tension on the opposite end in the snapping process.

Less "chalking-up" is necessary, if you put less tension on the string, and snap it very lightly on the first snap while there is a heavy residue of chalk on the tine. Then on each successive snap, slightly increase the tension on the string and snap it a bit harder each time. On the final snap, just before the string needs rechalking, the line should be pulled very tight and snapped as hard as possible. Never reduce the tension enough during any phase of this process to allow the string to sag.

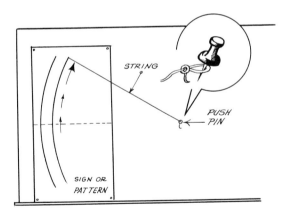

FIG. 32. With this procedure, you can use a string of any length and scribe an arc of any number of degrees you wish.

LAYOUT OF ARCS.
The vertical width of the average drawing board is usually 4 feet or less. This does not always provide sufficient distance to prepare the wide variety of arcs required.

Fig. 32 illustrates a procedure that is well known to

most experienced signmen. By placing the paper on end as shown, at the end of the board, you can use a string as long or as short as you wish to make an arc in almost any degree desired by utilizing the length, rather than the depth of the work bench. A pushpin, as shown, is an excellent device to use as a center for the string and will not pull out very easily, especially if it is pushed into the board slanting away from the pull of the string, as shown.

Push-pins are handy for many things. When pushed into a surface at an angle slanting away from the force of the pull, they can be used for snapping fairly long guide-lines. This use is limited to the required tension. These pins are too small to withstand the pull needed to span a large highway bulletin.

CHALK LINE PADDLES.

To keep chalk lines in good condition, try the method as shown in Fig. 33. Saw

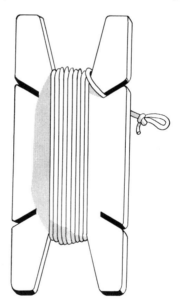

FIG. 33. Chalk line paddles: Saw paddles out of thin hardboard and make saw-cuts in four places as shown. String can be secured into closest saw-cut after winding. Make several sizes to fit your needs.

paddles out of thin hardboard and make saw-cuts in four places as illustrated. The line can be secured into the closest saw-cut after winding. It is advisable to make a number of sizes according to the length and the thickness of the chalk lines.

COMMENTARY. So we see that even an insignificant item, such as a length of string can become an important tool in the hands of a sign painter. String is frequently used in the many procedures of sign painting.

Indeed, the stately erectness of many of our fine buildings, in construction, partially depended upon a simple factor. Stretched between two stakes, or tied to a plumb-bob, was a humble item. A length of string.

So, in the process of sign painting never underestimate the importance of the most simple gadget. Try to learn several methods of doing every job, regardless of how insignificant such methods appear to be. Then when an obstacle arises to prevent the use of one method, you can readily use a different approach. Above all, do not discount the value of old tried and true methods of sign painting—techniques that have endured the tests of time. For example, do not refuse to adapt to the use of a mahlstick just because the guy down the street says it "ain't necessary."

It is to your benefit to keep an open mind and never neglect to accept new approaches and techniques, if they prove to be effective. Learn the basics that have been with us for years, and learn the new as well. Only by doing this can you hope to develop your own versatility to the high point required of the modern day sign painter.

Chapter 20
How to Cope With Obstacles

A number of photographs will be used to illustrate the instruction to follow. These pictures were not chosen because they present outstanding examples of sign painting. An instruction book for beginners should not be used as a medium to "show off" work of the author.

It would be ridiculous to present to the novice a display of highly complicated examples of sign work that can only be accomplished after one has acquired the high degree of skill that develops through long experience. Such presentation could be compared to the father showing to his small son a beautiful selection of new bicycles and then telling him that several years must pass before he could own one.

Therefore, the photographs in this book were chosen mainly to demonstrate certain points of instruction. Also in this choice, great care was taken to present only such work that either is, or soon will be, within the realm of your possibilities. This policy applies to all instruction within this book.

THE COMPLICATIONS OF LAYOUT.

Although signmen prefer to work upon surfaces that are in good condition and free of obstacles, this is not always possible. As long as there are such things as hinges, doorhandles, cracks, ventilators, pillars, eaves-troughs, wires, insulators, etc., it will be necessary for you as a beginner to learn how to adapt and adjust your procedure to cope with such handicaps.

Veteran signmen develop many ways to handle just about any situation, and this knack of learning how to surmount these difficulties is acquired through experience. The essential requirement is to "think out" the job to be done before proceeding with the work. Whenever you are confronted with a tricky job that presents unusual difficulties, spend some time to consider the entire job. When you have determined the most practical way to carry the job through from start to finish, then proceed.

Let us consider the straight-body trucks, vans, etc. with their ever-present hinges, handles, door-cracks and other obstructions. Occasionally both sides of a truck are much the same, but more often they are not. Quite frequently, you might apply the layout to the uncluttered side of a truck, only to discover as you move to the opposite side that it has an abundance of obstacles to contend with. Only then will you realize the impossibility of even coming close to duplicating the layout you have just placed on the first side. This cannot happen if you study the COMPLETE job beforehand.

The old argument that "nobody ever sees both sides of a truck at the same time," while true in concept, is not always acceptable. Most truck owners expect good continuity on their sign work, especially when established trademarks are involved. Considering the variance of contour on each side of the truck, they do not expect exact duplication, but they do desire as much similarity as possible. If the customer is a fleet owner, he is apt to be very much concerned in regard to the consistency of identification.

Therefore, in most signwork it is advisable to begin with the side or surface that presents the greatest difficulty, because it is what you are able to accomplish here that determines how much freedom of layout you will have on the remainder of the job. This is true of all multiple signwork if duplication is required.

In the process of truck lettering, there is another advantage in doing the difficult side first. With careful planning, you can arrange the lettering to completely avoid some of the big awkward hinges, or prevent the necessity of "nursing" certain letters across wide cracks or beads. When trademarks or patterns are involved, you can often void contact with these obstacles by slightly shifting the pattern in either direction. It is not always possible to miss these objects completely, but you can frequently adjust the patterns so that the more complicated parts of the layout will rest on a smooth portion of the surface.

If you lay out the plain side of a truck first, you establish a precedent. You then cannot expect to shift the pattern or change the layout sufficiently enough on the "obstacle side" to achieve a satisfactory degree of similarity. It is good procedure to first lay out the complicated side. The plainer surfaces to follow will be adaptable to layout adjustments and provide the flexibility necessary for maximum uniformity.

Perhaps the best routine to follow on jobs such as this is to combine the use of patterns with direct, or free-hand, layout. It is then possible to avoid many of the obstacles or so-called "deadheads."

The photographs of the two vanette-type trucks, as shown in Figures 34 and 35 are excellent examples. These two trucks alone show the tremendous difference that can exist on the two sides of any particular vehicle of this type. Although these two trucks are quite similar on the driver's side, the opposite side of each truck is completely different in design.

FIG. 34. Side 1.

FIG. 34. Side 2.

The best advice for you, as a novice, would be to thoroughly study the layout arrangements on the passenger sides of these two trucks. Perhaps it will be of some help to briefly describe the procedures used to letter these trucks.

The truck in Fig. 35 was repainted at a body shop. There were two patterns on file from the original lettering job. The pattern for the main panel on the driver's side was suitable for use on both trucks. This pattern included all the lettering shown on the panel above the words, "Shawano, Wis."

FIG. 35. Side 1.

FIG. 35. Side 2.

The word, "Lennox" is a registered trademark, so a separate pattern was prepared for this word within the process of making the original pattern for these main panels. When the layout was completely drawn on the main pattern, a second piece of paper was placed underneath this pattern, directly beneath the word, "Lennox." In the perforation process, more pressure was applied to the pounce wheel at this position to penetrate through the double layer of paper. This resulted in a separate pattern for the single word, "Lennox." This extra pattern was then trimmed down to a strip just large enough in size to comfortably contain this single word.

This is good procedure whenever trademarks or special designs are involved. It is almost necessary to place such a trademark upon other areas on a vehicle. It is easy to fit a small, separate pattern into a congested area. To use the main pattern in an effort to spot this single word into correct position would be an awkward maneuver and could damage the pattern.

Following is the procedure used on the truck pictured in Fig. 34: After consideration of the vehicle, I could see that the complicated side offered small opportunity for similarity. The only similarity possible was limited to the word, "Lennox" and to the bottom line.

The window arrangement allowed but a small panel for the firm name, city and state. All the layout work on this side was applied directly to the surface, except for the word, "Lennox". This demonstrates the convenience of the separate pattern for the isolated use of a trademark. Note how the lettering was arranged to avoid all hinges, cracks, etc. The letter L in the word "Oil" is the only character that bridges a crack.

Further details in regard to this layout are unnecessary. A careful study of the letter arrangements will be self explanatory. The requirement of this customer was that the letters in regard to "24 Hour Service" be as large as possible and absolutely predominant.

Admittedly, a better and more correct layout could have been applied by placing certain letters over cracks as they occurred. The reasons for the use of the layout just described, will soon be explained.

The truck shown in Fig. 35 presented less of a problem. Since I had lettered this truck before, there was an order blank on file, listing the previous procedure used, the size and location of the patterns, the time spent on the job, etc. To this order blank were clipped snapshots showing all detail, so there was no need for forethought or plan of layout.

You will note that the windows spanning the top of the passenger side cause the need for a completely different layout than that used on the Fig. 34 truck. Outside of the word, "Lennox," there was no possibility for similarity of layout. Careful study of the obstructed sides of both these trucks should be of great benefit to you in regard to copy distribution.

The plain sides of both trucks presented no problems. The pattern was transferred to the main panel on each truck. The rest of the lettering was layed out free-hand directly to the surface. You can see that both trucks are similar on the driver's side. There is no reason for the variance of letter-style as used in the words, "Shawano, Wis." This was due to my own negligence.

CUSTOMER CONSIDERATION. Very early in your career as a new operator, you should develop the knack of understanding and fulfilling the individual needs of each customer. Every client has a different set of circumstances and conditions to be considered.

For example, let us analyze the over-all conditions in regard to the trucks just described.

This firm operates a sizeable number of pick-up and van-type trucks. The very nature of the business subjects these trucks to an abnormal amount of accidental abuse. This would include the scratches, gouges and other incidental damages that result from the constant loading and unloading of furnaces, pipes, eaves-troughs, tools, bundles of roofing, tar-paper, etc. The splattering of tar from roofing work adds to this abuse.

The proprietor is wisely concerned about the firm's public image. Therefore, he tries at all times to keep his trucks in presentable condition. This is not an easy task. Because of the excessive wear and tear, these vehicles must quite frequently be repainted and relettered.

This customer also has the natural understanding of advertising that is so much appreciated by signmen. On a prestige vehicle, such as a station wagon, he will suggest the use of small, dignified, conservative lettering. However, he considers his work vehicles to be traveling billboards. Because of their full-time use, he realizes the value of the constant advertising potential of these vehicles. His usual requirement is that all available space, front, back and sides, be lettered with bright, flashy colors to obtain the greatest possible advertising impact. He does not quibble about price. He desires neat and attractive sign work, but does not expect each truck to be a shining example of sign painting, correct in every detail.

Considering a set of circumstances such as this, the unscrupulous sign painter, who is short of work, might purposely complicate the procedure and jump up the price accordingly. As a beginner you might be tempted to do likewise.

Such an approach would be ridiculous. Any man who can operate a successful business and is intelligent enough to maintain his equipment as described, certainly is not a fool. To take advantage of his situation would indeed result in a good profit. But this would be a one-time profit and of short-range benefit. It is doubtful if he would again ask for your services. This is one of the reasons why so many small operators must fold up in less than a year and go to work for somebody else.

The proper line of thought in this case is to consider this man's problems. The neat appearance of his trucks is a distinct advantage to his firm. But, the constant cost of maintenance is a disadantage. Your first concern, as a signman, should be to minimize this disadvantage.

You can do this only by using all the knowledge at your command to efficiently letter his trucks in the quickest possible manner. Since his only desire is for a reasonably neat piece of advertising, this is not too difficult. This eliminates the time-consuming need to letter over hinges, cracks, etc. This is also the reason, previously mentioned, why the layouts on the two trucks were arranged to avoid obstructions.

The same layout procedure was used on both the rears and fronts of all these trucks. Since there were more vehicles lettered in addition to those pictured, this planned avoidance of obstacles alone, considerably reduced the lettering time.

This is the type of thinking that results in long-range benefits. By cutting the working time to a minimum, it is possible to reduce the price without loss of profit percentage. The repeat business and the volume of work available from this account should be considered. Of course, this also does away with the chance to make a "big killing" on one job. But which do you prefer—one big profit and the loss of a customer, or the continued patronage of a reliable firm?

Earlier, it was mentioned that this client did not quibble about price. Because of this, you might wonder why there should be so much concern about the economy of the work. The very fact that any fair minded businessman does not quibble about price is because he has faith in your integrity. Even though the price charged for lettering each vehicle might fluctuate considerably, he will not complain. If you have treated him fairly in previous dealings, he will be confident that you have done the job in the most efficient manner possible. This is what customer consideration is all about.

The most generous customer is not apt to applaud you for "robbing" him. There might be some truth in the classic statement, "There's a sucker born every minute." This literally applies to every infant until such time as mama removes the nursing bottle in favor of baby foods. Seldom does this statement apply to adults. Whether myth or fact, if Mr. Barnum spoke these words, he was referring to his circus patrons. But then, it is assumed that you do not plan to operate a circus, even though there will be certain days and occasions when you will have cause to wonder about this.

THE ADAPTION OF LAYOUT. The planning
of a layout to avoid contact with obstructions should never be carried to an obnoxious extreme. This type of letter arrangement should remain within the limits of good layout. Alternative procedures such as this, are generally used for reasons of convenience and economy. If a layout must be grossly distorted to avoid an obstacle, this method immediately becomes a bad habit.

In regard to shifting of patterns and change of layout, there are professional sign painters who refuse to deviate as much as an inch to miss an obstacle. Perhaps this trait of sticking precisely to the layout, regardless of consequences, is commendable. However, this is a matter of preference and you must ask yourself these questions: "Is it better to adhere to the layout and have a portion of a letter or design cross a large hinge, causing it to present a grotesque appearance when viewed from an oblique angle?" Or, "Is it better to adjust the pattern slightly to avoid such distortion?" Consider within this last question the extra time consumed to maneuver the letter S for instance, across and around a hinge instead of avoiding it whenever possible.

Quite frequently, while waiting for a stop light to change, I have been parked directly behind a large truck. It is natural for a signman to observe the lettering on the rear of such a truck. Even this short study can tell much about the character of the sign painter who lettered the truck. On occasions, I have seen cases where as little as 1 inch of either side of a letter had been nursed over a large, complicated obstruction. Yet, this obstacle could have been completely avoided, by simply condensing an overly-expanded letter W within the same line of lettering. Examples such as this, demonstrate the plain bullheaded character of the person who lettered the truck. Also, I have noticed excellent examples of flexibility on such occasions.

Specifications might sometimes be so strict that the sign-man must adhere to them. It is not always possible, or even advisable, to avoid lettering over hinges, etc. This applies especially to established trademarks. So, you must learn to letter and to stripe over all obstacles. The general rule then is to paint the design so that it appears properly formed as you observe it from a head-on position, or at 90 degrees. Naturally, it will be distorted when viewed from all other angles. This cannot be avoided.

You can expect to be confronted with other problems in the process of layout. Fig. 36 illustrates the rear of a truck with a number of obstacles. Let us assume that this is but one of many trucks that you letter for this customer. Suppose that, normally, the trademark or copy area is positioned a bit lower on the other trucks in this fleet; that this is an odd truck, with an extra large door handle, situated higher than usual.

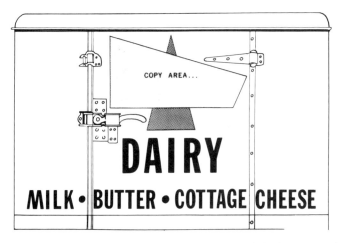

FIG. 36. Extra large door handle requires careful placement of logo or copy area to avoid obstacles. Letter D of "Dairy" is under door handle where it will be subject to abuse, but some-times such things cannot be avoided.

The suggested procedure would be as follows: It is better to raise the pattern to permit the trademark to miss the complicated handle, than it would be to place it in the customary position and paint over the hinge.

Note also how the rest of the lettering is arranged to miss the vertical "turn-bar" leading from the handle, and to avoid other obstructions. With careful forethought to layout it is possible to avoid some of these nuisance areas, but not all of them. Suppose that the copy area in this example would be an oval design, such as an ellipse of 60 degrees. This would then have to cross the upper hinge on the right.

If the oval required painting, this would not be much of a problem. But let us assume that the trademark was some form of film or decal. It is not only difficult to apply a decal across a heavy and prominent obstacle, but the material must usually be cut at these points to eliminate air-bubbles. The field color shows through at these points and must be touched up with paint.

Small patches of decal material, whether they be water-type or film, seldom stick very well on hinges, handles, etc. My preference is to apply the decal and cut out the entire section that covers the obstruction and discard it. Then I paint these hinges and handles by hand to match the color of the decal. If the obstructions are uncomplicated and do not protrude very much, then I would not advise this, since the decals or films can then be applied successfully.

FIG. 37. Oversize F permits spacing letters so as to miss the crack between doors.

Also note that the letter D is directly beneath the door handle. Ordinarily, it is advisable to avoid the placement of lettering beneath door handles. From constantly using the handle, the truck-driver's hand or glove will soon abrase this area. There are occasions when this cannot be avoided.

The sketch in Fig. 37 shows one method of laying out a word in which the center letter would ordinarily have to span the door crack. If the doors fit well and the crack is narrow, it is then best to stick to good fundamentals and center the word in normal position. In this case the second letter M would properly intersect the crack.

However, on secondhand trucks and on a few new ones, this crack will be quite wide. Especially if the doors have been abused, or are out of line, this crack may be an inch wide. It would be difficult to bridge such a crack with a letter. Therefore, this can be avoided by using a large capital letter to compensate for enough space to permit centering the word and arranging for the crack to intersect between the letters. The letter F as shown, is about the maximum size one would use for this purpose. This should not be any larger than necessary when using a standard, unflexible alphabet.

The "Muehl's Furniture" photo shown in Fig. 38, illustrates the same principle. Here, however, the large letter F, although out of context with the rest of the word "Furniture," is designed to appear a planned part of the trademark and is purposely made much larger. Actually, the word "Muehl's" alone is normally the trademark.

FIG. 38. Oversize F here appears to be part of the "Muehl's" trademark and offers spacing of letters to miss the door closure obstacle. Then "n" of "Shawano" would normally fall across the obstacle; extra space between words enables avoidance of that problem.

In the word "Shawano," the lettering would normally occur under or over the door closure at center. By allowing more space between the two words, it is possible and practical to move the word "Shawano" far enough to the left to avoid this.

It is not my contention that the signmen who adhere strictly to the fundamentals are wrong. Certainly, it is wise to stick to sound basics whenever possible. You must judge for yourself when it is practical to bend procedures a little for reasons of economy and profit, without sacrifice of attractive results.

LAYOUT ON AN OBSTRUCTED WALL.

Sometimes the nature of an obstruction on a sign will be such that it might be best to begin the entire layout at this point. This was the case in painting the "Washerette" wall bulletin shown in Fig. 39. The problem, as you can see in the picture, was the concrete-block pillar that juts out from the building.

FIG. 39. *Concrete block pillar projecting from wall posed a problem in this painted wall sign.*

There were two specifications made by the owner. First, he had noticed and liked a few words of this "off-beat" script that I had painted elsewhere on another sign. He requested that the same type of script be used for the word "Washerette." Secondly, he seemed to favor reds and greens on a white field.

The word "Washerette" had to span the length of the wall. At first glance, as a novice, you might wonder why the pillar was not completely avoided. Your first inclination might have been to place the word "Washerette" to the left of the pillar, and then to lay out the words "Open 24 Hours" in one or two lines in the space to the right. This would have been poor layout indeed, because the word "Washerette" is too long to be squeezed into a space of this proportion. Also, in this case, a companion sign of the same size was to be painted on the other side of the building where no pillar existed; hence there was no logical reason to divide the sign into two parts.

The best way to help you to understand the "hows and the whys" of this job would be to explain my logic and the procedure of the job:

Fortunately the copy was simple. Upon studying the size of the wall and the position of the pillar, I realized that one of the letters in the word "Washerette" would have to rest completely upon the pillar. This projected too far out from the wall to intersect with a letter. So I wrote the word "Washerette" upon a piece of scratch paper to help determine which letter would most naturally occur at this position. This proved to be the letter E as shown. The letter R might have been placed here instead, but the pillar was a bit too narrow to contain this letter.

My first step in layout was to lightly draw the letter E as shown, upon the pillar. All of this preliminary layout work was done very lightly with a round stick of soft charcoal. Then, working backwards, starting with the letter R, I sketched the rest of the letters back through the letter A. The letter W was not done at this time. Next, moving to the right of the pillar, I indicated the three remaining letters.

The distance between the final letter E and the right edge of the wall provided me with the necessary position for the initial letter W on the opposite end of the sign. The initial, capital letter of any word of script is usually quite flexible and can be adjusted considerably to fit within the available space. This is the reason why the letter W was not applied previously. It is also much simpler to center a word in this manner. Liberties might be taken with the initial letter that would not be practical within the body of any word.

After the letter W was indicated there was a fairly accurate marking of the position in regard to the entire word. Since it is difficult to lay out letters backwards and maintain a graceful sweep, I next more accurately went over the entire layout in the normal manner of writing, starting with the letter A. In this way it was possible to make the necessary corrections and to provide the smooth, flowing motion that was difficult to accomplish on the original temporary backward layout.

It should be mentioned here that on the other side of the building there is an exhaust vent that protrudes from the building about 6 inches. Upon originally planning the layout, I figured that this would occur approximately above the last letter T in "Washerette." The extra low dip of the second letter T was accordingly planned beforehand in order to avoid this vent.

The bottom part of this sign is quite routine. You will note that the pillar is avoided by arranging the trim work to bridge the abutment. To draw the circle housing the numerals, 24 and the side-arcs for the trim flanges, I drove a small masonry nail into the wall at center and used a string looped about this nail for a compass. The small nail hole is no more serious than a normal pit common to concrete blocks and was filled with paint later.

Through necessity, this wall was not painted in proper sequence. The bottom portion was lettered first, contrary to normal procedure. Since most mothers who patronize washerettes bring their children along, there were quite a few youngsters playing close to the work area. Therefore I first painted those portions on the sign that were within reach of their busy little hands. In this way the paint along the bottom had time to dry up a bit while I lettered the word "Washerette" and was still there to watch them.

It is a "brave" man, indeed, who will nonchalantly drive away to leave a freshly painted sign at the mercy of a dozen little kids.

The colors of this sign are as follows: "Washerette" and the field-color of the 24 circle are painted bright red. The other two words are lettered with dark green, and the trim work and apron along the bottom are painted with a very bright green bordering on chartreuse.

Chapter 21

Understanding the Alphabets

No attempt will be made within this instruction to present a large selection of alphabets. That would be a tremendous task. In addition to the hundreds of alphabets now in existence, there are countless variations and modifications of the same. Newly designed alphabets are regularly being developed and accepted by the trade.

The space within a general instruction book would not permit the presentation of a variety large enough to be of much practical value. Any effort to compile and design a good selection of alphabets would require a separate book.

Fortunately, there are a number of excellent alphabet books available. As a supplement to general instruction, it is suggested that you purchase such a book. You will have need of it for many years. Even the long-time professional must occasionally peek within the pages of an alphabet book to refresh his memory.

Therefore the instruction to follow has been planned to help you to understand better the mechanics of alphabets in general.

It is essential to know how to take full advantage of an alphabet. You must develop the ability to properly execute the lettering, the knack for modification, the wisdom to avoid the common errors, etc. Too frequently, the novice sign painter fails in his quest for professionalism simply because he does not have a thorough understanding of the fundamentals. Although letter-styles change with the times and new alphabets develop, the basics of good lettering remain in regard to uniformity, consistency, etc.

The veteran sign painter, through the years, usually develops at least one alphabet that is almost his own. This is, in most cases, what might be considered a "steal" or a variation of the existent alphabet. An alphabet such as this comes about almost automatically over a period of time and is developed mainly to pick up speed.

An alphabet developed in this way will seldom be found in lettering books, at least not entirely, although some of the letters might be similar to certain standard alphabets.

Because alphabets of this type are primarily developed for speed and economy of time spent, the lettering is not always as precise in continuity as the standard alphabets. Actually these alphabets might be called orphans because they are usually common only to the individual who develops and makes use of them.

The average old timer will usually have two or three personal alphabets that he has developed so that he might have an "ace-in-the-hole" when speed is very essential. In his bag of tricks, he might have one alphabet consisting of capital letters only, another containing both upper and lower case, a fast individual script, etc.

Usually none of these would be considered fine examples of lettering as such, but are quite attractive, acceptable and serve the purpose for which they are intended—to gain time when time is a factor.

Shown in Fig. 40 is an alphabet that falls into this category. This might be an "orphan" in consideration, but I call this my "Utility Alphabet." Also, I do not claim to have invented it because it is, in reality, merely an adaptation of a one-stroke Gothic alphabet done in Italic style.

For some years and for reasons of speed, I had used a rough adaptation of a straight-up Lydian-type alphabet in upper and lower case. However, the advertising man for one of my biggest customers did not like upper and lower case letters, but preferred all capitals. His reason was and still is that caps are easier to read, especially at a distance. Neither did he approve of the casual, fast-type alphabets, but desired a solid, conservative letter-style without any of the frivolities so common to casual lettering, such as broken letters, freak scripts, etc.

Since a large portion of their work consisted of display panels containing an abundance of copy, it became necessary for me to devise a suitable, yet fast, alphabet.

For example, it is common for this company to bring to me a dozen panels, 3 by 4 ft. in size, to be used in upright position, with each to contain different copy.

Customarily there will be a heading such as, "You, too, can show a bigger profit!" This might be followed by 10 to 20 lines of heavy, "catalog-type" copy.

On a sign such as this, any attempt to break the monotony or to impart a unique quality to the sign must be made within the heading. Therefore, I make the heading larger and extend all effort to "flash-up" this part of the sign with a snappy script and as much color as possible. There is no opportunity to do this with the copy to follow. Within the particular heading just mentioned, I might work a design of a "dollar-sign" into the area to tie in with the words, . . . "a bigger profit."

At first, in an effort to please this customer, I tried lettering the bulky copy with a conventional straight-up Gothic letter, with all the corners neatly pointed, but I soon found this to be too slow. The time spent in this effort raised the cost to the customer to a prohibitive figure.

ABCCDE
FGGHJK
LMMNO
PQRSTU
VWXYZ

FIG. 40. "Utility" Alphabet.

Very soon, I began to use the alphabet as shown in Fig. 40. Because this was adapted to my particular method of working, it was very fast for me to do. Other signmen might find no speed advantage in this alphabet at all, especially those who are left handed.

Many beginners will find this alphabet very helpful to be used for speed and utility, so I will direct your attention to a few of the mechanics involved. Note that the "stroke endings" are a bit round in nature and not pointed off. On this plate they are done quite precisely, but it is permissible to allow these strokes to remain rounder still on the ends if you prefer.

In fact, if you are working with an exceptionally good brush, the original start of many of these strokes might be good enough and will not require further "doctoring" with the brush. The tops of the strokes in the letter "H" for example, may be accurate enough upon application, if care is used, and only the bottoms will need touching up.

Also study the upper left corner of the letter "B." The stubby little round serif at this point avoids pointing off the letters. The vertical stroke is made first; then the brush is moved to the top, and the little serif is quickly applied. The brush is then pulled around twice to make the double loops to form the rest of the letter. Pulling the first vertical stroke at the bottom a bit to left, as you bring it to an end to form the oblique corner, also speeds things along.

This little stubby serif is found on other letters to follow, such as the letters, D, E, F, P, and R.

The first letter C is made with two strokes of the brush only. This accounts for the peaks on the stroke ends, which is the natural way in which a curved stroke terminates, if the brush is properly manipulated. The same result is evident in other curved letters. It is this feature that causes the lack of continuity or consistency mentioned previously. To have some letters end with sharp peaks and others with blunt ends is ordinarily not considered good lettering procedure. But there are occasions when it is expedient to sacrifice a bit of conformity in the interest of speed.

You will notice several alternate letters or modifications. The use of these is a matter of choice. If you use the second letter C with the extra downstroke, you must then follow through with the same technique on the letters G and S.

The letters shown in Fig. 41 demonstrate the variance between letters now being discussed and the more correctly formed casual styles. The first letter S on the right is as it should appear in the "utility alphabet." Do not, in any case, confuse this type of letter with the casual letter S shown second from left. This casual type of lettering belongs in an entirely different alphabet, as does the style of letters C and G. There are many versions of this casual type of lettering, although most are quite similar in sweep.

The word "casual" is quite deceptive because it suggests ease of execution, but do not let this fool you. Most of the casual lettering, currently so popular, is not simple to do at first. Rather it is a "studied" casualness and requires a great amount of skill in brush handling. Most casual alphabets are developed by lettering artists who possess a thorough knowledge of letter formations. The primary object is to develop a letter that can be made with the least number of strokes. To do this, the letters must be formed to take advantage of the natural way in which a brush begins and ends certain strokes.

FIG. 41. Alternate letters.

A complete knowledge of lettering and much practice is necessary to do a casual letter properly. The very casualness; the graceful sweeping lines that suggest ease of lettering, is the result of extreme excellence in brush handling. This can not be achieved properly until you are quite proficient with a brush. To attempt it sooner results in a clumsy, belabored mess. Once you have learned and have mastered several of the casual type alphabets, you will find them to be extremely fast and highly attractive.

Regarding the full alphabet shown in Fig. 40, it should not be used as a basic alphabet. In my case, I use this and other personal adaptations to gain time. Upon lettering a truck, I might use it for the street address, the name of the city and state. It is especially suitable for license numbers, weights, etc. or for incidental copy. Perhaps you might use it to a greater degree when your customer's budget requires economy or for an overload of copy.

In the use of all alphabets that you might personally develop, try to maintain as much consistency as possible. Do not stray too far from good lettering principles. Confine their use to necessity and classify them for what they are—utility alphabets.

ABUSE OF THE ALPHABETS. The word "modified" is often used in the description of an alphabet. The newcomer to the sign trade should understand right from the start that there is a vast difference between modification of an alphabet and "butchery" of an alphabet.

In my dictionary, the definition of the word, "modify" means, in essence, to somewhat change the form of, or alter somewhat. There is no harm in modification and most sign-men do this to some extent with all the alphabets. This gives a personal touch to their lettering and sometimes the modifications, when skillfully done, actually seem to improve the original alphabet.

The experienced sign painter might modify an alphabet or a number of reasons. He purposely might do this for better readability, to save space, to gain speed in lettering, etc.

Without actual purpose, he will develop certain modifications through the years due to the way he holds the brush, starts his strokes and other lettering techniques peculiar to his own style. The latter modifications come about almost automatically.

No two sign painters work exactly the same, although there can be a marked similarity in their lettering. No matter how one is trained or by what method he begins, he will eventually end up by doing his lettering in the manner that is easiest and most natural for him, thereby developing his own technique.

Most of these modifications, whether done purposely or automatically, are excellent when executed by a skilled sign painter. A word of advice to you, as a novice: Do not deviate too much from the "mother-alphabet." This generally results in a hodge-podge of stunt lettering and such result will definitely stamp your work as that of an amateur.

Good modification is usually slight and if it is radical, it must be well planned and in keeping with the over-all characteristics of the original alphabet.

When we speak of "butchering" an alphabet, I can think of no other alphabet that is more abused than the Old English alphabet and its variations.

For example on a recent trip, I noticed throughout the entire drive, a number of signs upon which the word "Antique" consisted of all capital letters. This is a taboo of long standing in the sign trade. In all the Old English variations, the capital letter should only be used as the initial letter, and the rest of the word should consist of all lower-case letters. There are rare exceptions. Certain words can consist completely of capitals. Before using such a word you must carefully consider the formation of each letter within the word. The word, "'Season's," so often used at Christmas time, is one such word.

It is difficult to read the Old English text on any sign at best, but when using all capital letters it is almost ridiculous. (See Fig. 42)

In preparing this illustration, I have modified the lettering to one of its most simple forms, yet it is still awkward in appearance and difficult to read. Several other common mistakes have been included within the word that I noticed on several of the previously mentioned signs. Note the extra top cross-bar on the letter A. This would not correctly be present on a one-stroke, modified version such as this.

ANTIQUES

FIG. 42. Old English in all capitals is extremely difficult to read.

Also notice the double-stroke on the letter S and extending upward. This type of S belongs in a completely different version of the Old English alphabet. If this type of S were to be used here, then certain other letters of the word would also have to be given the more complete, fancy, double-stroke treatment.

Incidentally, some of the "Antique" signs that I beheld were actually given the full-blown treatment of the "Engrosser's Old English," complete with all the fanciful curlicues, fine lines, etc. Indeed a sign to behold, but not one to be read; in fact not much more readable than a foreign language.

Obviously, most of these signs were prepared by amateurs, beginners, or poorly trained sign painters. This brings up another question. Why is it that so many feel that the only way to show antiquity on a sign is to use an Old English letter? Whenever required to show antiquity upon a sign, or an aura of old-world dignity, the first thing that pops into their head is Old English, yet the veteran signman will only use this alphabet sparingly.

In regard to "Antiques," for example, the competent signman would be more apt to use one of the Trylon-type letters, such as "Barnum" or "Playbill," also referred to as "Woodblock." This would be simpler to do, be more legible, and would provide the "old-world" atmosphere far better than does Old English or any of its variations. There are occasions when the customer demands the use of Old English and the sign painter has no choice.

Recently I saw a sign upon which the sign painter actually insulted the Old English alphabet. The sign was in front of a Gift Shop. It was not convenient for me to get a picture, so see Fig. 43 for an approximate example of the manner in which the word "Gift" was handled. Note the big capital T used as the final letter of the word. Why this big capital letter was used is still a mystery to me.

FIG. 43. *Insult to Old English alphabet.*

There is also no valid reason for the spur on the left edge of the letter G or the thin vertical line on the letter T. The actual sign was poorly lettered, with clumsy, ungraceful strokes. To add to the confusion, the remainder of the copy on the sign was done in a nondescript block letter. Most of this lettering was shaded with a very deep gray, instead of a dainty pastel shade of some variety. The entire sign provided the mood one would have when visiting a morgue, not the gay, expectant feeling that a person would associate with a visit to a gift shop.

During the process of learning how to modify lettering, you should adhere to the predominant characteristics of the original alphabet.

Fig. 44 presents seven examples of the lower-case letter a. All of the first six can be used successfully within a line of modified Old English. The first one is perhaps, the most correct and most commonly used style. No. 2 is actually taken from the Goudy text, but is slightly modified by making the peaks more pronounced. In this way it is more adaptable to be used in connection with Old English as a substitute for No. 1. When correctly rendered, the Goudy text would have these peaks, but would tend to be rounded off a little more at these points.

No. 3 is a letter that I use frequently. I do not know its origin, but it is quite adaptable. No. 5 is adapted from the "Cloister" alphabet, while Nos. 4 and 6 are modifications based somewhat upon "Engraver's Old English." You will notice that all six have one thing in common: The broad strokes and thin lines, plus the peaks, all of which are associated with the Old English alphabet. No. 7 was added as a little "fooler." At first glance you might consider this to be as suitable to use as any of the first six letters. The round top rules this out, because it is not in keeping with the flat, sharp strokes and peaks common to Old English.

FIG. 44. When lettering to modify an alphabet, you must stay with the basic characteristics of the original alphabet. The first six examples are suitable for use within a line of Old English. The seventh is not.

This is, however, a neat letter and is taken from an attractive alphabet called "Pen Scribe." (I first noticed this alphabet as prepared for SIGNS of the Times magazine, in the issue of December, 1962, by J. I. Biegeleisen, in which he gives credit for its design to Carlyle and Oring.) For sheer beauty, this alphabet has a fine potential when properly used.

FIG. 45. Two acceptable versions of Old English discussed by Gregory.

Sometimes letters are modified merely because of a personal dislike for a certain letter. Other times, the modification is to save time in lettering. The first letter S as shown in Fig. 45 is perhaps the most commonly accepted in the modified version of Old English. However, in my case I find it a bit difficult and time-consuming to execute this letter correctly. Therefore, I use the radically modified letter S (No. 2) whenever it is practical, mainly because it can be quickly and easily executed. On high class work, it is advisable to stick to the more authentic version, No. 1.

To sum up, it is well to say that the Old English alphabet is indeed beautiful in character and has a definite, established place in the sign trade. Its beauty depends on its gracefulness and upon completion should not have a belabored appearance. No attempt should be made to use it on a regular job until you have mastered it to a respectable degree. This dignified alphabet can be converted to ugliness through poor execution.

The traditional good taste and beauty of Old English is completely lost when used in the wrong place. Recently, a number of large cattle trucks have been passing through town lettered with Old English. To me, this is as incongruous as lettering a sleek, stream-lined funeral hearse with big, yellow, cartoon-style letters and outlining them with fluorescent red. This is a case where, somewhere, a sign painter fell in love with this one alphabet and has decided to work it to death. It is a safe bet that the stock cars in his area have been lettered likewise.

There are times when a customer might demand to have Old English lettering placed on a beat-up garbage truck. You would then have no choice but to do so, or to refuse the job entirely. This might have been the case with the signman who is lettering these cattle trucks. Perhaps he had to do it for one customer, and then other truckers demanded the same.

Old English, even in its most modified form should be confined to headings on church signs, funeral parlors, diplomas, Christmas signs, perhaps a bank or colonial sign, etc. All good lettering should be used in keeping with its intended purpose and tradition.

VARIATIONS OF THE ALPHABETS.

The sign painter of today is confronted with an astounding variety of alphabets. When I first began dabbling around with signwork over 40 years ago, most lettering consisted of the basic alphabets. To attest to their durability, many of these are still being used today. The variety was small compared to present standards.

Most of the old timers of that era frowned on any deviation from the old tried and true alphabets. Fortunately, progress cannot be stopped in any trade. The younger sign painters and the more broadminded old timers, began to take liberties with letter formations. Other signmen copied these modifications and added some of their own. Soon, a completely new alphabet was born. Although the original alphabet might have been Roman or Gothic, it could no longer be considered as such because of the changes. Therefore, it became a separate entity and was given a name. It can be assumed that this modification procedure was the mother of many of the present day alphabets.

It is conceivable that in a decade or two a new group of signmen will follow this same process with other existent alphabets. After a period of evolution, this will result in additional new and individual alphabets.

The implication here is not to suggest that all alphabets were developed in this way. Many of our alphabets were purposely designed from scratch by lettering artists through many long hours of tedious thought and labor over a drawing board.

Regardless of how these variations came about, the beginner today should be thankful. Never before has there been a broader scope of lettering to choose from than there is at present. Speaking to you, as a novice, it is only through change, experimentation, etc. that we progress. Although beginners at the moment, there is certain to be among you those who will be creative enough to develop the alphabets of tomorrow.

The alphabet to be used as a base for this discussion of variation was chosen because it lends itself to many modifications. (See Fig. 46) Since I do not know who developed it, credit cannot be given to the originator of this alphabet. However, variations of this alphabet have been in use for many years. This type of letter was especially popular on the early American scene.

For some years it was practically non-existent and only during the last few years has it again become a very popular and widely used alphabet. There seems to be some confusion among signmen in regard to its true name. It is referred to on occasion as Trylon, Barnum, Playbill, Woodcut, etc. If it is expanded considerably, it is called Western.

Most frequently it appears to be referred to as "Playbill." This alphabet has rather heavy, thick-and-thin characteristics, including very wide serifs at top and bottom. "Barnum" does not have exactly the same treatment. The strokes and serifs are much thinner, and some of the cross-strokes in the Barnum version are curved such as the upper cross bar of the letter T.

The complete alphabet, as shown in Fig. 46, might be very close to the original. The thick-and-thin treatment must be followed when using this version. Some signmen prefer to place the thin vertical stroke of the letter M on the left side of the letter rather than on the right as shown.

FIG. 46. *Traditional Playbill has lent itself to numerous variations and was especially popular on the early American scene.*

Numerous signmen, including myself, do not like the lack of a serif on top of the letter A, so they place one at this point as shown in Fig. 47. Note that the vertical strokes actually converge at an imaginary point within the top serif. This is done to prevent the letter from appearing squat in shape. The top peak in the letter opening is also rounded off to make the intrusion into the serif less noticeable and for better design.

The true letter G as shown in the master alphabet is a bit difficult to make. Some signmen also feel that it appears clumsy. Therefore, they modify it as shown in Fig. 47, and in this case the letters C and S must also be modified. It would be poor procedure to remove the extra vertical serifs from the letter G and fail to do so on the letters C and S.

Concerning the letter N, the reason for this modification is practically the same as for the letter A. The lack of a serif on the bottom right of the N seems to cause an unfinished naked appearance. The addition of a serif, as shown on Fig. 47 is simple.

In this Playbill alphabet, the letter that receives the most criticism is the letter Q. The complaint is that it is ugly and confusing to read. The illustration shows two alternate treatments. The second example is used most frequently, most likely because of its simplicity.

The letter R is in my estimation, a beautiful letter just as it is on Fig. 46. However, on some of the master alphabet plates of Playbill, the letter R is used instead as it is shown on Fig. 47. It would therefore become an alternate rather than a modification.

FIG. 47. Modifications of Playbill.

The straight downstroke on the indication of the second letter R in Fig. 47 can only be employed if the entire alphabet is being used in a wider or extended form. If used throughout the entire copy area, this slab-serif would require maximum space.

Finally, we consider the modification of the letter S. The example on the illustration is self explanatory. In preparing this letter, I purposely flattened the inside curves of top and bottom serifs. Note how these are almost horizontal, with merely a slight curve at each corner. This is in direct contrast to the same curves of the letters C, G, and Q, in which these curves are almost half-round. The inside curves of all the round-type letters can be given the same treatment as used on the letter S if you choose.

You will note that the thick-and-thin technique was abandoned on the modifications. The thin strokes are all of equal width. This must then be carried through in the use of the entire alphabet. It was done in this way to provide you with the possibility of a modification of the complete alphabet. It is much faster and easier to do this, than to do the thick-and-thin. But, then it would be an adaptation of, rather than a true version of either Playbill or Trylon.

When you paint the letters pertinent to this type of alphabet, you will develop your most natural technique. My preference is to letter, fill-in, and finish each letter as the work proceeds. My procedure is to use a quill of a size which I can execute the thinner lines with one stroke, outline the slab-serifs, and fill these in with the same brush. This results in a smoother letter, a minimum of brush strokes and avoids the hazard of working over a profusion of wet strokes off to your right and below. This would be the case, should you paint all of the thin strokes first, and then go back over this jumbled up area to complete the work. By completing each letter immediately, you avoid the lumpy looking finish on the letters at such points where the paint piles up from delay of the fill-in process. On highway bulletins, of course, one would use fitches or flat cutters.

This type of alphabet is one that you should definitely add to your repertory. It has a flexible quality that allows for dozens of variations. Watch the magazines, newspapers, etc. and look through the back issues of SIGNS of the Times magazine. You will find many variations. With the addition of various peaks on the letter-strokes, a curlicue or two, fancy curves to the tops and bottoms of the serifs, you can design a gala letter for many occasions. You will be amazed at the number of alphabets that evidently had their origin with this Playbill-type letter. If I were to be asked to suggest an over-all title for this alphabet, it would be "Traditional." I do not know its origin, but it immediately suggests one word to me: America. It is almost automatic to associate this alphabet with the good old days, solidity, the old-west, parades, circuses, picnics, antiques, hamburgers, hot dogs, vacations, rustic resorts, county fairs, elections— you name it.

In fact if this country were to ever adopt a National Alphabet, I would nominate this little old alphabet as strictly "All American."

COMMENTARY. How many alphabets you commit to memory depends upon your individual needs. It is advisable to memorize the lettering that you use on a steady basis. It is not too essential to memorize alphabets that will rarely be used. Many excellent professionals will consult an alphabet book when required to do authentic Old English. Most veterans can efficiently letter simplified versions from memory, but few bother to learn the complicated style because the need for this is infrequent. Those who do have a constant need for Old English, will naturally realize the advantage of learning it by heart and do so.

The extent to which you memorize alphabets must therefore be based upon your personal preference and the frequency of use.

Chapter 22

The Side Factors of Lettering

The professionalism that you seek in the process of learning the sign trade cannot be found solely within the major fundamentals. It is the knowledge of the side factors that can contribute so much to your effort.

Throughout the remainder of this book, there will be revealed to you an abundance of professional tricks of the trade. These will be described to coincide with your progress.

At this point it becomes necessary to describe several of the major side factors in order to keep pace with the formal instruction.

CONSIDER THE AMPERSAND. The ampersand has a rather dignified name for a mischievous little character. When a customer says, "Don't print the entire word 'and,' but use one of those little 'doo-hickeys,'" he is referring to what is more commonly known as the "and-sign," technically, the ampersand.

Scarcely a day passes that the signman (or sign lady) does not make use of this symbol. It is therefore unfortunate that it is, more often than not, omitted from alphabet plates. A check on this will show many alphabets presented in their entirety, along with the dollar sign, the exclamation point, and everything else but the ampersand.

The professional can quite easily improvise a symbol to fit within any alphabet. To the novice, this must be a bit confusing, and perhaps it accounts for the conglomeration of unsuitable ampersands apparent at times.

The ampersand, like a summer-cold, seems to have no end and one could easily develop a hundred or more acceptable versions of this symbol.

Through observation it seems that most signmen will experiment with many versions of this symbol and eventually will adopt the use of perhaps a favored half-dozen. Indeed, a person can often recognize the work of another signwriter by his unique ampersands. They identify the job just as surely as though he had signed his name to the work.

The ampersand can at once be a blessing and a curse. At times it appears to be out of place no matter where it might be positioned. This occurs, especially, when one must use two lines for the copy. A good example would be the words, "Transfer & Storage" to be lettered in two lines on a narrow truck door. Your question might be, "Should I place the "and-sign" at the end of "Transfer," or on the line below, ahead of the word, Storage?"

In this particular case it would be best to place it on the second line, ahead of "Storage," which has one less letter than the word "Transfer," thus allowing more space.

At other times the ampersand can actually be an object of beauty, improving the layout. One has only to page through certain high class magazines to realize how important this symbol has become. In the past the ampersand was usually subdued and treated as a necessary evil. The new breed of adman, has, in recent years, emphasized the ampersand and turned it into an asset through good design, causing it to be an integral part of the ad. Many signmen are following suit.

Illustrated in Fig. 48 are a number of commonly used ampersands. We shall briefly describe their pros and cons. Let me point out that although I do know most of these and others by heart, the fact is that I did learn some of them from fellow signmen. Others, I picked up through

FIG. 48. Some commonly used ampersands.

general observance of magazine and newspaper ads, etc. I like to think that a few of these are absolutely original, but I hesitate to "trip" myself. It is not uncommon for each of us to see a technique, letter, or symbol, salt it away in our memory and many months later drag it out of our subconscious minds thinking it to be original.

So, cautiously, I'll say that I have a sneaking suspicion that I did develop several of the ampersands illustrated.

The opinions that I express to you about the examples shown here are strictly my own, and do not think that any statement is the last-word or the reflection of the entire sign trade. Other signmen may sharply disagree with these opinions and I respect their right to do so.

The technique of one signman, although highly skilled, does not necessarily have to appeal to another sign painter of equal ability with a different approach. It is only through friendly disagreement, criticism, etc. that any trade or profession can improve and progress.

Your best approach would be to study the ampersands pictured and to choose the examples that have the most appeal and those that appear to be most compatible to the manner in which you manipulate the brush.

Proper placement of the ampersand is important. Fig. 49 illustrates how you would position example No. 1 of the ampersands within a line of copy. For most purposes it is proper to apply the symbol about 25 per cent smaller than the adjacent lettering. If No. 2 had been used here, the lower right downstroke would not have extended down to the lower guideline. It would, instead, touch neither guideline and would occupy a position close to mid-center between the two letters.

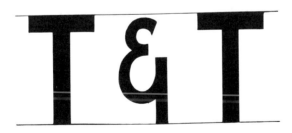

FIG. 49. *Proper placement of ampersand is important. It should be about 25% smaller than the adjacent lettering.*

Ampersands such as Nos. 4, 5, 6, 19, 20, etc., look best when resting flush on the lower guideline. This is because of the nature of the downstroke, which is similar to the oblique downstroke of the letter H. These are restive types of ampersands, and therefore must obviously rest upon the guideline. This type would not look well floating around in center.

In addition to No. 2, you could position at center such symbols as Nos. 10, 11, 12, 13, 14, 15, and possibly 21. This means that the central body of the symbol is at the center. The various downstrokes can terminate at the bottom guideline or a bit below.

Discussing the selection from the beginning; Nos. 1, 2, 3, 4, 6, 11, and 13 are all suitable for most everyday lettering such as one-stroke Gothic. No. 4 presents a slightly unfinished appearance. No. 11 is also to be used in one-stroke Gothic, but has a "stunt" characteristic that is not always desirable.

No. 5 is to be used with thin, condensed lettering such as Condensed Ribbon, Huxley and other similar alphabets where the curvature is of the same degree.

No. 8 is designed for use with blunt-serif letters of bold nature such as Cooper and other similar fonts. (This type of alphabet is often referred to by old timers as, "soup-bone" or "ham-bone.")

The thick-and-thin type alphabets call for ampersands such as Nos. 9, 10, 12, 14, 15, and 16. Some are for italics, and others for vertical lettering. Almost any of these can be adapted to either script or the printed letter. In this example they are in their thinner or dainty form, but all of these can be proportionally changed to be as thick as necessary when using a bold or heavy stroke letter.

No. 17 is to be used with Old English type alphabets and should be as high as the capital letters.

The symbol, No. 18, fits well with most casual alphabets and is also adaptable to the "broken" type Italic letter styles.

For very heavy, bold poster or comic-style lettering use No. 19. This can be slanted for Italics or modified at will in regard to boldness.

No. 20 is one version of an ampersand compatible with "Broadway," which along with similar alphabets is enjoying a surge of popularity.

No. 21 is also quite popular at this time with perhaps a dozen versions, all quite similar. It is usually used in the same size as the adjacent lettering, but can be reduced.

Now we come to what I call the "monstrosities." These consist of Nos. 22, 23, 24, 25, 26, and 27. The deplorable fact is that these ampersands are perhaps more authentic than any of those so far discussed. My sign knowledge goes back only to 1929, but we had to learn to make use of these at that time. They were then, and in some cases are still considered to be true ampersands. My impression is that they are clumsy, ungraceful and about as modern as a covered wagon. It is regrettable that they did not go out of existence along with the prairie schooners.

For years I have looked upon this type of ampersand as a respectable numeral 8 that had either broken its back, or had become too lazy to stand up without a prop. No. 26 is a real freak and might be called the "lazyman's and," a poorly executed number 3 done in reverse.

No. 22 is about the only one that I would accept by today's standards unless I were under duress.

Finally, let us consider No. 28. This is the ampersand from the "Playbill" alphabet. I have no quarrel with it, except to say that I prefer either of the two alternates, No. 29 or 30.

There are hundreds of ampersands. We have considered but a few.

THE USE OF THE WORD "AND" INSTEAD OF THE SYMBOL.

It has been established that the ampersand or "and-sign" is an important factor in the performance of good lettering.

You must not rule out the importance of learning how to use the word "and" in its entirety. Just as the ampersand has its variations, so too does the complete word. Although the symbol is used more frequently, there are occasions where the use of the complete word will be more advisable and, indeed, almost necessary to maintain a better balance of layout.

This situation occurs many times while lettering trucks upon which the lettering must bridge the cracks between the doors or other obstacles.

Fig. 50 presents a classic example. Here you see a group of words that must bridge the crack between the two rear doors of a van-type truck at center. Since "Laundry and Dry Cleaners" is a fairly common line of copy, most veteran sign painters have lettered this many times. They have done so, just as I have, by using either the ampersand or the complete word without any significant difficulty.

But let's consider the several various approaches and the pros and cons of each. In the study of the illustration it is important that you understand why it is most logical to use the complete word rather than an ampersand. At the moment this may seem to be of small consequence. As you progress with your development as a sign painter, you will frequently encounter the same, or at least similar situations. This example embodies several of the basic principles incidental to proficient layout procedure.

An ampersand could be used without any difficulty here if the letters were vertical, or "straight-up" instead of being in Italics. You could then divide the line by arranging the lettering so the door-crack would occur between the letters D and R in the word, "Dry." In this way the letters, "Laundry & D" would be positioned to the left of the crack, and the letters, "ry Cleaners" to the right. The ampersand could then be placed at center between the words, "Laundry and Dry."

If the letters were to be without shading then both the letter D and the letter R would be placed as close to the crack as possible to avoid too much space between the letters. Should the letters require a drop-shadow on the left side, you would then have to position the letter R further to the right of the crack to allow for the shading stroke.

This would cause a greater space between the letters at this point. For uniformity it would be necessary to allow approximately the same amount of space between the rest of the lettering. Sometimes the crack between doors will be quite wide. In this case you would have a maximum amount of space between each letter. Therefore, the letters would need to be quite tall and thin to fit within the limited horizontal space.

LAUNDRY and DRY CLEANING

FIG. 50. *Group of words arranged to bridge crack between two rear doors of a van type truck. However, when necessary, it is better to paint a letter over a crack than to overly arrange to miss the crack entirely and use erratic spacing.*

To arrange a layout so the crack intersects between the letters is difficult when Italics are involved. You will note on Fig. 50 that it would be impossible to arrange for the crack to occur between the letters D and R without leaving considerable space. The limited width could not accommodate the rest of the copy at this spacing ratio.

If you were to use an ampersand in this particular layout, parts of both the letters D and R would have to be lettered across the crack. This is not a great problem if the doors are well-fitted and the crack is narrow. Sometimes this crack will be pronounced and difficult to cross.

The pleasant alternative is to proceed as shown in the illustration. Use the complete word "and" to separate the words. The word "and" is flexible. It can be condensed or extended as required to compensate for any awkwardness that might otherwise occur in the layout.

With this method you can avoid a number of obstacles in all lettering. It must be stressed that when necessary you should letter over a crack. It is bad procedure to avoid such an obstacle when conditions do not permit and then attempt to compensate for this by using erratic spacing within the rest of the word. Any effort to miss an obstacle becomes secondary, if such a maneuver results in the sacrifice of good layout.

When using the script form of the word "and" in connection with printed letters you must adapt its style to harmonize with the adjacent lettering. It would be ridiculous to employ a heavy, thick-stroke letter as a conjunction for a dainty, thin-stroke style of lettering.

To aid you in selecting the proper forms of the word "and" to adapt for your needs, I have prepared a group of samples. (See Fig. 51) This selection, although not large, should be diversified enough for you to choose a style that will be suitable to use in conjunction with nearly every printed letter you might be using.

All of these samples are of the thick-and-thin variety, but if you are using a one-stroke letter of uniform width, you can modify most of these to what is commonly referred to as a "pencil-script." This signifies that the strokes maintain a fairly uniform width throughout. This pencil-script is not illustrated, but can easily be executed by following the same basic forms as illustrated. Eliminate the thick-and-thin characteristic and twirl the brush so that the resultant stroke is of uniform width.

It is suggested that you make the strokes of the word "and" slightly thinner in width than those of the adjoining printed letters by using a smaller brush.

Sometimes a slightly thick-and-thin characteristic such as in No. 13 is necessary, because this is too bold to use a full stroke. This particular example might best be used with any of the heavy, bold display-type Gothics, or other heavy letters, whether they be of uniform width or not. This applies also to Nos. 9 and 10.

No. 1 is a very common script and is compatible with the thick-and-thin Roman styles. The thickness of the stroke in all cases should be modified to be consistent with the adjacent printed letters. The strokes are peaked off, so this must be considered. If the printed letters are round in nature, then use No. 2.

No. 6, because of its extended form, is excellent to use when you must fill up extra space. When space is limited, a condensed style such as No. 7 should be used. Use No. 8 in conjunction with any of the top-heavy letters, thickening or thinning the strokes to conform with the printed letters.

FIG. 51. Script of the word "and" must harmonize with the adjacent lettering. These samples can aid in selecting proper form.

Casual printed letters require the use of scripts such as Nos. 9 and 10. Detailed explanation is not required to further describe these examples. By now, your judgment should be sufficiently developed to enable you to choose the style that is most adaptable for your immediate purpose.

No. 5 has never been acceptable to me, although it is popular with some. It is a bit too frivolous and its unique formation draws attention away from the principle message. Some sign painters will latch on to a stunt gimmick such as this and use it for every purpose. Usually this is an attempt to cover up other shortcomings. Stunt letter-arrangements of this type should be used sparingly and with some regard for the nature of the sign involved.

No. 12 is one adaptation of many done in the same style. Its most proper use is perhaps for tall, vertical display cards. When placed upon a line by itself, it can provide attractive "white space" and contribute a certain flair to an otherwise drab sign. This is one of the "way-out" lettering styles. If it were to stand alone, it would be scarcely recognizable as the word "and." It must depend partly on the adjacent lettering to establish its identity.

The sign painter must use care in deciding how "far out" he might go with these extreme styles of lettering. A retailer will expect a piece of advertising to attract a certain type of customer. You must design every sign that you paint with this in mind.

For example, a window card with the fast, ultra-ultra script, scarcely distinguishable as English, might be acceptable and indeed, admired in the window of a high-class store in a large city. The clientele is accustomed to this type of lettering.

Place this same card in the window of a budget-priced department store in a small, obscure town out in the "sticks" and the viewer might say, "Gosh, it's pretty! But what does it say?" — then walk on, mumbling, "Maybe it's upside down."

Currently, the trend of advertising is toward simplicity, especially with the big nationally advertised products. These advertisers have realized the fallacy of presenting advertising that appeals only to the urbane. Their goal is to reach the greatest number of buyers.

So, plan your sign painting with consideration for your local environment.

FUNDAMENTALS OF SHADING. A veteran sign painter once said to me, "Don't worry too much about the shade. Just make a good letter and you can slap the shading on just about any old way."

That was a stupid remark. The reference to good lettering was fine, but careless shading can ruin a sign, regardless of how expert the lettering might be.

It is true that a skilled sign painter can apply shading very rapidly. As a novice, you might think that it is being done haphazardly, but upon close observance you will note that it is quite accurate. This ability is acquired through a complete understanding of the principles of shading, plus hours of applied practice.

Since it is essential that you do understand the process of good shading, we will now consider the most basic fundamentals. The most common type of shading, and the one that you will most frequently use, is similar to the example shown in Fig. 52. This will consist of a one-stroke shade on the left side and the bottom of each letter. None of the strokes will touch the letter as shown, but will be kept away from the letter a slight bit. You should leave a space between the shading strokes and the letter edges not to exceed an eighth of an inch. In this way you can shade the letters before they are dry and more rapidly bring the job to completion. Even when the lettering is dry, this technique of shading is the most popular and rapid of all methods.

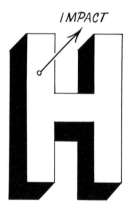

FIG. 52. Shading to left and bottom gives maximum impact to display that is viewed from right.

Some refer to this as a cast shadow, but it might more correctly be termed a block shadow. This is exactly what you do in this process—cause the letters to present a block-like appearance.

The requirement for all correct shading is to maintain

the proper position of all the angles. A 45-degree angle is ideal for this fast and simple shade, and it is advisable to strive for uniformity on these slants. Shading is never applied merely to fill up space or to add another color to a sign. It is used to provide the additional impact that the letter has upon the eyes of the viewer. You should never paint anything upon a sign unless you have a calculated reason for doing so.

At first you will find it rather difficult to shade amidst wet lettering. It will then become apparent why so much stress was placed upon developing the ability to use a mahlstick and to work hand-over-hand. Numerous signmen apply all of the lettering with the hand-down method, and then switch to the use of the mahlstick or the hand-over-hand method for the shading process. This is the only practical method for the application of trim work around designs or lettering when the paint is still wet.

If you can letter only with the hand-down method, there are several approaches that might reduce the risk of smearing the wet lettering. If you are lettering a truck, and there is a considerable amount of lettering to be done, proceed as follows: Determine which portions of the truck will require the most intricate shading. Apply a direct layout or transfer the pattern to just one of these areas and letter this immediately. Follow this procedure on the next portion that will require shading, always arranging to leave those letters that are not to be shaded until the very last. In this way, by the time that you have finished all of the lettering on the vehicle, the very first portion that you lettered will have had the maximum amount of time in which to dry. This portion might be dry enough so that you can apply the shading without problem. While shading this, the second portion will have additional drying time, etc. until the job is completed. On a job such as this, careful planning in regard to the sequence of work can often permit you to continue the work without any waiting periods.

On a smaller job, such as two cab doors of a truck, there is seldom enough lettering to gain much drying time. Therefore if it is a one-man job, you will be forced to shade around wet lettering. Proceed as follows: Apply the layout and letter the top line of copy only, on each side of the truck. Then shade both of these lines before proceeding with any of the lettering beneath. Next, apply the second line of lettering to both sides of the truck and immediately shade each of these. Do this progressively until the job is completed. This method involves much washing of brushes and switching of colors, but at least you can avoid messing up the line of lettering beneath the one upon which you are working, as would be the case if you were to do all of the lettering and then try to apply the shading.

For your own sake, do not accept the work-sequences just described as permanent methods of procedure. These are suggested only as a means of getting the work done if you are still limited to "hand-down" method of lettering. Should this be your personal circumstance, would it not be advisable at this time to supplement your versatility by learning the additional hand-positions? It would not then be necessary to "bend" professional procedure to adapt to your individual lack of versatilty.

Illustrated, are several of the most commonly used forms of shading. The heavy, block-form as shown in Fig. 52 is what might be called a precision shade and should be done as accurately as the lettering. Since no space is left between the shade and the letter, it is best to do this when the lettering is dry. On smaller, single-stroke work, you would proceed the same as you would on ordinary "stay-away" shading as described, but on larger letters it is advisable to use the double-stroke method to build up the shading in proportion to that shown on the illustration.

Most shading is placed on the left and bottom, since this seems to be the easiest and most natural application for the average lettering artist. However, certain conditions make it more acceptable to place the shade on the right and bottom, as shown in Fig. 53. Sometimes this is mandatory in the reproduction of trademarks, upon which the shading is in such position. At other times the shading is converted to the right side so the letters will provide the greatest impact upon the eyes of the viewer. This is especially true on highway bulletins. Since most highway signs are on the right side of the road, all emphasis on the sign should be concentrated in such a manner that the copy is "pointed" toward the reader, or to the left. When the copy is shaded as shown in Figure 52, the actual impact of the wording is "pointed" away from the reader and most likely toward the middle of a hayfield. (The arrows show the point of impact).

This situation is, of course, reversed when the sign is on the left side of the highway. It is also customary to read or look at things from left to right, so the eye seems to receive the impact of the letter more forcefully when it is shaded on the right. Many of the large advertisers evidently follow this line of thinking, because most of the trademarks, logos, etc. seem to be shaded on the right hand sides.

IMPACT

FIG. 53. *Shading to right and bottom gives maximum impact to display that is to be viewed from left.*

Like many sign painters you might find it awkward to place the shading on the right. It is so natural for me to apply the shading on the left, that I only reverse the process when duplicating a trademark, or when it results in the best possible impact upon the viewer.

Fig. 54 is a perspective shade. At first glance you might think that this is the same as the shade used in Fig. 52, except that it is a bit heavier. There is a pronounced difference between the two. The slants or angles of the shading in Fig. 52 are all drawn at a 45-degree angle. If you were to place a straight-edge on the angles and draw continuous pencil lines downward, the lines would all remain parallel and never converge.

If you should place a straightedge on the angles of the shading in Fig. 54 and draw pencil lines downward, you would discover that the lines would all converge or come together at a common vanishing-point at a comparatively short distance below and to the left of the letter.

Outstanding effects are possible with this form of shading. It is especially adaptable if you want the letter to appear to be popping-out of a great distance directly into the vision of the viewer. This treatment works effectively on extra-wide shading effects. If you have not had any training in simple perspective, the layout for this type of shading is simple. All you must do is to place a small pencil mark or dot at a desired point below and to the left of the letter to be shaded. Then the straight-edge is placed on this dot and manipulated to intersect with each corner of the letter above. This provides the basis for every slant. The width of the vertical and horizontal strokes can be drawn to the size you desire. The horizontal stroke will naturally occur at the point where the vertical shading stroke intersects the slanted line running from the corner of the letter to the vanishing point. As an aid to your understanding of this type of shading layout, use the illustration, Fig. 54 and with the help of a straight-edge determine the original vanishing point used in the preparation of this example. The result will show an acceptable position to place the vanishing point.

FIG. 54. *Perspective shade makes the letter appear to be "popping out" of the background.*

You can move this point to provide your own variations. The perspective depends on the placement of the vanishing-point. For instance, if you placed this common point above and to the right of the letter, indicated the angles accordingly, shaded the letter on the top and the right, then the letter would appear to be descending toward your vision from the upper right.

When drawing the slants in this shading process, it is important that one end of the straight-edge connects with the vanishing-point for each and every line that leads to the letter regardless of degree. The perspective is distorted if you deviate from this absolute rule.

Fig. 55 is a drop-shadow, and of all shading treatments, it is the one that most accurately conforms to our accepted definition of the word shadow. The shadow as shown, is in nearly the exact position a natural shadow would be if the letter could, in effect, be raised from the surface and allowed to cast its own shadow. This is an impressive shading technique. Without a pattern it is quite difficult to use this shading process, but it can quite simply be accomplished with the use of a pattern.

FIG. 55. Drop-Shadow is the treatment that most closely lives up to the accepted definition of the word "shadow."

First, tape the pattern to the surface and pounce over the perforations as usual. Do not remove the pattern until you indicate its position. Apply chalk or pencil marks at the two top corners, for example. Such indications are referred to as "registry marks." This is not necessary if the pattern is the exact size of the panel being lettered. Remove the pattern and do the lettering. When the lettering is dry, apply the pattern the second time, but move it slightly down and to the left, using the registry marks as a guide. Pounce over the letter perforations again, and this will indicate the position of the drop shadow.

The thickness of the shadow depends on how much you move the pattern in relation to the position of the lettering. The black shadow and the dotted-line indications on Fig. 55 show the amount of pattern movement required to result in the example illustrated. You can pounce the pattern in both positions before starting to letter, if you choose to do the lettering and shading without waiting for the lettering to dry. This requires considerable skill and the double-pattern lines are confusing.

Since this is a natural shadow, the best effect is obtained color-wise by darkening some of the field color to use for painting the shade. For example, use khaki on yellow, maroon on red, etc. It is permissible to use completely different colors, but then the natural shadow effect will be lost.

Fig. 56 illustrates a shading method that is fast and works very well on display cards and on some sign work. This is an "upside-down" shade. Simply turn the card or sign upside down after it is lettered and shade as you

FIG. 56. Simply turn a card upside down to render a shading method that works extra fast.

normally do on the left and bottom. This actually can be done on any sign that can be turned upside down without too much effort. It is a very fast process, especially if you stay away from the letters slightly. In most work, you would not bring the shade completely flush with the letters as shown in the illustration.

COMMENTARY. In regard to shading the most common mistake made by the novice is a poor choice of color. Except in the use of a few freak alphabets, the shading should never predominate the lettering. A positive color should seldom be used as a shade when lettering on a light colored background. One bad example of this would be a white truck, lettered with black and the shading done with red, or worse still, with dark blue.

If a positive, or dark color such as either of these is used, it must be applied with utmost accuracy. The shade must be absolutely precise, as shown in Fig. 52 with each letter blocked out at perfect angles. The shading must be flush against the letters and accurate. Any attempt to use the random-type of "stay-away" shading with positive colors, such as red, blue, black, etc. on a light field, is ridiculous. Because of the sharp contrast, every slight flaw stands out with sharp clarity. The shading must be equal in perfection to that of the lettering.

Most of the shading used in the everyday course of your work is applied to emphasize certain portions of the copy. In regard to this, the contrast between the field-color and shading should not be too pronounced. One color selection that is always appropriate for shading letters on a light field is a darker shade of the same color used for the background. Whenever it is possible, choose a pastel color that harmonizes well with the entire job and use this for shading on light field colors. These colors can be darkened for greater contrast.

The same consideration in regard to color of shade should extend to the lettering on dark backgrounds. It is not uncommon to see red trucks lettered with aluminum or white and shaded with lemon yellow, etc. A dark shade, such as black, maroon or dark blue would be much more attractive.

Suppose you were lettering with black upon the doors of a bright yellow truck. What would be your first choice for the color of shade? Would it be red, blue, or green? If so, why not reconsider? Shade the letters instead with white, khaki or light-orange and discover how much easier it is to develop a more attractive job.

The novice frequently has the tendency to use thin shading strokes. Usually these strokes are much too thin and are used in order to fit within the space between the letters. When shading letters about 3 inches high, it is a safe rule to use the same width of stroke for the shading as that used on the lettering, or a slight bit thinner. Shading-strokes that are too thin, add little to the attractiveness of any job, and fail to place the necessary emphasis upon the lettering.

A final word of caution—avoid those long, exaggerated peaks at the stroke-endings of the shade lines. These ugly peaks are suitable on Japanese crockery, but not on sign work. Square off the stroke-endings neatly and sharply, but avoid that extra flourish on the peaks. This does not demonstrate your skill with the brush. Instead, this stamps the work as either that of an amateur or a sloppy veteran.

SPACE SAVERS. "Make all the letters big!" How often do we sign painters flinch upon hearing these words, especially when the customer orders a small sign and then produces enough copy to fill the space on a highway bulletin?

Each sign painter might react differently to this common problem. One reaction might be to accept the job as presented, and then later, after the customer leaves, "blow a fuse," stomp around the shop, and finally cram the copy upon the sign regardless.

The novice may skeptically accept the job and later, in bewildered fashion, try to squeeze every letter onto the sign, making each as large as possible.

The experienced and competent sign painter will do neither of the above. He has long since learned the absurdity of the old adage: "The customer is always right." He knows that these words might well apply to a supermarket, but not to the operation of a sign plant or art studio. He understands how to handle a customer in a friendly, diplomatic manner. Additionally, he has learned many techniques for manually saving space within the actual performance of doing the job.

Situations such as the one just described will become a common part of your life as an active operator in the sign trade. Sometimes by learning how to handle one problem you will automatically develop a certain finesse for solving others. So the following information is slanted toward you as a less experienced sign painter in the hope that it will be a stepping-stone for you in the effort to understand public relations. Also the manual knowledge will be provided to solve the immediate situation.

In addition to learning the technical part of sign painting, it is essential to learn how to deal with customers. Maintaining good public relations is highly important to your success as a signman. When a man enters a market to buy a pound of coffee he is certain to favor a certain brand. In no case would the store manager try to convince him that he had chosen the wrong coffee. The customer knows just as much about coffee as the manager, so the customer is indeed right.

Conversely, when a client comes to you, he is the layman, while you are the professional. Therefore, he has every right to expect competent advice, and you should be able to give it. To do this, you must develop a thorough knowledge of the trade.

Consider the man with the small sign and the abundance of copy. The first and most logical step is to go over the copy with him and edit the wording. Chances are that you can immediately eliminate repetitive words. Also, words of little or no importance may be crossed out. Explain to the customer in your discussion how this will result in a more attractive and readable sign.

Level-headed people will take your advice, but occasionally you will encounter a real "hardhead" who wants every word to remain as is and may even decide to add a few. Nothing can be done about this. You have the choice of accepting or rejecting the job.

The second, but no less important step in handling a sign with too much copy begins with the actual layout of the sign itself. The copy as agreed upon is before you and common sense tells you that an attractive sign cannot be produced if you are to "make all the letters big."

This is where you take over and forget about the customer. In fact you now edit the copy the second time. Do not hesitate to abbreviate within reason; to use a word of script to break the monotony; or to enlarge an all important word or phrase. At first, you might be a bit apprehensive about taking such liberties, because it might displease your customer. Most always, it has the opposite result. He is apt to say, "I'm glad you did that. It looks sharp!" Soon, he will trust your ability and when submitting future work will say, "Use your own judgment." The rare customer who complains about these well planned changes is not worth any consideration and you will be better off in the long run without his business.

Over a period of years, experienced signmen and artists memorize or develop hundreds of methods of condensing copy, words, abbreviations, etc.

Illustrated are a few of these, presented in the hope that you might use them, and through their use develop adaptations of your own. Through constant observation, you can become familiar with many others.

The lettering in Fig. 57 comes about through sound judgment. If a sign is placed in front of a home, saying, "This Property For Sale," about all the observer will see is

FIG. 57. Subjugate the less important.

"Property For Sale." Yet the phrase would appear awkward without the word "this." So, it is proper to use the word, but to subjugate it, since it is unimportant. Note that the word "this" in script form takes up scarcely more space than any two of the printed letters. Yet, it provides a pleasant area of white-space and a bit of flair. Your own style of script can be used in this situation, perhaps providing a higher and wider sweep to the capital letter T.

When a sign is immediately on the property to be sold, I see no reason for the definition "This Property." The words "For Sale," followed by other essential copy would seem sufficient. Unfortunately some real estate men do not agree.

FIG. 58. In some instances the o of "Co." can be nestled within the C to advantage.

The abbreviation of "Co." is self-explanatory. (**Fig. 58**) This can be adapted to many other alphabets with proper modification. The letter O cannot always be nestled completely within the letter C.

FIG. 59. While an ampersand could be used here, there is a unique touch in the vertical arrangement of the "and."

The treatment of the word "and" in "New and Used" as shown in Fig. 59 is actually not used to save space, since an ampersand could do as well. However, an ampersand would not provide the unique touch that is so necessary to a crowded and otherwise drab sign. As with all "stunt-treatments," it is not advisable to use this more than once on any one sign face.

"Smith, Inc." illustrates a condensation of the abbreviation "Inc." (See Fig. 60). Interesting color effects can be arranged. Should the lettering be black, outlined with orange, then the cross-bars above and below the word "Inc." might be painted solid orange, etc.

SMITH INC.

FIG. 60. The abbreviation of "Incorporated" can be contracted.

Note the absence of a comma. This is optional. Liberties might be taken with punctuation sometimes in the interest of appearance. A good example is the following combination: "Co., Inc." This is proper punctuation, but many signmen eliminate the comma.

FIG. 61. By diminishing the letter L, the E can be extended to balance with the S.

The word "SALE" as illustrated in Fig. 61, might contradict previous emphasis on letter uniformity, but there are certain instances where one can and should deviate.

Ordinarily, the letters L and E should be of equal width. To place a big, bold letter-style within a limited space, such as this, it is advisable to diminish the width of the letter L. In this way, the letter E can be made wide enough to correspond to the width of the letter S for proper balance. Suppose, in this example, that the letters L and E were of equal width; they would then be completely out of proportion to the letters SA.

The width of all four letters could be cut down to provide more space for the letter L, but then the desired boldness would not be possible. This same principle can be applied to the letter T in other words. The top cross-stroke can be cut to a minimum to afford more space for bolder letters.

Within the procedure of any layout work it is not uncommon to commit an error and to cheat a little to come out right. In such case, start cutting the space immediately and try to gain enough space to allow for a full-sized letter at the end. Narrowed letters are much less noticeable within a line of lettering. Do not dwindle off the letters to a crowded ending with the last letter considerably narrower than the preceding letters.

It is more desirable to begin a completely new layout; but sometimes for various reasons this is not convenient.

Chapter 23

The Fundamentals of Script

When preparing an instruction book it is difficult for any author to determine the most proper sequence in which to present the material. It would be an ideal situation if the information could be presented in accordance with its importance. In a trade as complex as sign painting, with its limitless tangents, there are occasions when five or six completely different subjects become of equal importance at the same time. Obviously, it is impossible to charge through the pages discussing subjects six abreast! So, with each change of subject, one is faced with the same decision: "What comes next?"

Right at this point there are numerous tangents of equal importance that should be considered. To complicate matters, certain procedures are dependent upon factors not yet discussed, so these must be pulled into play whenever necessary.

So, although other discussions are of equal importance at this point, they must be momentarily set aside. It seems most logical to now explore the basic fundamentals of script. You can learn as little or as much of this as you feel is adaptable to your present point of progress and refer back to this part of the book as occasion demands.

Script has fascinated me since my very early days as a sign painter. In fact, it seems that most sign writers, veterans and beginners alike, show a special interest in the various forms of script. This is indeed a healthy attitude, because the ability to competently execute several forms of script is a distinct asset to the signman. It is my hope that you have this curiosity in regard to script.

Almost every beginner might be following a slightly different technique in the development of his ability. For brushes, he may be using red sables, flats, quills, or a combination of any of these. In addition, he might be practicing his work in one or three ways; with the hand-down method, with a mahlstick, or hand-over-hand, or a combination of all three.

Consequently, the teaching of script or writing about it

for a broad group of readers can be most difficult. There is no "cut-and-dried" method that a writer can grab on to and say: "Here, young fella', this is the way to do it. This is how to hold the brush. This is where you start your first stroke, etc., etc." Since script, in many ways, involves all of the personal traits of handwriting, it naturally becomes to a great extent, a matter of personal design. Outside of the standard forms, such as the true Spencerian and several others, you will find that script affords the most freedom and broadest scope of all lettering forms. Therefore, the individual technique of every signman is bound to show up in every line of script that he executes, even in the standards.

In view of all the foregoing, the explanations, examples, and procedures to follow will be offered in the broadest sense, taking into consideration the fact that you might be using different tools and methods. My intention is never to imply that my way is the only way, or even the most correct way, but one way in which you can do the job with acceptable results.

Early in this book you were presented with a simplified script and advised to practice these letters in your own individual style. The sequence of stroke was to be done in the manner most comfortable to your individual method of holding the brush while practicing on the printed letters. There will be no attempt now to lay down the rules for a set sequence of stroke. If I were to show you how I do my scripts, such as stroke number one, stroke number two, etc., it would tend to confuse you rather than be of help to you. For example, a capital letter of script that perhaps required a dozen separate strokes in my years as a beginner, is now done more swiftly and gracefully with perhaps three or four strokes of the brush. During 40 years of lettering, through gradual elimination of a stroke here, and a stroke there, it is natural for any signman to reduce his stroke pattern to an absolute minimum. How then, can an author expect the beginner to accomplish in a few short months what it has taken another years to develop? My logic is that, as in hand-writing you should use all the strokes necessary for you to do a neat script and gradually develop your own individual technique. It is only in this way that you can eventually develop the effortless sweep needed to accomplish your personal renditions of script.

Script is a personal thing. It must be done without effort. Therefore, although I can help you in many other ways in regard to script, I can do little to aid you with your personal hand movements. This is what causes script to be so fascinating.

Although the manipulation of the brush must be developed largely by yourself, this does not mean that you should not watch other experienced signmen at work on script. Much can be gained by studying their techniques. Neither should you ignore the fact that the more detailed stroke by stroke method of teaching might be a great help to you. If this type of teaching is available to you, it is possible that you could do very well by following another's methods, either completely or by using them partly in conjunction with adaptions of your own. There are many little tricks and rules that experienced men follow. This type of observance along with constant practice can bring your work up to a professional level.

BRUSHES FOR SCRIPT. For script, sign painters in general use round pencil-quill brushes, or flats and may combine either of these with the use of "highliners" for the finer lines as they occur in a line of script. It is not uncommon for some expert signmen to use two brushes for one line of script; one for the thicker line and a thin highliner for the very thin elements. Others can do this same work with but one brush, by increasing and decreasing pressure on the brush, plus expert shaping of the brush upon the palette.

One little innovation that has served me well for many years is in regard to trimmed-down lettering brushes, which I use instead of the usual "high-liners."

To make a highliner out of a lettering quill, do as follows: Choose a good brush that has not been a "hairloser"—one that has been an excellent lettering brush. You need not use a brush that is still good enough for lettering, but one that has reached the stage where it is no longer efficient enough for this purpose. Hold the brush in a vertical position as shown in Fig. 62 and, using a sharp razor blade, trim some of the hair away, either by twirling the brush against the blade, or the blade against the brush in a circular motion. Cut very gently and sparingly, just cutting away a few bristles at a time, until you have it cut down to the desired size. Hold the blade at a complete right angle to the brush and cut right at the heel of the brush where the hair joins the quill. Try to cut away an equal amount of hair all the way around, so that the remaining portion of the hair will be in the center.

It is my practice to keep in my sign kit about three each of No. 4, 6 and 8 quills trimmed down to various thicknesses. These brushes, depending upon the extent to which they have been trimmed, can be used for outlining, highlights, underscoring, striping, and as the second brush for any of the various fine- line scripts. These brushes can be trimmed very little for fuller lines and also trimmed extremely for very fine lines. A No. 8 quill, for example is an excellent size to trim down to various degrees, and can be used for many purposes.

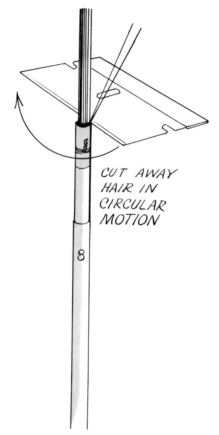

CUT AWAY HAIR IN CIRCULAR MOTION

FIG. 62. *To make a highliner out of a lettering quill, hold the quill vertically as shown and trim some hair away by twirling the brush or the blade.*

After I trim such a brush and try it out for the size of stroke and workability, I use a little gimmick to retard unnecessary loss of hair. Just around the very heel of the brush where the hair joins the quill I apply a very small amount of liquid solder. With a round toothpick, I even this solder into place to circle the brush. This circular layer of solder does not exceed a sixteenth of an inch at any point. When dry this solder, which can be purchased in most dime stores in a small tube, will withstand most solvents.

Several of my sign painter friends in other cities mentioned having trouble with outlining and highlighting, etc. After trimming down several brushes in this way and using them, they wrote to me saying that these were the best brushes they had ever used for these purposes. This is not so much a matter of saving money as the satisfaction of working with a better tool. To me the time spent in trimming and preparing a brush such as this is actually worth the price of three new brushes. But at least I have the type of tool necessary to do the job to my own degree of satisfaction.

Newcomers to the trade are inclined to use brushes far past their peak efficiency. To use a brush that does not perform well is false economy. Almost all new brushes will lose a few hairs during first use. This hair loss will stop and the brush will provide long, satisfactory use. Others will continue to lose a hair or two with nearly every stroke. You can lose more time patching flawed strokes and picking hair off the surface of finished strokes than such a brush is worth, so the best advice is to junk it. If it has a badly trimmed or jagged edge do the same.

Some fellows maintain that they can trim the end, but this is seldom successful. The barest fraction of hair trimmed off the tip of a brush can cause it to be too blunt. Also, when paletted from a different direction the chisel-end will be at an angle, instead of straight across. It will have a chisel-edge only in that position of the hair at which it was trimmed. I have trimmed the end a slight bit with success on rare occasions, but more often I have met with failure.

Although most brushes that are flawed in manufacture cannot be re-trimmed to work efficiently, it is worth at least one try. If a new brush has a slightly ragged edge, try to trim the edge as follows: Dip the brush in bulletin color and palette the hair into its most natural chisel-shape. Then hold the brush in the left hand with the hair flat against a piece of smooth, hard cardboard on a firm surface with the hair in chisel-shape. Be sure that you can see the hair-edge plainly, and then with a new single-edged razor blade press down on the sair across the chisel-edge, trimming just enough of the hair-tips away to eliminate the ragged edge, do not use a see-saw motion with the blade. Just press.

If the brush still has a knife-edge, and the brush is straight across when paletted from any direction, then it is possible that you have salvaged a brush. If the end has been blunted to any extent, it is useless.

I have read and been told about dozens of ways in which to trim a brush, including such procedures as placing the tip over a sharp edge of a piece of glass and striking the edge with a sandpaper block, etc. The results have been doubtful, to say the least.

The brushes that wear down gradually without excessive hair loss and become too narrow for good lettering can be put away to be used later to make stripers and high-liners.

As soon as a brush no longer enables you to do fast, efficient lettering, it is best to start using a new one. Your time and the quality of your work are worth more than the price of a brush.

It is true that some signmen will use brushes for several months that other men have discarded. The quality of the work done by such men and the slow speed with which they do it usually attests to the foolishness of using inferior brushes.

The very best sign painter cannot do first class work with second rate brushes, so as a novice you should most certainly use good brushes. The least expensive place for a poor tool of any kind is in the trash barrel. Change brushes often. You can't paint with the handles.

THE PLACEMENT OF SCRIPT.
At this point you might have spent considerable time in the practice of script and reached the stage where you can do it quite well. Yet, when you look at the completed job with a critical eye, you will be a bit disappointed, because the script still does not present the snappy, professional appearance that you are striving for. Even the further advanced sign painter can sense this sort of frustration, if he has not had considerable experience in the application of script.

Do not be too disheartened when this occurs, because you might have lost the "professional touch" for a very small reason. The difference between the amateur appearance and the professional snap can be very slight. This is especially true if you have practiced diligently and can do a neat, well-formed script. This variance might hinge entirely upon some little trick the experienced man knows that you do not.

Sometimes the mere placement of a word of script within

the layout can be the factor. There are some words that are perfect for script, while other words do not look well in script form no matter how expertly they might be done. Some words will look best when placed in slanted position, and others will be more adaptable to a straight horizontal position.

To help you to better understand how to place script so that it will show up to its greatest advantage, let us study a few of the illustrations.

Fig. 63 is one treatment of the word, "Pleasure." This word was chosen, because it begins with two of the taller letters and then dwindles to completion with only the smaller letters. There are many words with this over-all contour, such as "Please" and "Clearance," among others.

Note that in Fig. 63, the word has been placed hori-

FIG. 63. *This word written in script horizontally has an unpleasant slant downward to the right.*

zontally or straight across. This causes an unpleasant amount of space to the upper right as shown by the slanted, dotted line. The entire plane of the layout appears to be running downhill to the right, which is an unattractive beginning for any layout. Blank, or "white-space" is very necessary to design a good layout, but not in an awkward position such as this.

Now study Fig. 64, and you will immediately notice the attractiveness that has been gained by placing the same word in slanted position. The dotted horizontal line shows that the over-all plane of the layout is better. The slant raises up the smaller letters to compensate for the letters P and L, which are much taller.

There is no iron-clad rule that words such as this must be placed on a slant. Sometimes, when used within a copy grouping or paragraph, they must be horizontal. It might be necessary to position the word straight across to accommodate other copy. But, in most cases, whenever a word has all of the taller letters at the start, more balance and grace can be achieved by slanting the word as shown in Fig. 63. This is especially true if such word occurs at the top of a display card, or happens to be the principal word within the content of any layout. Then it is most advisable to not only increase its size in proportion to the incidental copy, but also to place it on a slant.

FIG. 64. *An upward slant of the script to the right will improve the appearance.*

There is seldom any problem in regard to placement when a word ends with a tall letter such as the word "Pleasant" illustrated in Fig. 65.

In some work, script has the disadvantage of taking up a great amount of space in comparison to the printed capital letters. This fact applies when using upper and lower case printed letters. The sign painters stick to capital letters much of the time, especially on crowded signs. Much space is used when the copy contains lower-case letters that extend both above and below the guidelines, such as the letters T, L, G, Y, and others.

FIG. 65. *But if a word ends in a tall letter it will look nice on a horizontal line.*

The word "Cottage" is a good example of this. If the sign consists of crowded copy, then every bit of space saved becomes important and proper placement is essential.

Fig. 66 shows the best method of placing the word "Cottage" so that it requires a minimum of space. You would slant the word just enough to bring the bottom of the letter G up to the same position as the bottom of the initial letter C.

Please note that in Fig. 67 the word "Cottage" has been positioned straight across and consumes more space because of the drop of the letter G. When the word is placed on a slant, as in Fig. 66 it requires no more vertical space than the letter C.

FIG. 66. *Angling script of this word upward to the right makes more efficient use of space.*

Incidentally, the type of script used in the word "Cottage" is an example of what might be called a "sign painter's script." It is bottom heavy because the strokes have a slightly reversed position as compared to the strokes commonly used in the more standard scripts. The two most basic strokes used in this formation are shown in the circular inset in Fig. 67. There are additional strokes involved, of course, such as the thinner stroke on the right side of the letter O, etc.

FIG. 67. *Written horizontally, the word takes up more space. The inset shows the two most basic strokes used in the formation of this script.*

This script is very fast and simple to do. The basic strokes are best achieved by paletting the brush to a chisel edge, and holding it slightly counter-clockwise to the position you normally use when lettering. The thinner strokes can usually be made with the same brush by shaping it a bit smaller on the palette and reducing the pressure throughout the stroke. This is one of the many scripts where increase and decrease of pressure on the brush is required to form the letters properly and to letter with good speed.

With experience, you will discover that many attractive types of script can be executed by changing the position of the brush in your grip. This is also true with the reservoir type pens, especially with the C and D styles. For uniformity, you should continue to hold the brush in much the same position and grip throughout the line of script upon which you are working. The only change of grip would be for the several odd strokes within such a rendition.

For the basic strokes, if you hold the brush at a different slant or position as you proceed, you will end up with two or three various styles of lettering in one word of script.

One technique that many sign painters favor is that of "dwindling" their scripts toward the end of a word. This is especially adaptable on long names or words. In doing this, draw the cross guidelines a slight bit narrower toward the end of the word. For example, the vertical measurement of the shorter letters might be $3\frac{1}{4}$ inches on the left and diminish to 3 inches or less on the right. This does lend a graceful flair to script, especially when it is being placed on a freehand arc or on a fancy swirl.

THE MECHANICS OF SCRIPT.

It was previously mentioned that certain words are more suitable for script than others. After working with script for some time, this will become apparent and you will notice that even some of the letter combinations are awkward in appearance.

It is safe to assume that most signmen have an aversion to doing certain types of words and letters in script form. My personal dislike is for words that have all the higher letters in the beginning or within the center of the word and none at the end. In regard to individual letters I have an aversion to letters such as b, j, k, p, q, among others when they occur within the body of a word of script. This depends somewhat upon the flanking letters. My favorite type of words are those that terminate with one of the taller letters, such as "Fresh," "Festival," "National," etc.

The adaptability of a name for script treatment can be a source of consternation when dealing with customers. One customer might have a name that looks beautiful in script, and you letter this on the doors of his truck. Another customer, after seeing this, will ask that his name also be applied in script. His name might be one of those that will look terrible in any form of script. It is generally impossible to explain to him that his name will not result in the same attractive appearance as that of his friend. Too frequently a sign painter is required to letter a name in script, knowing full well that it would look much better in printed form.

FIG. 68. *Keep slants at same angle. While the slants of the script on this sign are not machine perfect or the strokes perfectly uniform in width, it is accurate enough for a professional looking sign. This was accomplished free-hand and optically with no triangle or other aid to guide.*

One of the more important requirements for a neat script is keeping the slants at the same angle throughout. On the photograph in Fig. 68, note how the slants in the name "Redmann" are pretty much the same throughout the word. Now study the comparative drawing in Fig. 69, upon which the slants have purposely been distorted. Immediately you will discover how the grace of the same word of script can be lost, because the slants are not uniform. The dotted lines show the true angle to which all the letters should conform. You will note that the letter R is slanted correctly, but

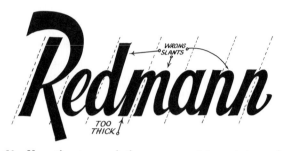

FIG. 69. How the grace of the same word in script can be lost
when slants are not uniform. Dotted lines show true angle to
which all letters should conform.

when you consider the letter d, you can see that the slant
is definitely out of line. This fault is repeated throughout
the word. The thicknesses of the strokes are also variant.

Study the photograph, Fig. 68, and you will note that
the slants here are not machine perfect either, nor are the
strokes completely uniform in width. This was drawn freehand and optically, with no sort of triangle for a guide,
but it is accurate enough for the economy demanded in this
particular job. Most experienced signmen depend upon their
well-trained sense of proportion in this sort of a layout and
use no other aids.

You might at first find it difficult to keep your lettering
uniformly slanted. Since you would not buy different transparent triangles for every slant you might need, try this:
Draw the first letter of the layout to determine the slant
that you desire. Next cut a piece of cardboard in the shape
of a triangle so that the angle corresponds to the slant of
this first letter. Use this cardboard device to check the
slants for accuracy as you proceed with the layout. Do not
discard this cardboard triangle. Punch a hole in one end
and hang it on a nail handy to your layout bench. Eventually, you will have enough triangles hanging on this nail
to provide just about any slant required.

The word "Redmann" in the sign illustration is the actual
name of the customer. The Indian pictorial is a play on
his name. The script is lettered with a well-used No. 8 gray
pencil-quill throughout. (On a similar script, you might
prefer to alternate with a smaller brush for the finer lines).
The Indian is painted in full color and plenty of it, on a
pale blue field. The sign panel itself, which is lettered on
both sides, is overlaid plywood and painted white. "Red-

mann" is lettered in bright red with a primrose yellow shade. The sky-blue panel is "dry-brushed" at the bottom as it nears the lettering to avoid a sharp break where it joins the white field.

The word "Redmann" again shows the amazing flexibility of script. At first it was difficult to squeeze this word into this narrow width while still retaining a respectable height to the letters. It was finally done, however, even though the letter n's are a little odd looking, and a bit of congestion is evident throughout the word. Note also how the bottom part of the Indian design has been arranged to take advantage of the upper contour of the word "Redmann."

The absolute maneuverability of script is again demonstrated in the photograph, Fig. 70. The word, "Peaceful" swirls upward to provide a spot for the word "Acres." This word of script lends a bit of grace to this sign that printed letters could not provide. The word "Acres" in its "Playbill" type letter adds a bit of "olden-day" charm to the overall appearance.

FIG. 70. *Flexibility of script is demonstrated here in the way the word "Peaceful" swirls upward to open up space for the word "Acres."*

It is my custom to "pick my own work to pieces" not only for your sake, but for my own as well.

In this case the downstroke on the letter P in "Peaceful" slants a bit too much to the right on the top. It is true that on a swirled line of script the slants cannot be at the same angle, but the letter P is not as correctly slanted as it might be. Note also that the downward serif is missing on the bottom of the letter S in "Acres"; the curved stroke of the letter R is too thick and could have had a more accurate and attractive curve. The last two errors are the result of plain carelessness, and the constant attempt to pack too much work into one day.

It is possible to do any word of script in such a way that it is attractive. Careful layout and execution are necessary for this. But unless I am working according to strict specifications, I find it easier to choose, whenever possible, those words or phrases for script that will be most suitable for the sign upon which I am working.

If you must lay out a tricky word of script and it has a stiff unsuitable appearance upon your first attempt, try placing it in a different position. You might place it on a slant or along a sweeping freehand arc.

Readability also is a big factor in script as in all lettering. There are few limitations when lettering display cards or other signs that are primarily to be viewed from a short distance. Highway signs are a different matter. If readability is your main concern on any sign designed to be readable at a distance, then the bolder scripts are best. Condensed scripts, or very thin-line Spencerian type scripts, are not very readable at any great distance. Seldom is script as easy to read at a distance as block letters.

The customer's wishes largely govern your choice of lettering. For instance, a bank or a funeral home might suggest a thin-line script or a light-stroke Roman letter. Formal establishments such as this are more interested in presenting a very dignified and conservative image in their advertising than they are in readability. As far as advertising is concerned, this is excellent thinking, so do not argue with it. Note how quickly a bank, for example, will change to bold advertising when the occasion demands and when it involves no chance of harming its conservative image.

Therefore good judgment is almost equally as important as good lettering. Script is not merely used to enhance the beauty of a layout. Its adaptability can be a great asset for getting the most out of any given amount of space. This adaptability also should be used in an effort to maintain good taste. The script should complement the business that it advertises. A dainty script should advertise beauty salons, flower shops, etc. A powerful, bold script should advertise heavy-duty equipment, contractors, etc. This type of thinking is the prime requisite of all advertising.

In regard to Fig. 71, no printed word could be arranged

to fit into this space quite as comfortably and, at the same time, contribute the extra flair to this otherwise "hum drum" sign. The capital letter D, for instance, could have been made in a number of other ways, but note how this particular sweep of the top stroke as it follows the general contour of the curved word above it. This gives the entire sign a flowing motion. A printed letter in this position would have resulted in a purely mechanical sign.

The letter Y ends with another graceful sweep, which seems to carry the eye right on down to the bottom line. All layout work should be designed with an attempt to carry the viewer's eye as effortlessly as possible from one line to the next.

FIG. 71. Script will fit into spaces where lettering would not be nearly so perfect.

This type of script is one of the most commonly used with its variations. It is sometimes referred to as Spencerian Bold, but there seems to be very little resemblance in this script to true Spencerian. This was lettered entirely with a full No. 8 gray quill. It is my preference to do this type of script with one brush, filling in as I proceed. By holding the brush properly and taking advantage of the "spring" of the brush, the thinner strokes can be done quite easily. In my experience I have never found it possible to do a flowing type of script with the "heel" of the brush. In fact I doubt if I could do any kind of a script by bearing down and using the full weight of the brush.

If you are using flats, you might prefer to do a word such as "Dairy" by using a ¼-inch flat to outline the script and fill in the larger areas with a larger brush. The size you would choose for this outline, of course, would depend on the amount of skill you have developed or are capable of employing.

Should you prefer red sables, then you would perhaps use a No. 6 highliner and a No. 10 or 12 long red sable lettering brush, alternating these as you proceed. In regard to red sables, it is agreed that they are splendid tools, but I was taught as an apprentice to confine their use mainly to tempera colors and showcard work. I still believe this, but if you can use them for general sign work, do so. For general sign work, I would find it difficult to do a graceful, free-flowing script with the very best of the red sables. However, I have used these brushes successfully in years past when doing freelance display card work for the better department stores.

FIG. 72. *Conveniently adaptable to the space available, script provides the opportunity for the g to "snuggle" in with the line of letters below.*

The word "Dillenburg" on the truck door in Fig. 72 is another commonly used script, its major difference being that it is done in what might be called "backhand." Note again how conveniently this script treatment has been adapted to the available space. This is a good example to demonstrate the meaning of the statement, previously made, that script was a matter of personal design. This is evident in the manner in which the letter G extends down to occupy the space at the end of the word "Vault." Actually the word "Dillenburg" sort of forms a frame for the second line, "Burial Vault." This results in a cohesive layout.

This word of script was lettered with a well broken-in No. 8 gray quill, so it was not as full as the newer quill

200

used to letter the word "Dairy." Depending on the size, graduation of strokes, etc., it is often advisable to employ a brush that has been used for some time to letter script. It is easier to paint the thinner strokes than it would be if a newer and fuller brush were to be used. The word "Dillenburg" also could be lettered by using a No. 8 quill for the heavy strokes and a No. 4 for the thinner lines.

The "Mason's Flowers" truck as shown in Fig. 73 demonstrates a simple, but interesting layout. The lightweight, graceful script used in the word "Flowers" is in keeping with the daintiness of flowers and also with the dignity this floral company tries to convey in its advertising. The advantage of using one word of script in this layout is apparent. Try to imagine how quickly a printed word in this same position would "kill" the beauty of the layout. Just this one word provides the necessary flair.

FIG. 73. *Light and graceful flair is provided for this florist truck.*

A No. 4 quill was used for this entire word. This involves skill in brush manipulation. Pressure must be used for the heavier strokes, and this must be reduced considerably for the thin lines. In fact the very thin lines are painted with practically the very tip of the brush, holding it a bit slanted so the normal chisel-end makes its initial contact with the surface on a slight angle. In this way the hair is pressed into compact form resulting in a thinner stroke. To do this it is essential for the brush to be well charged with paint and well shaped on the palette. The paint should be free-flowing and there should be no "drag" on the brush when doing a fine line script of any kind. If it is possible, the thinner strokes should be made with one stroke of the brush. To go over such strokes the second time usually thickens the stroke, and some of the "free-wheeling" motion is bound to be lost.

Many signmen would use a long haired highliner of some type for this thin-line script. Sometimes I would use a trimmed down No. 6 or No. 8 for this same script instead of the No. 4. This would depend on the quality of the No. 4's on hand. It is not always easy to find good quality quills, especially in the smaller sizes.

Color selection is important as usual. The field color of this truck is very pale blue. The ovals are alternately, medium blue (brilliant blue with a bit of white added), blue-green, and dark blue. The ovals are cut-in around the letters, which remain the pale blue of the field color. The word "Flowers" is black, shaded with pink, and the lettering on the door is medium blue. A round "FTD" decal was later applied immediately to the left of the lettering on the door.

THE FREE-STYLE SCRIPTS. In addition to the
standard and other commonly used scripts, every competent sign painter—through long experience—develops a flair for doing the unusual in the execution of script. In fact this flair becomes so personal to each signwriter that it is not uncommon for one tradesman to recognize another's work merely by the technique used in his various scripts.

It seems that almost every sign painter will develop one or two scripts that are very nearly his own. He might do this after seeing a few words of script in a magazine that he particularly admired. Since the sample in the magazine will not provide the entire alphabet, it becomes necessary for him to use that portion of the alphabet that is provided as a nucleus and develop the rest through use of his own skill. This is really not too difficult, because any given alphabet of script will usually maintain the same stroke pattern throughout.

As a newomer you will naturally not be able to do this immediately. You must be prepared to spend time at practice and gain experience before you develop the ability to do the flamboyant scripts. It is very important for you to plan to do just this if you hope to become a top man in the art of lettering. Close study and constant observation of the existent scripts and all lettering can be of much help to you in the gradual transformation that changes you from an amateur into a professional.

Years ago it was easy to get by with the working knowledge of several good standard scripts. At present, however, there is an ever increasing trend in all forms of advertising to constantly come up with a "new look." What is popular today might be "old hat" in a few years. Therefore you must keep your talent flexible so that you can flex with the times. At no time has it been more important to be original and to be able to develop your own lettering than it is right now.

A good example of an exceptionally "snappy" letter is shown in the word "Malco" (See Fig. 74). Rather than attempt to explain the detailed procedure for you to follow in doing these scripts, it seems more advisable to relate the logic and the methods that I used. In this way you can adjust your own efforts accordingly.

FIG. 74. This rather flamboyant script was adapted from ten letters clipped from a brochure. Gregory developed the rest of the alphabet from these. While they are not exactly the same as those of the originator, they are good enough to utilize.

Originally I only had available ten letters of the script used in the word "Malco." These were clipped from a brochure and consisted of two capitals and eight lower case letters. I developed the rest of the alphabet from the original ten; probably not the same as those done by the originator, but good enough to follow through. Incidentally I would like to mention that the person who designed the original lettering in the brochure was a true expert in the art of lettering. Seldom have I more greatly admired any piece of commercial artwork.

When developing alphabets from skimpy samples such as this, I usually lay out the word of script in full and accurate detail before doing the actual lettering. Gradually, after doing the script over and over, I find that I can automatically do the lettering in a more freehanded manner with merely a suggestive and much less detailed layout. Also through usage, I discover what type and size of brush is most adaptable to its characteristics.

For instance, in preparing the word "Malco" for this

illustration, I used a No. 4 gray pencil quill with black bulletin color, doubling the strokes for the heavier portions of the letters. The thinner portions of the letters were made with single strokes and the variance of stroke was achieved through increase and decrease of pressure on the brush in addition to proper paletting. The original was prepared 10 inches in width and has been reduced for presentation here.

The word "house" as shown in Fig. 75 is another example of script with the same characteristics and as it was actually used on a highway sign. An interesting point to note here is that the letter H is not capitalized. It is quite common and many times preferable in modern adver-

FIG. 75. *The word "House" is in the same script as the word "Malco." Here the initial letter is not capitalized.*

tising to use lower case letters on an entire word or throughout an entire sentence. Such procedure can often provide just the right amount of originality for which you are striving. As with all gimmicks use good judgment and do not overdo things such as this. This particular type of script, with variations, seems to be very popular and can add the necessary punch to an otherwise weak sign.

A trick frequently used by old timers, although not original, does show what can be done by taking advantage of the natural beauty of script. Abbreviations such as "Inc." and "Co." are sometimes awkward to place within a good layout. The example shown in Fig. 76 is one way in which a word ending with a letter y can be handled to provide a graceful frame for an abbreviation such as "Inc." (This example was also done with a No. 4 quill and bulletin color with the original being 8 inches wide). This procedure need not be confined to the letter y since there are a number of letters that can be adapted to serve the same purpose.

The same technique can be applied to the initial letter of a word. An example of this is apparent in the words "Ken Beyer" as shown in the photograph of the truck door in Fig. 77. This can be done successfully only when the

FIG. 76. *Abbreviations, such as "Inc." and "Co." are sometimes awkward to place within a group layout. This example shows how a word ending with the letter y can be handled to provide a graceful frame for such an abbreviation.*

first name or word is very short. You could scarcely expect to do this with the name "Ferdinand," for instance. This method works effectively when the customer uses his initials rather than his full name.

FIG. 77. *Here a first name is nestled within a flourish of the initial letter of the last name.*

You must be the judge as to when it is feasible to do fanciful lettering such as this. In this case the customer involved never haggles about price, nor does he have any suggestions as to how he wants his equipment painted. Invariably he will say, "Here's the truck: this is what I want on it. Paint it in the way you think best." These are the kind of customers for whom you can do a more complicated job with the assurance that the extra effort will be cheerfully paid for as well as appreciated. If all customers were like this, there would not only be better examples of sign work in existence, but our trade would be more of a pleasure.

You need only work in this trade for several months before you discover what all experienced sign painters already know. It is useless to outdo yourself for certain customers. Price is their only concern and any extra effort on your part is not in the least appreciated or even recognized as such. For this type of customer it is best to do a fast, neat, plain block-type letter, avoid the frills, and when you hand him the bill, he won't have to raise his eyebrows quite as high or drive away grumbling that you are a "highway robber." Actually in my experience, I have overheard people such as this express their foolish philosophy. Upon hearing an appreciative customer offer a compliment on the work, these "purse-squeezers" offer warnings such as, "Don't brag up the work, or he'll jack up the price!"

A word of warning—never do a sloppy job! There is a difference between doing a neat, economical job and a slapstick piece of work. One bad job out in public, especially on the doors of a truck, etc., can result in more adverse publicity than you can overcome with a dozen topnotch jobs.

Inventiveness plays a big part in all sign work and particularly so in the development of "off-beat" scripts. You can often put a real "sock" into a sign with one word. Consider the one word "Sign" for example. This word consists of but four letters. I would guess that this word has perhaps been made in more ways than any other. Since every sign company tries to be unique with its own design, it is interesting to notice the tremendous number of techniques that are applied throughout the country to this one simple word. There seems to be no end to the variance of presentation.

When considering the scripts we must not overlook the possibilities of "backhand" scripts, because this opens up a great field for unique script treatments. In recent years "straight-up" and "backhand" scripts have been used extensively and are presently extremely popular.

"Gun Caddy" as illustrated in Fig. 78 is an interesting bit of backhand script. This is just one of the many variations possible and shows that a unique effect is easily achieved. One splendid factor about the backhand scripts is that if accomplished properly, they seem to have a most pleasant rolling motion with graceful loops and swirls. There seems to be no end to the personal innovations the sign painter can employ with this form of script. This particular "Gun Caddy" illustration was originally designed as a trademark and was done with pen and ink. The style, however, is most adaptable to the use of a brush. In everyday use, it would be advisable to use a more practical letter y. A one-shot design such as this is usually drawn pretty much the same as a pictorial. The very purpose is to place within the design something that will be unique Therefore the letter y in this case was designed as shown to give this one set of letters an individuality of its own. The rest of the lettering can be adapted for normal purposes.

FIG. 78. One of many variations of back-hand script which, when accomplished properly, appears to have a pleasant, rolling motion with graceful loops and swirls.

It is hoped that as your skill increases you will put some extra effort into your work with the scripts and other "off-beat" lettering. All too often an otherwise good sign painter will be somewhat weak in executing the scripts. To be a really complete sign painter you must at least be able to do several of the standard scripts. Later you should consider developing a few adaptations of your own or at least be able to adapt to those invented by others. Advertisers are no longer satisfied with the commonplace.

No attempt has been made here to include a representative group of script styles in complete alphabet form. The same philosophy applies here that was used at the beginning of our discussion of the printed alphabets. There are a number of excellent books available that present large selections of the various alphabets in complete form. To supplement this over-all instruction, it is suggested that you purchase at least one good book on alphabets and use it in connection with this instruction.

Chapter 24

The Demands of the Trade

In regard to general sign painting, it would be difficult to single out any other trade that requires the workman to know quite a bit about so very much.

The very large sign plants can conveniently employ signmen who specialize in one or several phases of the work. The smaller shops must necessarily hire men who have a broader working knowledge of the sign trade. Until such time as he can enlarge and hire men, the one-man shop operator must personally be able to handle the "whole ball of wax."

Thousands of businessmen in smaller cities throughout this country still need and depend upon the services of the small operators. The roots of our democracy are nourished by free enterprises, both large and small. Should this cease to be a fact, these same roots will perish because of starvation.

As a new operator you naturally cannot expect to amass this over-all knowledge in a few short months. Rather you must sort of "grow" into the sign trade on a step-at-a-time basis. Therefore all that we can hope to do here is to take one thing at a time in an effort to speed this development.

PAPER SIGNS AND BANNERS. It is doubtful if you will go through your career as a signman without being required to produce paper signs.

Frequently we see paper banners in store windows that are poorly made, the reason being that work of this nature is usually for temporary use and is done at a low price. Therefore the sign painter decides to slight the work to show a profit. It is advisable to mention that there are occasions when it is possible to actually paint paper signs with too much precision. Sometimes a merchant purposely desires the fast, "knock-out" appearance on his signs. This would apply to those cases where he definitely wants to impress upon the buying public that his sale was caused by an emergency. In such cases, he wants the signs to have a rushed and hurried appearance to emphasize this fact and to psychologically impress the viewer in this way.

In normal circumstances, however, most merchants require neat work. It is not necessary to slight the work to any major extent in painting good banners if proper procedure is followed.

There are several satisfactory methods to use for painting paper signs and each has its merits. Procedure might vary, depending on the advance notice provided by the customer when the work is ordered. Unfortunately some folks wait until the last minute and expect delivery the same day.

Some signmen use red sables and tempera water color for all paper signs. I can see nothing but disadvantages with this method. The red sables carry a minimum of color eliminating the possibility of long, fast strokes. Also the tempera colors wrinkle the paper. Being water soluble, if the window condenses with sweat the colors dissolve and become a mess.

It is much more convenient to use a good brand of permanent poster colors. These colors dry fast with a flat velvet finish and are not affected by water. The colors are bright and can be thinned with common solvents such as turpentine. These colors cannot be thinned with water. You can either use gray quills, which have much more body and snap than brown quills, or the flat "greyhound" type of brushes.

If you do not have poster colors, you can use regular bulletin colors and the same type of brushes used in poster colors. Bulletin colors must be thinned considerably to work satisfactorily on paper. Some sign painters place a small quantity of bulletin color in a small can without thinning, place a small can beside this containing gasoline. They alternately dip the brush into both the gasoline and the paint, palette this mixture on a "thin-as-you-go" basis, and letter the banners in this way. This paint takes longer to dry, and the letters also take on a mottled appearance. This method will work, however, and it has an advantage over tempera colors, because the colors are waterproof and are much brighter than showcard colors.

A novel way to present this instruction would be for you to "look over my shoulder" while I now do an actual banner job. In this way I might describe a few short-cuts:

The order is for three signs, each measuring 3 by 12 feet, to go across three large front windows of a prestige furniture store. Each window has a metal divider at center so each sign will be in two parts, half on each side of the divider. Six separate signs, each 3 by 6 feet, must be painted. The copy is to be: "Red Tag Anniversary Sale" and the only specification is that a red tag motif be employed. Rather than divide any of the words at center, it is convenient to put "Red Tag" on the left-hand sheet facing the street, and "Anniversary Sale" on the right. For brevity, we shall discuss only the Red Tag portion of the sign (see Fig. 79).

FIG. 79. Gregory details his procedure in lettering this banner.

First I unroll a length of 24-pound white poster paper on the drawing board and measure off 12 feet, indicating this point with a pencil. Using a T-Square flush against the bottom ledge of the drawing board, I mark a vertical pencil line for a square cut. Next I hold a hardwood yardstick firmly along this line, using it as a straightedge, and cut the paper with a sharp single-edged razor blade. This sheet is thumbtacked into place, and another length of paper is rolled over the top of it, making sure that the left edges are flush. The right-hand edge of the bottom sheet will show through enough to use as a guide for cutting the second sheet at the 12-foot point. The third sheet is rolled over this and cut in the same manner. Now there are three 12-foot lengths of paper on the board, so I measure the center of these at the 6-foot point, and indicate this with a pencil mark. After drawing a vertical pencil line at this point, I cut through all three sheets at one time with the razor blade. This results in the six 3 x 6-foot sheets of paper needed for the job. Five of these sheets are removed from the board and the remaining sheet stays in place for the layout.

With a 6H pencil, I make a tentative layout, starting with the outline of the tag. Placing a sheet of 22 x 28-inch cardboard on the paper, I move it about until it is in an attractive position, hold it in place and mark the left, right, and bottom edges of the tag. This provides the "square-start" needed to measure the top part of the tag. After satisfactorily completing the rest of the layout, I go over all of the lines, quite heavily, with a No. 2 pencil. The 6H pencil was originally used because this leaves a faint line and corrections are scarcely noticeable.

Next I successively place the remaining two sheets of paper over this master layout and trace the two Red Tag units needed. The heavy pencil lines on the first unit show through enough to accomplish this. This tracing is done very quickly and lightly. Although I prefer this method, there are other ways of doing this. The first banner could be lettered without the second heavy pencilling procedure, and when dry, copies could be traced by placing paper over the finished banner.

Some sign plants are fortunate enough to have a large, transparent sheet of glass or plastic with light behind it to provide a transparent surface for multiple sign work. However, the intent of the instruction is to explain methods to be used with a minimum of equipment. Most beginners do not have these advanced facilities.

To proceed with the job, all three "Red Tag" signs are now ready to be painted. Using an aerosol type spray can I spray light yellow all around the word "Red." This is done very quickly and provides impact and color. There is no need for any further hand shading or trim. You will note on the illustration that the approximate position of this sprayed area has been indicated with gray-toned shading. The entire sign at this point would appear as it does on the "ed" on the illustration. Pay attention to the sequence of the broken type of layout lines. Most signmen find it easier to use a dotted or broken line for layout work, especially on curves.

This sign is removed and hung over a wire, which is permanently strung across the shop for this purpose. The other two signs are sprayed in the same way and hung on the wire to dry.

While these are drying, I follow the same procedure with the other three "Anniversary Sale" signs, using a heavy script for "Anniversary," and a bold, cartoon-type letter for "Sale." By the time these are ready to hang up to dry, the original three are dry enough to letter. Using poster colors, I first paint the front part of the string with a khaki-yellow, then dip the same brush into a bit of red and deepen the khaki upon the palette to paint the section of string that runs through the back of the tag. A No. 8 gray quill is used for this.

With bright red poster color, I letter the word "Red" with a No. 20 gray camel-ox hair jumbo quill and fill in the centers with a 1½-inch white bristle cutter. The tag is to be reverse or "cut-in" lettering. Using a No. 20 quill, I paint around the letters in the word "Tag," the hole at top-center, the string, and paint the outer edges of the tag. The remaining areas are filled in with the cutter. Fill-in work should always be done as soon as possible after the cutting-in process. This provides a smoother, less mottled surface. Do not proceed too far ahead with the cut-in work before filling in.

The sign is complete, and the remaining two are done in the same way. Next I proceed with the three "Anniversary Sale" sections. For this I use a bright blue poster color. Poster colors are not described in supply catalogs by the same numbers common to bulletin colors nor by the same name. So I use ultramarine blue, which, in the brand of poster colors that I use, would approximate the color of brilliant blue No. 156, lightened with a bit of white. The red that I use in poster colors is described as medium red and it compares somewhat with bright red No. 104 in bulletin colors. It would be more convenient for all signmen if the paint companies would all use the same numbers and description in regard to at least the basic colors. They suggest referral to color charts, but many times the supplier does not have such charts in stock. Then one must order through the mail and take a chance on descriptive names that mean nothing, such as pea-green, peacock blue, etc.

A few tips on paper signs in general: The aerosol sprays can be the biggest time saver. Hand shading and trimming can be eliminated. After the spray paint is dry and before lettering, it is a good idea to wipe over this paint with a dry rag. Some aerosol paints leave a pebbly, chalky residue. It is difficult to letter over this. The rag eliminates much of this.

Extra color flash can be executed with spray cans in a minute or two per sign. As time goes by you can accumulate a good supply of various cardboard masks, panels, stars, etc. For example, carefully cut out a star from a sheet of 6-ply cardboard. Placing the star itself on the sign and spraying around it will provide a reverse star. The piece of cardboard from which the star was cut can be held on the sign, sprayed, and a positive star results. This double use can apply to most shapes or decorations you might cut out.

There is practically no limit to the effects that can originate with the use of spray cans. You cannot expect the same preciseness, however, that is possible with air brushes.

If you must move a large banner off the drawing board without help, before it is dry, slip a long lath-like strip of wood under the top edge, thumbtack the paper to this, and you can move the sign off the board with less danger of the paper folding or smearing.

You can use 16 or 20-pound paper if you prefer, but 24-pound results in better appearing and more durable signs. The small difference in price can be recovered by charging more. Many store owners will use undated signs several times and they appreciate this maximum durability. Also the heavier stock is easier to work with and, upon delivery, the banners have the expensive appearance that allows for an increase in price. Do not mistakenly think that because you prolong the life of any sign that you are beating yourself out of repeat business. The reputation that you build up over a period of years will doubly compensate for any repeat business you might get through producing an inferior product.

The described use of the No. 20 quill and the cutter does not imply that you must use such tools. By all means use the brushes that work best for you. The procedure remains pretty much the same, but if you can improve upon it, then do not hesitate to do so.

LETTERING WITH ALUMINUM.

The question is often asked why there are so many trucks and windows lettered with aluminum. There are several reasons for this; the chief one being that with the use of aluminum, the signman can provide his customers with fairly attractive and serviceable signs at comparatively low prices.

The popularity of aluminum dates back many years when it was used as a sign medium to a much greater degree than it is now. In those days, many of the fine paint products we now use, such as bulletin colors, one-coat enamels, etc., were not available. Thus the signman came to depend upon aluminum, because it was easy to work with, covered well, and enabled him to do a job with good speed and result.

There are two basic methods for doing an aluminum job, either by lettering with paint ready mixed or by the "dust on" method.

Let us assume that you are to letter an exterior window job with the ready mix method. It is best to prepare a small quantity of the mix in the shop, preferably not much more than you will need. This mixture dulls somewhat if it stands for several days. Unless you have a similar job to do the following day, it is advisable to mix a fresh batch for each job.

Place a heaping tablespoon of superfine aluminum lining bronze powder into a small jar. To this add about a teaspoonful of a good grade quick gold-size or spar varnish. Replace the cover on the jar and shake it thoroughly. This mixture is sometimes too thick, so add a few drops of turpentine, and shake again. A little experimentation will be required, because sizings and varnishes vary in thickness. There are very good proprietary bonding agents which you can find by looking in supply catalogs. The description will usually state if it is adaptable for mixing with bronzing powders. A few drops of clear fibroseal added to any bronze mix, along with the gold size, will toughen the mixture and speed the drying process.

Many beginners and some veterans have a problem with self-mixed aluminum. In almost every case this trouble is because of the bronzing powder being used. The most important factor in achieving a bright smooth letter is to buy the finest-ground powder available. Superfine aluminum lining bronze is ground as fine as a high grade kitchen flour. The cheaper, coarsely ground powders result in a grainy mix that rolls under the brush and a professional job is impossible. If the powder appears to be the least bit grainy then it does not even pay to attempt a satisfactory mix. If the mix does not cover well and is transparent, it is too thin and more bronze must be added.

There are other ways to prepare an aluminum mix. Some signmen prefer to use a paste form of aluminum. Others use a patent mix prepared by the manufacturer. Choose the mix that you find to be most suitable. My preference is to mix my own and many other signmen of my acquaintance do likewise.

Proceed as usual with the window job. Clean the glass thoroughly and lay out the sign with a piece of chisel-edged chalk. A more precise layout is possible through the use of one of the glass marking pencils now available. These come in a variety of colors and can be sharpened to a point just as any lead pencil. Do not use the big, heavy black grease pencils.

These better type marking pencils adapt very well to glass and the marks can be removed with a damp chamois skin. The same marks are difficult to remove from painted surfaces.

The best method is to lay out all the guidelines with the marking pencil and then lightly indicate the lettering with chalk. Layout adjustments can then be made without problem since chalk is easily removed. After the layout is satisfactorily accomplished, if the chalk lines are not precise enough for your purposes, then use the marking pencil to indicate these lines more accurately. Lightly dust off the original chalk marks and proceed with the lettering.

Because aluminum is a light textured mixture in comparison to the heavy synthetics, many signmen prefer to use a softer lettering brush such as a brown quill. This is a matter of personal preference. I have never found this to be any advantage and have good success with the use of the gray quills.

Shortly after the lettering is completed the entire sign can be wiped over lightly with a very clean, damp chamois. This depends, of course, on the drying quality of the size used in the mix, but usually this can be done almost immediately. Otherwise you can normally remove the marks from the first few letters completed at the start of the job. Then while you shade and trim these, the rest of the lettering can dry.

Do not attempt to remove any marks with a rag. Sometimes just the weave of the cloth or the tiniest seam will scratch the lettering. A good grade, damp chamois skin can be used to remove layout marks from almost any surface even when bulletin colors or enamels are used. As soon as the paint has dried to a slight tack, a chamois skin can be used, but this must be done with great care and with a very light touch.

If this type of aluminum lettering is done on a glass that will receive a lot of abuse and washing, such as the door of a public building, it is advisable to apply a protective coat to the letters. Apply a coat of clear automotive enamel to the letters, extending this application at least 1/16 inch over the edges of the letters. This provides a margin of safety and the edges of the letters will not break down so readily due to the rough use of a squeegee, etc. This is commonly referred to as "pencil varnishing" in the trade.

It is almost impossible to letter with aluminum in direct sunshine. The fast setting nature of the medium, speeded up by excessive heat, causes a "pile-up" of paint. The brush becomes caked up with paint in the "heel" and must be rinsed in solvent at frequent intervals.

The dust-on procedure consists basically of doing the distinct advantages. Most importantly the job will endure much longer and does not necessarily require a protective coating. However, the initial cost to the customer is, or should be, considerably higher.

The dust-on procedure consists basically of doing the lettering with a size and, when nearly dry, dusting on the bronze powder in dry form. In regard to this sizing, there are so many possible mixes that work well that it is difficult to say which is best. Quick gold size or top quality spar varnish are perhaps the most common. My preference is to use gold size with a small quantity of yellow bulletin color added. This provides a better measure of visibility than does clear sizing.

It is essential that the surface to be lettered is scrupulously clean. Bronze powders adhere to hand smudges, finger prints, grease marks, etc.

From this point on, the job is lettered as usual with the sizing, except that you must avoid leaving a series of hand smudges around the lettering area.

The time that elapses between the application of the lettering and the dusting process depends upon the type of size used and drying conditions. Generally on smaller jobs, the entire sign can be lettered before applying the bronze powder. A handy method to determine this is to paint a swatch of sizing on the glass, away from the sign, and use this as a test patch. This is later removed. Do this at the start of the lettering. Test the patch occasionally with a finger. If the tack is such that your finger squeaks as you pull it along the sizing, then it is time to apply the dust.

Right here is where the most know-how is needed in regard to the efficiency of the completed job. The dryer the size, the brighter the letters will be, but if the sizing is too dry the aluminum will soon wear off causing the sign to look shabby. If the sizing is too wet, the letters will be dull and mottled. You will soon learn through experience how to judge the correct amount of drying time. The sized letters should be just tacky enough to absorb some of the bronzing powder but not smear. The letters will not be as shiny as a dryer job, but more durable.

The method of dusting is as follows: Dip a soft powder puff into the dry powder and pat it on to the letters with a firm pounding motion. After the patting process, rub the powder puff briskly, but lightly, over the lettering with a burnishing motion. The excess powder is then removed with soft, fluffy rags. You can then proceed with the shading or trim work. A little tip: An empty metal shoe polish can is a good container for the bronze powder. Use a powder puff small enough to fit within this can. This can remain in the can with the bronze powder when the lid is snapped back on to the can after use.

The lettering process for trucks and other signs is essentially the same. Although the lowly aluminum job is not as popular as it once was, there is a definite place for this work in the sign trade. For example, consider the contractor who has a fleet of trucks and uses any one unit only for a year or so before trading. His only desire may be to comply with the law and identify his trucks for legal reasons and at the lowest possible price. This is one example among many where aluminum lettering can be used to advantage, because of speed, economy, serviceability, and attractiveness.

It seems advisable at this point to describe a trick of layout. The layout procedure as outlined in Fig. 80 can be used on a variety of signs, word groupings, patterns, etc. This example illustrates how you might lay out the name of the city and state on a truck door. The average novice usually begins to mark out the layout from the left and continues to mark and rub off until he eventually manages to place the layout at center.

The three separate illustrations in Fig. 80 demonstrate how you can mark out and center any line of copy with a minimum of adjustment.

Your first step in this example would be to count the letters. Usually in counting letters, the M and the W are counted as 1½ and the letter I is counted as ½ a letter. In this case, the W and I could automatically be counted as

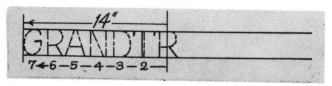

FIG. 80A. First step of layout procedure: Mark the letter R at center; then layout the letters T, D, N, A, R and G backwards toward the left as shown by the numbers. Measure from the center line to the left edge of the letter G to determine the left margin. Place a vertical mark at this point. Here it is 14 inches from the center.

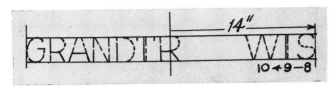

FIG. 80B. Next, measure 14 inches to the right of center to determine the right margin. Starting with the letter S, lay out the
word "Wis.", also backwards, as shown.

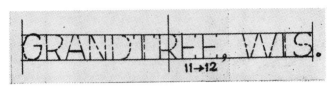

FIG. 80C. Then mark in the letters EE as shown to complete
the layout.

two letters (1½ plus ½ or 2). The space between words is
also counted as a letter, so you have a total of 13 elements.
Thus the letter R would be the center letter, so you can
proceed as shown in the illustration.

This method works out particularly well on a two-word
grouping, because the space between the words provides a
certain amount of latitude. If the space is a bit wider than
a normal one-letter space it doesn't matter. If the resultant
space is too narrow, in this case the two letters E could be
narrowed slightly, and the W condensed a bit to provide
more space between the two words.

It should be mentioned that few veterans count the
letters. Instead they do as follows: With a pencil they
quite accurately mark the line of copy upon a scratch pad,
using letters about ¼ inch high. This marking would be
much the same as the words "Grandtree, Wis." as shown in
the final drawing. This small form marking is then meas-
ured to find the approximate center. However, until you
develop the ability to do this, it is advisable to count the
letters.

TEMPORARY LETTERING INSIDE
WINDOWS. In addition to the less progressive veterans,
it is surprising how many of the newer sign painters fail to
master the art of lettering backwards. Frequently the question arises as to what is the best way to letter an exterior

window sign in zero weather. This can be answered with another question: "Why not letter it on the inside?"

When circumstances demand, most window signs can be done on the inside of the glass. You might argue this by saying, "Yes, but this would require more time and suppose my customer does not want to spend enough to cover the difference?" This would be sound argument if applied to warm weather painting. However, in freezing weather a good signman should be able to do the job on the interior nearly as fast as he could on the exterior.

Normally it would take longer to letter backwards, but on the interior this is offset by the advantage of working where it is warm. The hands are flexible, the paint flow is predictable, and the finished sign is not subjected to rugged weather. On an exterior job, the hands would not be flexible and would need to be warmed frequently. You might have to step inside occasionally to warm up. Also there is the disadvantage of working with heavy clothing—the sleeve of the jacket interfering with freedom of arm movement. The paint thickens in the cold and is difficult to apply. So time-wise, I doubt if there is any advantage at all in working on the outside during very cold weather.

The important consideration is to train yourself to do reverse lettering as efficiently as possible. Most high class window valances are done on the inside in both winter and summer. To be an all-around commercial sign painter you must be able to do this type of lettering.

The procedure on reverse work is to prepare a perforated pattern and transfer this to the glass. If you are adept at lettering, greater accuracy can be attained by pouncing the pattern on the inside. If you work "hand-down," there is the possibility of rubbing off parts of the pattern. In this case, pounce the pattern on to the exterior of the glass, and as you letter, try to keep the pattern directly in front of you. Should you view the pattern lines from an oblique angle, the thickness of the glass between the pattern and the actual working surface is sufficient to cause some distortion.

Tempera water colors work up or dissolve into a second coat applied over them. If a pictorial is involved, this can pose a problem. This can be solved in two ways. Either paint the outline of the picture only on the exterior, and apply the colors on the interior, or outline the pictorial on the inside with japan color. The latter method works best. Mix a small amount of paste japan color with a fast dry gold size and thin with turpentine if necessary. Outline the pictorial first, and by the time you do the adjacent lettering

220

this outline will be dry enough to paint over. Before application of the colors, wipe over the japan color outline with a damp chamois, or sometimes the tempera colors will creep at the points of contact with the japan color.

Excessive blending is not necessary on cheap pictorials of this type. It is practical to employ the tone-type approach such as is used on the numbered paintings with positive color divisions. These divisions can be perforated on the pattern and should be kept at a minimum. Adhere to simplicity unless you can get a sufficient price to justify more detailed procedure.

So much for the pattern type of temporary sign. Now for convenience of explanation, let me take you along on a tempera job of another nature.

One of my customers has a store front with four 12-foot plate glass windows. His building is on the outskirts of town where the traffic is moving about 50 miles per hour. The windows are 75 feet off the highway, so the lettering has to be quite large. The weather is about 15 to 20 degrees above zero. He is planning a month long carload sale and all four windows must be covered with flashy, colorful lettering.

Since a water color job is requested, I explain that once lettered, the windows cannot be washed until the paint is removed. The important copy consists of large lettering such as "Carload Sale," "Prices Slashed," etc. There are numerous specific items listed with prices for secondary copy. This copy is intended for those who drive in. The large lettering only is to be readable from the highway and is to serve as a "come-on" to lure motorists into the store.

The windows have been washed for lettering purposes, so the work begins. First, for my own use, I draw a quick, rough "thumbnail" sketch of the entire four-window spread on a piece of paper. This is done in a matter of minutes and only to establish the general positions.

My decision is to place the secondary price items in 4-foot circles, so I draw these upon the window with a piece of chalk pushed through the loop on the end of a piece of cord. Occasionally I hold the sketch up toward the window with the reverse side towards me. A quick study of this helps to determine the general layout positions. Next I draw horizontal guidelines within the circles for the copy. The next step is to mark out the positions for all the guidelines that are to contain the rest of the copy. Since I am working alone, I snap these lines with a chalk line by taping the left-hand end of the string to the glass. A good sized piece of masking tape is used for this, and the tape is rubbed firmly with the thumbnail for good adhesion. I must not pull too hard on the string or it will loosen the tape, so I use just enough pull to tighten the string. A good sized knot in the end of the string will help keep the string from pulling through the tape.

My concern is to do as much of the work as possible without going outside, so I determine the center of each line and mark it. The centers also are marked on each line of lettering on the rough sketch.

With all the guidelines, circles, and centers marked on the inside, the exterior work consists only of sketching in the lettering. This can be done while wearing gloves. I take a half dozen pieces of chalk sharpened to a chisel edge and go to the outside. The larger letters are marked out very rapidly and precisely in heavy, bold speed-type letters. The entire outlines of these letters are marked. Any lines of built-up script also are carefully marked in detail. One-stroke letters are indicated with a single chalk mark type of layout. These are not marked in detail because the size of the brush will automatically form a letter of consistent thickness. Those who are new to backward lettering might find it helpful on the one-stroke copy to draw those letters in detail that are difficult for them to letter.

The layout is finished and ready to be lettered. For contrast and good color distribution, I will alternately use three different tempera colors for the lettering. Some copy groupings will be lettered with white, others with yellow, and the remainder with pale-blue. This blue is mixed by adding regular blue to white until a bright, attractive color results. These colors are thinned to a free-flowing consistency, not too thick.

A little tip: If you place a jar or can of paint on the stepladder platform, do as follows: Fasten a shallow tin can solidly to the stepladder platform or step with a small screw through the bottom (see Fig. 81). Place the paint container within this can to keep it from sliding off or tipping if the ladder is accidentally bumped or slips. The ladder can carefully be pulled about without removing the container. The stationary can may be attached or removed very quickly as desired.

It is in the actual process of lettering that I can pick up extreme speed and still do neat, knife-edge letters by using a brush that is not commonly thought of as a tool to be used in water colors. I use a No. 20 jumbo gray camel-ox hair quill for the entire job.

No doubt some signmen will think I "blew my stack"

when they read this. They might insist that a red sable is the only proper brush for this. At one time I felt likewise, but through experimentation, I discovered that a jumbo quill enables me to cut-in the large letters and fill them in at the same time. This results in neat, transparent letters

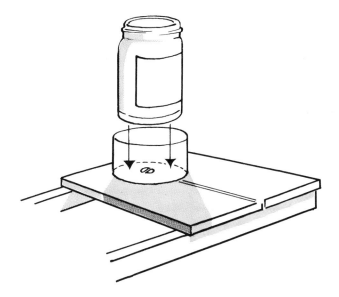

FIG. 81. *Fasten shallow tin can solidly to stepladder platform or step with a small screw through the bottom. Place jar or can of paint within this can to keep the container from sliding off or tipping and spilling its contents if the ladder is accidentally bumped or slips.*

with a minimum of muddy, piled up spots. This is a distinct advantage at night when the store lights backlight the letters and accentuate every flaw. Furthermore these jumbo quills, in all sizes, are not as stubby and carry much more color. This permits the application of long, uninterrupted strokes and since using this method my time of operation has been cut in half with better looking results. For the smaller lettering, I still use red sables, especially on letters from 5 inches on down. It is my practice to reserve several quills to be used expressly for this purpose. I never use these in japan or oil colors.

Several years ago, a signman from Chicago told me that he formerly avoided this type of work. Since I explained this method to him and, after using it, he now claims that he welcomes this same sort of sign work.

To get back to the job. First I do all the white lettering and then the yellow, followed by the blue. Next I outline or shade some of the predominant copy with bright red and some with regular blue. The secondary copy is left untrimmed. The circles are then painted with a heavy single stroke outline of bright red or blue using the color most adaptable to the adjacent lettering. These circular outlines can be painted in a casual, scalloped manner, or they can be applied with a steady, single stroke in accurate position around the outline of the circle.

When the lettering is dry, I wipe the guidelines off the interior with a soft, dry cloth and off the exterior with a damp, clean chamois skin.

The job is complete and 48 feet of 7-foot high windows have been lettered from top to near bottom in less than 5 hours. Before leaving, the proprietor inquires about the best way to remove the lettering when the sale is over. I advise him to scrape off the bulk of the lettering with new razor blades, clean off the residue with damp rags, and then wash the windows as usual. Any attempt to dissolve all this water color without first scraping off the bulk of the paint is a messy job. It is very simple to scrape off tempera colors from glass with sharp razor blades.

KEEPING PACE WITH THE TIMES.

In every trade or profession one must keep up with the trend of the times or soon fall into a state of mediocrity. As a sign painter you must accept and master new techniques to keep abreast with the constant changes in the field of advertising.

In no phase of the business does this more truly apply than to the knowledge and execution of lettering. You should develop a thorough understanding of the most basic alphabets before considering any of the others. The foundation alphabets consist of the Gothic or Egyptian styles, the Roman, including the sans-serif "thick and thin" treatments, and at least one or two of the basic scripts—not stunt scripts. In addition you should learn several fast-type alphabets so you can produce heavy copy jobs with good speed. One such example would be the Lydian alphabet, including its italic and cursive variations. An all-cap italic letter such as shown earlier in Fig. 40 also is adaptable to high-speed lettering.

Following this, you should then learn to modify these same alphabets to suit the space or purpose and extend this knowledge to their many variations.

Since most of the sign work you will ever be required to do, can and will be handled with the alphabets just mentioned, let me stress the following statement: Learn them and learn them well—so that you can practically do them by instinct. Once you master these, you can quite easily adapt to almost any alphabet that might present itself.

The past few paragraphs recap the instruction up to this point and apply only to the beginning of your career. While it is highly essential to learn the basic alphabets, do not let your progress end at this point. You must constantly modernize and be prepared to offer your customers the latest in sign design at all times. One of the occupational hazards in the sign business is that it is too easy to rationalize and rest on your laurels. For example, you might say, "Why should I learn these new fangled alphabets? My customers seem to be well pleased with my work the way it is, etc., etc."

Perhaps the most impressive way to answer this is to relate a story about a sign painter whom I knew many years ago. For convenience, I shall call him "One Track." When I was a young boy, One Track had the largest shop in the vicinity. It fascinated me to hang around his shop and watch him work. Indeed, he had an abundance of work with five or six sign painters in his employ. With pleasure I watched him letter his beautiful scrolls, curlicues, and circus-type signs. For instance, he would prepare a banner with bright red and blue letters. Later he would paint the bottom half of each letter with an inset line of black, followed by an outline of bright yellow, etc. I could see one of his signs along the street and immediately know that One Track did it, and again I would marvel at his excellence, hoping that one day I might be able to do such fine work.

The merchants flocked to him with their bakery and milk wagons, trucks, etc. Just before the county fair and other gala events, he worked day and night. His kind of work was highly popular at that time and his customers would seldom consider patronizing another shop.

This story could and should have a happy ending, but such is not the case. Shortly after this period, I left this vicinity and after many years of working as a sign painter, I returned. New, modern sign shops had been established and were doing excellent work, but there was no sign of One Track. After browsing about town I noticed a sign of his here and there. These signs had been painted in exactly the same manner now as they had been done 30 years previously. Instead of the glamour they once held for me, they now appeared to be as out of place as a horse and buggy on a freeway.

Upon inquiry, I found that old One Track was attempting to eke out an existence in a small second floor walk-up. What happened was this: He was going great, but refused to modernize and adapt to the trend. Younger signmen started shops and he laughed at their new fangled ideas and lettering. This worked fine for a while, because the older merchants growing old along with One Track still swore by his work. Gradually, though, the old merchants passed on, sold out, or turned their business places over to their sons. Old One Track refused to change and the younger generation just simply would not buy his old fashioned "gingerbread" any longer. The business world began to pass him by because he had made no effort to keep in pace.

Your first thought might be that his age had something to do with it. I prefer to think that in cases like this it is more likely to be the result of ignorance, lack of foresight, or just plain bullheadedness. There are scores of men in their late years who have kept pace with the times and are doing first class up-to-date work. In addition they have the great asset of being able to do the basic alphabets to perfection and have used this factor as a foundation for all the other lettering variations they have learned or developed. With great respect, I point to such men as Heinie Johnson with whom most of you are familiar. Consider his attitude and his talent. Also men such as George Peterson of Oakland, Calif. George is now in his mid-seventies, but his work compares with that of most modern younger sign painters. These men and countless others prove that age is no excuse for becoming obsolete.

So as a new operator, it is advisable for you to be receptive to new ideas, whether these appeal to you or not. Your success depends upon giving the public what it wants at any given time and not what it desired 10 or 15 years ago.

Occasionally this might involve using an alphabet or style that you will personally detest. One such style might be such as the one illustrated in Fig. 82, "The Krickets." At present this type of letter and variations are highly popular with the younger set.

This particular lettering arrangement was designed for a teenage dance band. The original drawing as shown was made for reproduction to be used in the printing of posters, newspaper ads, etc. A sheet of clear plastic also was lettered to fit over the dance band's drumhead. The automobile trailer in which the instruments are transported was lettered with this trademark along with other incidental equipment.

You can refer to this as "freak" lettering or by any other name, but if you are not able to do it, somebody else will. The young people "dig" this kind of stuff. Witness the big displays of "mad-mad" comic greeting cards enjoying excellent sales everywhere to young and old.

Frankly I do not like this type of lettering, but I do it because it results in lucrative orders. In fact the results can sometimes be comical. Several years ago I did my

FIG. 82. *Whether you like it or not, "freak" lettering of this sort is popular today, particularly with young people.*

first job of this type on an orchestra trailer for a teenage band leader. He brought, as a sample, the cover from a record album put out by a nationally known dance band. This band's name was designed with some "way-out" type of lettering. He asked if I could prepare the name of his band in the same style, which I did. Several days after the trailer was lettered, his dad showed it to a friend. The friend said, "Boy, is that goofy lettering—all crooked! Greg must have had a rough night before he did that one!" Fortunately the proud father advised him that I had been asked to letter the trailer in this fashion.

Let us briefly discuss this type of lettering. It is neither as simple or haphazard as it might appear. To achieve a pleasant effect, the letters must be grouped with some thought in regard to good balance. To come up with the casualness so necessary to the success of this type of lettering, you must acquire over-all knowledge of its common characteristics. This might be called an "ad lib" letter, because there does not seem to be any one basic alphabet. Therefore you must invent each letter as you proceed to most properly adapt to the space provided by the adjacent letters. The ultimate goal is always to end up with an interesting arrangement.

FIG. 83. *Meaning of the words influences styles of lettering used to make jobs such as this more expressive and more to the whims of the customers involved.*

To school yourself to do this type of lettering, it is advisable to buy a variety of greeting cards done in this motif. Since this lettering is quite popular you can find samples in many magazines, newspapers, and in television commercials. Study as many varieties of this type of lettering as you can, until you become familiar with the technique.

It has several advantages. Because of its condensed nature, it is possible to squeeze very large letters into a small amount of space. Perhaps this is why it is used considerably for television advertising. It also has a built-in alibi. If you do have a crooked line or a small mistake you can say: "It's supposed to be that way." This does not imply that you can slap out such lettering any old way. Good design is essential even though there is an allowance for slight error in the mechanical process.

The "Jet Stars" design (Fig. 83) is another example of a letter for which there is no prevalent or established complete alphabet. In designing a letter grouping such as this, you must consider the meaning of the words. In this case the word "Jet" immediately suggests speed. Therefore a streamlined letter was used to accent this fact. Note how the treatment of the letter A with the star below continues the jet-star effect and provides a complete uniqueness to the design.

This is an example of a one-shot job invented in a matter of minutes to suit the name. This was done swiftly and with as good a quality as possible to be within the limits of a teenage pocketbook. It could have been designed more carefully and accurately, but it proves that a fairly decent job can be done quickly and economically without resorting to sloppiness. Study the basics of lettering, because the origin of most other alphabets can generally be traced to the basics.

Chapter 25

Professional Procedures

Practically every sign painter, no matter how expert he might be, has his own individual technique. It was previously mentioned that although the lettering of some sign painters can be quite similar, it is doubtful if any two signmen work exactly alike. If one has at any time become familiar with the work of another sign painter it is often possible to glance at a finished sign and immediately know who did the lettering. It is not uncommon for most signmen to use a certain little recognizable technique throughout a lifetime.

Therefore you can very well expect to develop an individual style of lettering. However, there is a big difference between a good technique and poor workmanship. The important object is to have your work recognized because of its excellence rather than consistently repeated errors. To emphasize this point, let me cite two examples—the first good, the second bad.

Sometime ago a firm for whom I do much sign and artwork was setting up a big promotion many miles from here. A last minute need for an extra display developed, so they arranged to have this built and lettered in that city. Later they brought this unit to their local warehouse where I chanced to see the display. Recognizing the work immediately, I said, "I see old Jackson is still doing beautiful work."

The advertising man accompanying me began to laugh, somewhat surprised, and asked me how I knew that Jackson had done this particular job. I explained that most signmen could recognize the techniques of fellows with whom they had once worked. He was surprised further still when I said that I had not seen this man or his work for over 20 years and had no idea that he was in Wisconsin since I had worked with him in a different state. I then pointed out the characteristics that made it possible for me to pinpoint the source of the job.

The over-all excellence of the job itself immediately caused me to think of Jackson since few surpass him in the trade. Also he has a peculiar way of making the letter S, which is slightly topheavy. He makes the down stroke of the upper case letter T a bit thicker at the top, tapering it slightly toward the bottom. Both of these quirks, while not consistent with this type of alphabet, are done so gracefully by this man that they actually enhance the work. He also has a unique way of executing a lower case letter a which is completely individual to him.

This is a case in which the work was recognized by its excellence. It is easier still to identify the work of sign painters who have developed bad lettering habits. An example of this would be the man who uses a bad formation of the letter R as shown in Fig. 84. No matter what type of alphabet he might use, he always extends the down stroke of the letter R below the bottom guideline and chops it off at will.

FIG. 84. Some special characteristics, such as this over-extended downstroke on the letter R, might seem to have a nice effect in some situations. However, used to extreme in every sign a man does, they can become tiresome and overdone.

There are occasions when this stroke is extended in a graceful manner to achieve a stunt letter. But certainly a competent sign painter would not continue to apply this stroke in such a clumsy fashion for a period of 20 years or better. At one time somebody apparently told him that this was cute, so he now uses this technique on every sign that he paints. This same man has worked at the trade for many years but never bothered to learn the simple everyday fundamentals of lettering.

Some of the other poor procedures used by this "sign painter" seem to provide an excellent means of presenting to you the bad habits of lettering to be avoided.

Seldom does he letter a truck door without at least one line of lettering being off-center. To compensate for this

232

excessive space at either end of such a line, he applies a big, unsightly dot about the size of a silver dollar. Many of his signs with heavy copy are "peppered" with such dots in an attempt to cause "offside copy" to appear centered.

The remedy for this is simply to prepare a more precise layout. There also is a constant lack of consistency in his lettering. If the letter S should appear five times in one line of lettering, no two of these would be alike. It is essential in good lettering to make all companion letters as similar in shape as possible. For example, if you should curve the down-stroke of the letter R as it first appears you must then follow through and do likewise with the rest of these letters as they occur within the same copy grouping. Usually, in this case, you would apply the same treatment to the down-stroke of the letter K since the strokes are nearly identical.

It was mentioned that this man had not yet learned the fundamentals. This is most evident in the manner in which he letters the thick and thin Roman type alphabets. All of his thin strokes are slanted the wrong way, which also causes them to be on the wrong side as shown in Fig. 85. The rule to follow in regard to all thick and thin type alphabets is that all of the thin oblique strokes, slant from right to left; never from left to right. Remember this and your slants will always be correct.

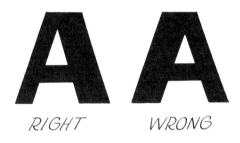

RIGHT   WRONG

FIG. 85. *Thin strokes should slant from right to left, never from left to right, and thick strokes vice versa.*

Most of the basic alphabets did not come into being by accident. In some measure their characteristics can be traced to the shape or nature of the primitive tools with which they were originally developed.

Evidently the Roman scribes and scholars used hand-fashioned reeds with flat knife-like nibs. Therefore the very formation of the first Roman letters with their thick and thin characteristics was a natural result of the way these ancient scribes held the lettering instruments. To develop speed they refrained from turning the pen as they printed these letters. Considering this fact, one can see why it would be almost impossible to have the thin element of a letter slant from left to right. Obviously the Romans did find it necessary to change the hand positions somewhat to form certain letters such as the letter N.

Other civilizations or cultures used trimmed quills shaped from various sized feathers. As these were pointed and afforded many degrees of flexibility, we could perhaps trace many of our scroll and text alphabets to their use. The orientals favored pointed brushes, which is quite evident in the unique shapes of the letters common to their techniques.

All of this does not imply that you must study the origin of lettering, etc. There are hundreds of excellent contemporary lettering artists. Many sources and examples of good lettering are available to you so you should have no problem if you have a sincere desire to learn.

The important point is to avoid the mistakes of our second example and not have your work recognized because of its imperfections. If you are conscientious, it might be inconceivable to you that a man could go on year-after-year making the same errors, but this is all too true. Workmen such as this develop the "good enough" attitude early in their careers and put forth no effort to improve.

This extends to such easily avoided mistakes as poor spelling. For many years there was a large sign on a brick wall of a building right on the main corner of the city. In letters 2 ft. high the word "Accordion" was misspelled, "Accordian." In another city, a few miles to the south and on a music store window in the heart of the business district, the same word was misspelled in the same way. Both signs were painted by the same man.

It is true that we are not all naturally good spellers, but you would think that any man who has the least amount of pride in his work would not hold it in lower esteem than the price of a pocket dictionary.

This painter had another very odd habit. When doing the layout work on a truck with white doors, he drew all of the cross guidelines with extremely heavy red grease pencil marks. When he finished the lettering, he made no attempt to remove these pronounced marks. Vision was no problem, since he did not wear eye glasses, so I will never know what prompted this strange and most obnoxious form of layout. As your experience with lettering progresses, you will discover many ways to ease and improve your work.

See Fig. 86 for a lettering tip that might be of some value. Note the reference to closing the peaks of the letters. This applies to such letters as the A, M, N, W, etc. In some alphabets this little trick actually lends grace to the letters, but its main advantage is that it is easier to shade the letters. When shading wet letters especially, it is difficult even for the expert to maneuver the strokes into these sharp peaks.

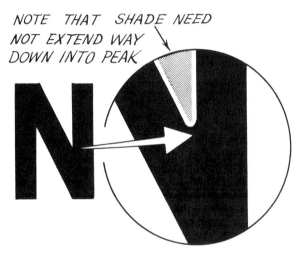

FIG. 86. When shading wet letters, it is especially difficult to pull the shade stroke completely down into the extreme peak. By closing these peaks slightly when lettering, the letterer can set up for more clearance between shade and letter with less chance of messing up the letter.

By slightly closing these peaks, the shade strokes can terminate farther out of the peaks where there is more clearance. A few signmen might frown on this procedure as being improper, but many expert workmen use this method in much of their work. These closures should not be more pronounced, proportionately, than the enlarged example on the illustration.

By the way, have you ever noticed that the letter W is in reality two letter Vs joined together? This is especially helpful in designing a well formed W in a thick and thin alphabet such as a sans-serif Roman.

When considering a layout it is advisable to choose a letter style that will adapt to the shape of the panel. Study the contour of the lettering as illustrated in Fig. 87. The choice of letters is not suited to the shape of this panel and the result is unattractive. The vertical space on a strip sign is limited and it is generally advisable to use capital letters only on such signs. Script and lower case letters can be used if the copy is free of letters that extend below the bottom guideline. If a line of lettering contains such letters as g, p, or y, it is better to use capital letters entirely.

Suppose you should decide to place the word "Advertising" on a thin strip sign. The capital A and the letters d and t extend above the line. The letter g would be the only letter to extend below the line. So just to accommodate this one letter you must reduce the height of all the other letters. The end result is that the line of lettering does not appear to run through the center of the strip. There is too much blank space along the bottom of the letters in comparison to the top. Effective readability also is at a minimum. This same rule applies to the bottom line of any sign. It is poor layout to use either lower case or script on the bottom line if some of the letters extend below. This results in a ragged appearance at the bottom instead of a preferable straight margin. Even on larger one-line signs, it is wise to avoid letters that extend below the bottom guideline. For example on a sign that measures 3 ft. by 24 ft., it would not be advisable to use such a word as "Signs" in either lower case or script. The lower extension of the single letter g would provide a poor balance of layout. Generally this letter g would very nearly touch the extreme bottom edge of the sign even if this bottom loop would be "snubbed off" as it usually is in these cases.

This applies to both script and lower case letters. In Fig. 87 you will note that the bottom loop of the letter g has been diminished as much as possible to fit within these

FIG. 87. *This is clumsy and unattractive because the alphabet chosen does not fit into the space. Where vertical space is limited and copy has letters which in lower case extend below bottom guideline, it is best to use caps to avoid the problem.*

236

limits, yet it looks cramped and does not have the graceful sweep common to this letter. The dwindled-off effect towards the right end is caused by the greater amount of space above the last three letters of the word. Visualize how much more adaptable capital letters would have been to this space.

ONE COAT COVERAGE IN LETTERING.

Whenever several signmen get together for a little chat, the conversation frequently includes a few pros and cons in regard to one-coat coverage with the use of high cover lettering enamels.

Paint products are constantly improving and there are now a number of excellent one-coat lettering enamels on the market. Some of the high quality white enamels cover quite well on one-stroke lettering, although the strokes might have to be "nursed" along a bit to produce acceptable coverage. The highly skilled lettering artist has the best chance for success in this process.

The paint must be thinned to an easy working consistency, so it is free-flowing. A common fault among inexperienced sign painters is to use paint that is much too thick for all purposes. Their logic is that thick paint will naturally cover better. Quite the opposite is true. Especially when lettering, thick paint will not flow from the brush, but will drag and pile-up. A thinner mixture provides a smoother letter and certainly better coverage. However, the paint cannot be thinned too much or the binding quality is destroyed. Excessive thinning causes the paint to dry with a flat finish. There also is a rapid color breakdown and as time passes the paint will chalk off.

Novice signmen often ask, "How do I get white to cover with one coat on a built-up letter?" The answer to this is, "You don't," at least not perfectly. Whenever a letter must be painted and filled in with a number of strokes, the overlaps of the strokes have double-coat coverage, while the remaining area that is only hit once with the brush will have a certain amount of transparency. Therefore it is common practice among signmen to double-coat such letters.

This can be done in two ways. If it is a rush job, letter it first with a coat of blocking-out white with a bit of bulletin color added. Just enough bulletin color is used to toughen the blocking-out white and provide better initial coverage. When this is dry, go over the lettering again with the finish coat. With this method, it is advisable to overlap the edges a slight bit with the tougher finish coat so the edges of the letters do not break down.

If time permits, it is better procedure to use two coats of regular lettering enamel. The advantage of this is the speed with which the second coat can be applied. When lettering the first coat do so in a careful, precise manner. Later when you apply the finish coat, you can then stay away from the letter edges 1/16 of an inch or less and pick up greater speed. It should be mentioned that it is not normally recommended to apply enamel over enamel. But to the extent of lettering, I have used this method on many jobs without any problem. Signs that were painted 6 or 7 years ago show no abnormal deterioration. The two-coat method, especially on built-up lettering, is superior to any attempt to pile on the paint in one coat. This applies especially to prestige work. I have known quality-minded signmen who actually will use three coats to provide the greatest possible degree of whiteness. One coat is generally sufficient on signs that are never viewed close-up such as highway bulletins, second story work, etc.

Perfectionists will frequently employ the two-coat method even on smaller, one-stroke lettering, especially on expensive signwork.

Individual signmen have various recipes for doping up white to achieve better coverage. Some add a bit of black to the white. Others add a small amount of aluminum or a touch of blue. Most of us have used these procedures. Better coverage does result, but only at the sacrifice of true white. There are other drawbacks. For example, the addition of a little blue will indeed provide better coverage, and if there is no other true white immediately adjacent on a sign or a truck to set up a close comparison, this mixture will appear to be white. However, as time passes and the lettering ages, the white will become bluer and bluer until it is definitely a pale blue instead of the original white. In short, it has a tendency to fade into a pale blue.

The use of pastel colors for lettering on dark surfaces presents no problem. These colors—especially pale blue, green, gray, and pink—will cover almost perfectly in one coat with careful application. This does not apply to creams, yellows, or ivories, which will usually require the same treatment as white.

Most signmen mix their own pastel colors. For example, if you need a pale blue, pour a small quantity of lettering white into a container. Very little color is needed to tint the white, so the blue can be added a slight bit at a time with the mixing stick. Pale blue has a tendency to dry to a much darker color after application. Therefore the blue should be mixed to a lighter shade than that desired on the finished job. The colors mixed should be compatible. Most bulletin colors can be used for tinting purposes. You might have a problem with pink, since it is a touchy color. Sometimes if bulletin red is added to lettering enamel it will not remain suspended after stirring. The red will separate and result in a mottled or marble-like effect. It can be used with constant stirring. If this does occur in the case of any color-mix, it means that the two products are not compatible and you might have to experiment until you do find compatible mixtures. Usually the same brands will provide the most stable mixtures. Trial and error will soon teach you which brands of paints can be successfully inter-mixed.

In regard to a one-coat yellow that will cover properly even when using a one-stroke letter, I must admit that I have not yet been able to discover such a yellow. Although I have managed to mix yellows to cover quite well in one coat, the result has usually been a dull or muddy shade and not the bright intense yellow that I desire. In correspondence with other signmen in regard to this, all of them seem to have the same problem. It seems that all of us have tried the same recipes, the same brands of paint, with questionable results. Yet I have inspected lettering on trucks from other cities and have seen excellent yellow lettering that appeared to be one-coat work, so some signmen must have the answer. At the moment, when I need a true yellow of original brightness, I continue to double-coat.

HOME MADE PAINT BUCKETS.

If you run short of paint buckets or find gallon pails too large for certain jobs, there are simple methods to use for making your own (see Fig. 88). Punch two holes in an empty tin can in about the same position of the holes in a regular paint pail. Use a piece of stovepipe wire for a handle, attached as shown in C on the illustration.

Old fashioned black stovepipe wire can be purchased in most hardware stores and is sturdy enough for smaller cans such as the family-sized tomato cans, etc. These cans measure about 4 in. across and are 4½ in. deep and suitable for many purposes. Two-pound coffee cans or 3-pound shortening cans are ideal for many uses, but it is best to use a double strand of wire for these sizes. If you do not have a heavy-duty punch, a low priced paper punch purchased from any variety store will punch these holes without problem. The punching-prong can be sharpened with a file when it becomes dulled. File straight across the face of the punching surface.

These buckets can be used many times over if you drain them after use. Pour the remaining paint back into the original container to drain as shown in drawing A. These

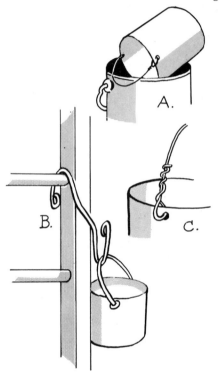

FIG. 88A. *A plentiful supply of paint buckets of various sizes can set up more convenient and economical work. Buckets can be used over and over if drained properly after use. This shows a can used on a job. Having had its contents poured back into the original container. it is now tilted upside down on a gallon pail, so it will drain dry to be ready for its next use.*

FIG. 88B. *The shape of the wire has several advantages over S-shaped hook commonly employed. It enables the bucket to be positioned solidly at the side, where it will not swing back and forth and will be out of the way.*

FIG. 88C. *Paint can is converted into a bucket by attaching a wire "handle."*

improvised buckets are so simply and quickly made that they can be discarded and replaced as necessary.

Example B on the illustrations shows a method for

bending a ladder hook to hold paint buckets. Use a fairly heavy length of wire for this and bend it approximately to the shape shown. Such a hook holds the paint bucket over to one side where it can rest against the ladder leg. It hangs quite solidly in this position, does not swing back and forth, and the brushes can be tapped out against the edge of the bucket.

Some painters commonly use an S-shaped hook slipped over the center of a ladder rung. This is a poor device because the bucket is not only in the way, but swings back and forth and is not in a solid enough position to work the paint out of the brush, etc.

When using the hook as shown the entire unit can be moved from rung to rung without separating hook and bucket. Grasp the lower part of the hook and bucket handle in the right hand and move the entire arrangement up and down as desired.

An empty bucket can be used in the same way on ladder work to hold other materials such as chalk, pencils, pounce bags, etc. It can be hung on the left side of the ladder with the contents handy for use. A carpenter apron, with its spacious pockets, is a handy piece of apparel to wear when doing ladder or swing stage work.

PROCEDURES FOR MAKING COPY

CHANGES. It is frequently necessary to change the copy on trucks and signs. This usually applies to changes of phone numbers, addresses, license numbers, etc. Quite often the use of decorative panels can be adapted to this type of work. Several practical procedures will now be presented to you.

You will soon discover that the average person thinks that sign painters have some magic formula or solution that we can use to wipe off the old lettering from the door of a truck as simply as one would wipe the dirt from a windshield.

Truck owners will breeze into your shop and say, "I gotta have the address and phone numbers taken off my truck and new ones put on. If you can do it right away, I'll wait."

Patiently you try to explain that the only method to remove the old lettering without completely wrecking the truck-finish is to use rubbing compound, which requires much time and elbow grease. You also mention that regardless of how carefully you perform the removal, the process will perhaps leave a dull, mottled area. It might also remove parts of the finish coat so the primer will show through in places where the old letters have been removed. You also explain that although the new lettering will cover the damaged areas to some degree, there is a possibility that the job will have a patched-up appearance.

What he does not understand is that paint is paint and, if you should use a remover potent enough to dissolve the lettering, it would at the same time dissolve the original finish of the truck. After you have convinced him that you have no remover that can distinguish between the lettering and the truck finish and that you have no secret formula, you can then sensibly discuss the best way to handle his particular problem.

If the truck is quite old, or if he trades his trucks frequently, then the use of rubbing compound might be practical. There are times when the lettering will rub off quite easily and scarcely damage the original finish. You might try it on one letter in his presence. If it comes off without problem, it might be wise for you to do the entire job in this way. Be certain to advise him that this process takes time and that he can expect to be charged accordingly.

However, if the lettering is difficult and stubborn to remove, he is there to witness the difficulty. You might be pressed for time or he might balk at the price of such removal. In either case, you might suggest to him that he buy a small can of "fast cut" rubbing compound, and especially if several trucks are involved, have his own men rub off the lettering. You can letter the trucks later.

Rubbing compound is cheap and I am generally pressed for time with a backlog of work. It is my practice to keep a large can of compound on hand and loan it to these fellows. I pick this up when I letter the trucks.

Most removals like this are difficult and it is a good idea to let your customer try the removal himself, unless you are short of work. Seldom will these people believe you when they leave the truck and later you tell them that it required an hour or two just to rub off the old lettering. Invariably when they take the compound along and do it themselves, their first remark when they return is, "Wow, was that a tough job getting that darn paint off! It took me all afternoon!"

He will not be so apt to complain about the price on the next "rub-off" job you do for him, and it will help dispel the fable that all a sign painter does is loll around in solid comfort doing nothing but lettering. This principle applies when you suggest to a customer that he scrape the old paint off his sign to have himself some money or to dig in his own posts for a highway sign. This is particularly effective psychology to use on a "tight wad." It is unlikely that he will again say to you, "Boy, some guys sure have it easy!"

Incidentally when using rubbing compound, it is best to use the fast-cut variety and to lubricate the rag with turpentine. Keep the entire section of lettering to be removed covered with this lubricated compound at all times. It seems to have a slight solvent action. After removal, be sure to clean the area with a commercial body cleaner, or lacking this, use a clean rag dipped in thinner, followed with a dry wipe.

If the truck owner has a fairly new truck, or several vehicles, suggest to him the use of decorative panels to cover the old phone numbers or address that must be changed. It is much easier to paint a different colored panel over the old lettering than it is to match the original paint of the truck. The use of panels causes the finished job to look like a planned effort rather than a patched-up mess.

I can think of no better way to describe the use of decorative panels than the ones used in the two illustrations and the circumstances leading up to their use.

Some years ago we were informed that all the phone numbers in our locality were to be changed in the near future. All customers were advised of the impending change when they contacted us to have work done. Most of these people told us to omit the number, but to leave room for it to be painted at such time as they received notice of their new number. Others requested that it be painted regardless, because the phone was important to their business.

At that time, our phone numbers were short, such as Phone 219," etc. The new numbers would consist of seven numerals, such as "526-2520." So on everything we painted, we allowed sufficient space for the longer number arrangements.

The illustrations show how changes of this kind can be made. This type of change need not be confined to a situation such as that just described, but can be adapted to various changes needed on any painted sign.

You will note in Fig. 89, for example, that this is a very common truck door layout. The dotted lines around "Phone 717" were not on the original lettering job. These lines merely indicate the position in which a simple panel was painted to blot out the old number.

FIG. 89. The old telephone number (717) can be covered up by a panel shape on which the new telephone number is painted. Dotted lines indicate location of panel with reference to the old copy.

The same applies to Fig. 90, which shows how a completely different layout might be handled. There is a lot of freedom in a casually shaped panel such as this. Note how it was designed to cover the small diamond "ding bat" used in the original layout. In regard to color, the panels should harmonize with the field color and also with the lettering on the truck.

When making changes of this type, you should use the method most convenient for you. You can paint these panels freehand with brushes or for an area such as shown in Fig. 89, you might prefer to use masking tape. If you intend to spray the panels, then you would use a spray-mask method.

Another procedure, and one that you might prefer to any others, would be to use one of the various types of marking films available. These films come in a variety of colors, also in transparent, and with several types of adhesive. The films can be cut to the shape desired with a No. 11 knife, lettered in the shop and applied to the unit when convenient. With this method, you do not have to paint any panels on the sign since the film will cover the existent copy. Most of these films are pressure-sensitive

FIG. 90. The old telephone number (941) is overlaid by casual shape with the new and longer telephone number. Dotted lines indicate placement of casual shape with reference to the copy it replaces.

and can be simply applied if you follow the manufacturer's directions. If their application suggests the use of a detergent solution in connection with their use, then do not attempt a dry application or you will have trouble.

When air bubbles occur, I prefer to make a very tiny cut with the corner of a sharp razor blade rather than to use a pinpoint. The air blisters can be effectively eliminated through these tiny cuts, which are practically invisible when the film is squeegeed upon completion.

Whatever method you use to effect copy changes depends on your own preferences, the equipment available to you, the extent of your ability, and, most important, your customer's wishes.

REPAINTING EXISTENT SIGNS. A common part of your work as a sign painter will be to completely repaint existing signs. There are several things to consider in this respect and you must use good judgment in these considerations. It is your advice and know-how that will be of benefit to both you and your customer.

Following is a good example. A trucker brought two detachable panels to me that he had removed from the doors of a truck. These consisted of two sheets of 26-gauge black iron. The original sign painter had evidently neglected to treat and prime the reverse sides of these panels, therefore these were badly rusted. The face sides contained areas where the paint had chipped off resulting in additional rust.

He wanted these sanded down and cleaned off and re-painted. What would you have done in this situation? (Just for the "heck" of it decide this before reading further.)

If you chose to abide by his wishes and repaint these panels you would be wrong.

Tactfully I explained to the customer that the time required to clean and prepare these panels would cost him considerably more than the price of new metal. Also because of the deeply pitted rust, it would not be long before they would again begin to rust. Since two new pieces of metal would cost less than a few dollars, you can see the fallacy of trying to clean these well enough for a successful repaint job. Furthermore the new panels would be of a more suitable material such as a galvanized type of metal or aluminum. He immediately realized the logic of this and ordered new panels.

You can use this example as a guide to good judgment when considering a large percentage of the repaints that will be brought to you. Always ask yourself this question, "Will the time that is spent in cleaning off this old beat-up surface amount to more than the cost of new materials?"

It is not uncommon for some signmen to spend $20 worth of time to salvage material that could be newly purchased for less than $10. Add to this the advantages of durability and appearance possible with the new material and you can see why repaint jobs are frequently impractical.

Fortunately the bigger percentage of signs brought to you will be suitable to repaint. In these cases you are faced with still another problem. Should you clean off the surface completely and start from scratch or should you merely sand it down and clean it up a bit?

To begin with, if it is a sign that you originally painted, it is easier. You know whether or not you followed good procedure when the sign was first painted. If it is a metal sign, you will know if you treated the metal properly and used a quality metal primer. Knowing this, and if the paint seems to be clinging tightly and in fair shape other than faded, you can repaint the sign without removing the old paint.

If you know that the sign, either by its imprint or otherwise, was painted by a reliable company, you can be reasonably certain that it was properly treated and primed.

In either of these cases, prepare the surface by sanding it thoroughly with fine sandpaper. Avoid cutting through to the bare metal. If bare metal does occur in spots through the sanding process, these areas must be spot coated with a flash bond or metal primer. Brush off the surface after sanding and wash off with a commercial solvent or cleaning liquid to remove all foreign matter, such as grease, tar, etc. The sign is then ready for repainting.

If you originally painted the sign and have a pattern on file there is no problem in regard to the copy. If such is not the case, and the sign is to retain the same copy, you will want to save the layout. The methods of doing this are determined by the procedure you favor using. For example, if the field color or background is light such as white or yellow and only one coat is needed, you can paint right over the sign. If this coat is applied with a brush, the old design should show through enough to be discernible. You can quickly pencil the lines of the original layout and re-letter the sign.

Should the sign require two coats then apply the first coat as usual and when this is dry, draw over the original layout with either a soft indelible or ditto pencil. When you apply the second coat, these lines should dissolve and show through.

When a roller is used, it is best to use the ditto-type pencil before any paint is applied. With a roller, one coat of paint will sometimes cover so effectively that the old lay-out will not be visible. This indelible procedure is especially practical on large signs, such as highway bulletins, walls, etc., unless it is a one-coat job and the lettering will show through of its own accord. If there is any chance that the coat of paint will obliterate the layout then you should take steps beforehand to save the layout. Sometimes the original lettering has been applied so heavily that the resultant raised effect of the letters will continue to show without any marking. There also are occasions where the original lettering and layout has been so poorly done that your biggest concern will be to get rid of it and replace it with a decent professional job.

Another method to use for saving a layout is to take a pattern. This is especially practical on smaller commercial signs. You can do this with regular heavy brown wrapping paper. Tape the paper in position and rub over the paper with a rag saturated with turpentine. This will cause the paper to be transparent. Other liquids can be used. Some signmen use gasoline, but this dries rapidly. It is preferable to use turpentine because it maintains its transparency for a much longer period. Trace the pattern while the paper is wet, remove the paper, and perforate the lines with a pounce wheel.

The pattern process has a great advantage because no matter what procedure you follow in repainting, you have the pattern to use not only for the job at hand, but on possible repaints in the future.

The procedure for signs with a dark field and light colored lettering also depends on the procedure you prefer. For many years, most signmen did this with the cut-in method. In doing this, you would merely brush the light colors across the letters in a rather rough fashion with, perhaps, a 2-inch brush. This is referred to as "spot coating" and no attempt is made to follow the letters—just cover them. When these applications are dry, you then would paint the field color around the letters with a lettering brush, filling in the larger areas with a much larger brush. The lettering usually shows through the spot coat so no pattern work or indelible pencil is necessary.

This last method results in an abundance of brush marks in the field color. Also there are overlaps of paint, so as time passes, the sign will not fade in an even manner. The double coat of paint that results at these points of overlap will endure much longer than the adjacent areas.

Many signmen now prefer to either spray, brush, or roll the field color upon the sign first for a neat smooth background. The sign is then surface lettered with the lighter colors in much the same way that you would letter a dark colored truck. This method became more popular with the advent of the better quality lettering enamels.

The indelible system is useless on this type of a job so you must either take a pattern or provide a new layout after the field color has been applied.

If you are repainting a neon sign, it is advisable to pull strips of masking tape around the glass housings to keep from messing them up with paint. Tuck the tape snugly into position around the glass where it meets the sign face so there will be no unpainted areas around the glass units when the tape is removed.

The most important decision you must make in regard to repainting metal signs is whether to merely sandpaper the surface and paint over the old layout or to remove the old paint entirely and begin anew.

The fact that a sign still has a presentable appearance with no bare spots or other visible indications of paint failure does not always prove that it is suitable to repaint as is. The paint might be oxidized to a point where it is little better than a clinging layer of dry dust. You can determine this by using a putty knife on a small area of one corner of the sign.

If the paint seems to be tough and somewhat elastic it need not be removed. But before repainting, it is advisable to check the entire sign, testing several areas to be certain that the condition of the paint is uniformly good. Should there be doubtful areas, it is best to remove the paint from the entire surface.

Sometimes the paint can be scraped off the entire sign without problem. On other signs the paint will come off easily in spots and in other areas it can scarcely be "hacked" off. If it is too difficult to remove by scraping, then use an effective commercial paint remover.

A common error in the use of paint removers is the failure to follow through with a thorough clean-up job after using the remover. A number of paint removers will leave a waxy residue. Although the surface will appear to be clean, this residue will remain dormant especially around screwheads and in cracks. Later upon paint application, this residue might be reactivated and sort of "boil up" from underneath. This can be an immediate or delayed reaction. Therefore after using remover, you must thoroughly clean the surface with a commercial cleaner to positively remove all traces of paint remover.

Some signmen consider gasoline to be a suitable cleaner, and in a sense it is, since it does remove tar and other substances. But gasoline leaves a film of its own that should be cleaned off. This film might appear as a thin powdery layer or in the form of an oily film that will not be receptive to layout marks. At times the powders used on pounce patterns will fail to "grab" the surface because of this film.

So it appears that an all-around commercial cleaner is best for a final clean-up. The types used in auto body shops are excellent. Some of these cleaners are quite potent so read the directions. Be especially cautious when cleaning the surface of a recently painted vehicle upon which the paint has not aged sufficiently. Do not assume that a brand new vehicle is immune to the attack of such cleaners. Some of these might have been painted more recently than you assume. Test the cleaner on a very small area at the very bottom where the body curves under the vehicle and a blemish will not be noticeable.

If the directions require you to apply the cleaner with one rag and immediately wipe dry with another clean, dry cloth, then do so. If the contact is prolonged the cleaner might craze, flatten, or even lift the surface paint. If there is any danger of mutilating the original body finish, then it is safer to use a mild detergent for cleaning and rinse this with clear water. My preference is to use the old fashioned Bon-Ami powder with the yellow label. This is no longer on the retail market, but is sold to institutions and, according to my last knowledge, could be purchased only by the case from the factory.

There is no special concern about the potency of cleaners in regard to bare metal. But some of these liquids do leave a film, which the manufacturer suggests should be rinsed with water. So it is mandatory to read and to follow the directions of any product. Too often an excellent product is maligned because it was not used according to specifications.

There are numerous methods of removing paint from metal such as the use of a torch, sandblasting equipment, or just plain scraping. Scraping will most likely be your first procedure. The most simple scraping job can become a chore if you use the wrong tools or even if the right tools are used in the wrong way.

The common putty knife is a handy tool if it is sharpened correctly. The first tendency is to sharpen a putty knife in the shape of a wood chisel, which is incorrect (see Fig. 91). This results in one sharp edge which dulls very quickly, digs into the metal, and will scrape quite ineffectively with a pushing motion only.

The proper way to sharpen any tool to be used for scraping metal signs is straight across as shown. If you lack an emery wheel, use a sharp, flat file to sharpen the edge. Instead of one frail edge, you will have a tool with two sturdier edges that will stay sharp much longer and also ease the work. With such edges you can scrape with either a pushing or pulling motion by changing the angle at which you hold the tool.

In the process of all scraping, whether it be on glass, metal, or other surfaces, try to confine the initial scraping to the large areas that are free of obstacles. Avoid hitting the metal edges of a window frame or the screw heads or joints of a metal sign. Such obstacles dull the cutting edges. Scrape the unobstructed areas first and finish by scraping more closely around the obstacles. This will reduce the necessity of sharpening to a minimum.

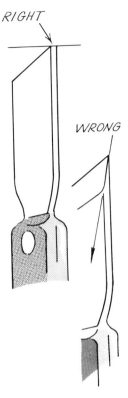

RIGHT

WRONG

FIG. 91. *The proper way to sharpen any tool for scraping metal is straight across.*

The commercial, heavy-duty scraping tools with the flanged, double blades at the end are sharpened the same as the putty knife.

An excellent scraping tool can be made out of a heavy machinist's file as shown in Fig. 92. Machine and welding shops usually have any number of old worn-out files in discard. Contact the machinist to cut down several of these to a length of about 5 inches. Have them sharpened straight across and insert the files into sturdy handles. A tool such as this will really knock tohe paint off a stubborn surface where a lighter instrument might fail. Since this is very hard metal, the tool will hold a sharp edge for a very long time, but it must be sharpened, when necessary, on a heavy-duty power wheel.

A little tip: When using a heavy tool such as this, especially on a sign mounted at a second story level over a busy sidewalk, it is wise to use precaution. A scraping tool can easily be knocked from your grasp upon hitting an unexpected screw head and fall to the sidewalk. To strike an innocent pedestrian on the head with such a tool could be an unpleasant and costly experience. Therefore I drill a small hole near the end of the handle, thread a length of stout cord through this hole, form a loop long enough to fit around my wrist, and tie a knot in the cord. This loop is long enough to wrap around my wrist and yet not interfere with the work. If I should lose my grasp, the tool dangles from my wrist instead of falling to the sidewalk. This is a good idea to use for any heavy tool when working above a busy street.

FIG. 92. Machinist's file is a good scraper.

Don't say that the dropping of tools is improbable. Years ago I was lettering a window at the same time that a fellow employee was tightening some bolts on a neon sign directly above me. For no apparent reason I happened to look up just as he dropped a 16-inch crescent wrench. Instinctively I had time to take a slight step backwards and the wrench cleared the end of my nose by a bare inch. Those close to me have remarked on occasion about my hard head. If I had not stepped back when I did, I doubt if I would be writing this book. There are few heads hard enough to withstand the solid bash of a 16-inch wrench. I had witnessed tools being dropped before and had dropped a few myself. At that time I would have laughed at the suggestion of a safety cord. But after this episode, I realized that one cannot take a 16-inch wrench too lightly. This made a heavy impression on my thinking and it was about that time that I began to use the safety cord gimmick on all heavy tools. Three days later I was working in a city

200 miles away from the dent made by that wrench in the sidewalk.

Back to the work: When a sign is cleaned down to the bare metal and ready to be repainted, there is no need to etch the surface. Chances are that the sign was etched at origin and if not, the natural oxidation process caused by long exposure to the weather has aged the metal to a point where it need not be etched.

The process of etching should be explained. Etching is a procedure used whereby a liquid chemical is applied to new metal to draw out or remove the elements within the metal that are incompatible to paint. There is a special etching solution for galvanized metal and another for aluminum. Also there is an all around liquid metal treatment for metals such as black iron, etc. Many years ago vinegar was commonly used for etching purposes. This provided what might be termed a "half-result." Although some signmen still swear by the use of vinegar, its complete effectiveness is questionable. There are a number of dependable commercial etching liquids available. It is advisable to use these in accordance with the directions. Most of these come in concentrated form and should be diluted as specified on the label.

Although etching is generally not required when repainting aged or weathered metal, it is definitely advisable to apply a coat of quality metal primer. This can be a regular paint-type of pigmented primer or a clear bonding agent.

Metal primers also are labeled with directions concerning their express use. Certain primers are recommended by the manufacturer as all around primers to be used on a variety of metals. Other companies produce a separate primer for each type of metal. Be certain when painting black iron or other rust-prone metals that you use a primer that definitely contains a rust inhibitor. Some metal primers do little to stop rust; therefore no mention of rust will appear on the label.

When the primer is dry, you then proceed with the painting and lettering as usual.

In regard to paints and materials, let me mention a few words of advice that can be of tremendous help to you as a sign painter. Most reliable manufacturers of sign supplies constantly engage in intensive research in an effort to provide you with the best possible products. They are most anxious for you to receive the full benefit of this costly research. They know that you must have the knowledge to use their products intelligently if you are to get maximum results.

Therefore they will furnish you, free-of-charge, with an abundance of literature all designed to help you. This includes booklets describing the use and characteristics of each product, step-by-step procedures, things to do and things not to do. Also available are charts concerning color intermixing, durability expectancy, temperature control etc., including samples of new products. Some companies arrange clinics in centralized cities where experts will demonstrate the best techniques for using their products. Portfolios are provided containing full information.

The important factor is to get your name on their mailing lists. Write to these firms and ask for the literature that you need or ask the salesman for this when he calls upon you. Follow these instructions conscientiously and your work will be easier.

Veteran signmen know the characteristics of most established products and also know when they can improvise or successfully depart from directions. But as a newcomer to the trade, it is advisable to adhere to the information supplied by the manufacturers until you develop experience.

SIMPLIFYING COPY CHANGES.

Some of the signs that you produce will be of a type that will require frequent copy changes. In many cases such changes can be anticipated and the original layout should be planned accordingly. This is one area in which preliminary planning can eliminate many of your problems and save money for your customer. Usually this type of sign will contain a certain amount of copy that is stable and not subject to change. Other portions of the lettering will require periodical copy changes. A short conference with your customer is all that is necessary to determine which portions of the copy will be subject to change. You can then group this lettering and isolate it within the layout and do so in a way that is adaptable to frequent change. There is an additional bonus provided by this procedure. Even with constant copy changes, signs planned with forethought will continue to present a finished rather than a patched-up appearance.

Most real estate firms face the problem of frequent copy changes on certain signs. Refer to the illustration of the "Hilgenberg" sign in Fig. 92. This will be used as a basis of the following discussion and is an excellent example to demonstrate the point.

The average real estate company will have a greater number of smaller signs upon which the copy seldom changes. These are for general use and placed in front of properties that require a normal selling approach. They also have properties for sale that demand a more intensified sales approach, which includes a stepped up newspaper campaign and more emphasis on signs.

These are usually expensive business-type properties that must be sold as quickly as possible. This requires bigger signs and, more importantly, a brief description of the property on each sign. Because most real estate firms work on a percentage and have economy in mind when considering sign work, they desire plain, readable signs of simple design and not too elaborate. Therefore this illustration was not chosen as a classic example of lettering, but rather as an economical utility unit.

FIG. 93. Descriptive copy in white on red on left can be repainted to apply to a new location whenever sign is moved to a new location. Major portion of sign with permanent copy does not have to be repainted at that time.

This sign consists of one 4 x 10-foot panel of ¾-inch medium density overlaid plywood without rear framework of any kind. The field color is white. The vertical panel on the left with the descriptive copy has a bright red field, surface-lettered with high-cover white lettering enamel, all one-stroke. The "Hilgenberg" strip has a black field with white lettering. The other copy is painted alternately with bright red, blue-green, and black. "For Sale" is shaded with primrose yellow.

There are several ways in which this unit could have been painted. Suppose you would paint the entire sign white with all of the normal copy on the upper part of the sign and then letter the descriptive copy across the bottom, also on the white background. You would not separate this on a panel of a different color.

Soon the property is sold, the sign is moved to a new location, and you must change the descriptive copy on the bottom portion of the sign. You would place a strip of masking tape across the sign above the descriptive copy and paint this bottom area white, requiring two or three coats to cover the old copy. After several copy changes such as this, the sign begins to have a patched up appearance with the bottom part appearing to be newer and whiter than the upper portion. In addition to the ever-increasing poor appearance, there is a maximum amount of work involved in this procedure.

Compare this method with the one shown in the photo. All of the stable copy is placed on a separate white background portion to the right. The descriptive copy is a separate entity on a red panel to the left. When a copy change is required, all that is necessary is to place a strip of masking tape along the right edge of the red panel and apply one coat of red. When dry, it is lettered with white. Because it stands alone as a separate panel there is no patched-up appearance and the working time has been reduced to a minimum.

Dark colors are suggested for this procedure because lighter colors require several coats of paint for effective coverage. The idea is to cut the number of separate operations to a minimum. When the signs are brought into the shop, this is not so important. But if you must paint the signs on location, each separate operation requires a trip to and from the sign.

This particular real estate operator arranges to have his own employees move these signs to new locations, posts attached, so this panel method works well since the copy must be changed on location. However, if they are to be moved any great distance from town, his men bring them to the shop for copy changes before relocation. This saves him the expense of the two longer trips that would be required to do the job.

Another method, and one that is most practical, is to use removable panels for the descriptive copy. For example, when this "Hilgenberg" sign was originally made, a separate piece of overlaid plywood could have been cut to the size of this panel on the left end. This panel could then have been mounted to the main panel in the same position by drilling holes through the small panel and the main sign and attaching bolts. Wing nuts could have been used for convenient removal and replacement. Then, whether it be summer or winter, these small panels could be brought to the shop for repainting.

For some reason, the average customer does not welcome the initial cost of the extra material needed for these removable panels. He seems to be partial to panels painted directly upon the sign face even though, in the long run, the panel method would be more convenient and economical.

This panel method need not be confined to the end of a sign. Whether separate panels are used, or if panels are to be painted on the sign, the same principle can be used at any position on any sign. You might find it practical designwise to make fold patterns of fancy scroll-top panels or other shapes and paint one of these within the layout of the sign. An oval or circle would be adaptable.

DON'T QUOTE PRICES BY PHONE. One of the pet peeves of sign operators is the customer who calls on the telephone and insists that he be given a price for refinishing a sign without giving the signman the opportunity to first examine the condition of the unit.

During the phone conversation, for example, you might inquire, "Is the sign smooth and in fairly good condition?"

"Oh, yes," he'll reply. "It's nice and smooth. All it needs is a coat of paint and to be relettered."

Later when he brings the sign it will probably be badly chipped or peeled and about as smooth as the hide of a razorback hog. The customer's idea of what constitutes a smooth surface is generally quite different than that of the signman.

To cut costs, customers will frequently paint the sign panels themselves and bring them to you only to be lettered. On the phone they will mention that the signs are brand new, freshly painted, and smooth. When you see these signs, the backgrounds will be in sad shape for lettering. It is amazing how they can ruin a sign face even on the choicest material. The paint might look like it was applied thickly with a whisk broom resulting in a corduroy finish. Or it might appear that the paint was smeared on with a cement trowel. The surfaces might be covered with dead flies, leaves, pine-needles, or chunks of paint, dust, or with bristles left by a cheap paint brush.

So it is impossible to quote an intelligent price for a sign sight unseen over the telephone. This might be done in regard to a completely new unit if you are to do the entire job. It is not advisable to quote a price on a repaint unless you originally produced the sign or might otherwise be familiar with its probable condition.

MORE ABOUT REPAINTS. We discussed metal sign repaints so we should now consider other surfaces. The signs brought to you will frequently be made from various types of plywood. There is a type of plywood available for just about every purpose, but unfortunately there are those who still use the wrong material for the wrong purpose. Later they condemn the material because it has not provided the durability they had no right to expect. It is not uncommon for such a customer to condemn you along with the material.

Therefore signs will be presented to you for repainting that were originally constructed with interior plywood and have been contrarily used for exterior purposes. Chances are that such signs will be in poor condition and not worth a repaint job. You must then explain to the customer that it is to his advantage to have new signs constructed of a material more suitable for exterior use such as overlaid plywood.

Interior plywood is an excellent product and can be used in many ways in the sign trade, but its use should be confined to interior displays, signs, etc. It was not manufactured nor intended for exterior use.

Most repaints on signs constructed of plywoods, hardboards, lumber, etc., are quite routine. If the surface is in good condition, it should be thoroughly sanded to remove any chalky film that exists. Next the surface should be brushed to remove the sandpaper dust. An old four-inch paint brush, washed out and dry, is an excellent device for this. Also a wide wallpaper brush will serve as a good duster. The surface should then be wiped off with a tack rag. If you lack a tack rag, saturate a rag with turpentine or thinner and use this instead.

If you want to save the original layout, you can use essentially the same procedure as that described in regard to the repainting of metal signs.

Should the sign require a change of design or different copy, you will then want the new field color to completely hide the old lettering. If this background is a light color, such as white or yellow, you might unnecessarily apply coat after coat of paint to accomplish this unless you first neutralize the old background.

Sign painters with limited experience will pile on a heavy coat of white block-out paint in an effort to hide the old copy. Some will actually apply two coats. This is extremely bad procedure and a waste of time and material.

A sign with a heavy intermediate coat will not be durable.

A better method, and one commonly used, is to neutralize the background. This is done by applying a thin coat of light gray block-out paint directly over the old sign face. This should be a very light gray. You can buy ready mixed block-out gray or mix your own by adding a bit of black to the block-out white you normally use. Do not pour the black directly into the white, but pour a small quantity onto the stirring paddle and mix it into the white. Add a little at a time until you have the desired shade of gray. You will be surprised to find how much more hiding power even the lightest gray will provide as compared to clear white. If this coat of light gray is applied properly it will generally provide an even color over the entire surface and the letters underneath will scarcely be visible. You can then apply another thin coat of white block-out paint over the gray. When this is dry, the finish coat can be applied. If the finish coat has exceptionally good coverage, or if the finish coat is applied with a roller, the second coat of white block-out paint can sometimes be eliminated.

Most beginners have a tendency to use all paints, especially block-out in too thick a consistency. Block-out paint should be thinned considerably, almost to the consistency of cream, and sort of "fanned" on to the surface in what is called a "skim-coat," instead of being piled on.

If drying time is not a factor, it is common practice to add a small amount of bulletin finish white to the block-out paint. Some old timers prefer to use a half and half mixture of block-out and bulletin white. This seems to toughen the paint and result in better adherence. A mixture such as this should not be used to such extent that the paint loses the flat, toothy finish common to block-out paint. These mixtures are a matter of personal preference. For my own use, I would hesitate to add more than 10 per cent of bulletin color to block-out paint.

In regard to any type of wooden-faced sign, if the surface has been sanded to the extent that bare wood is showing through, it is best to apply a coat of good quality wood primer just as you would on a new sign. When this is dry, follow-through with normal painting procedure. If this primer coat provides a flat surface comparable to that of block-out white you might be able to immediately apply the finish coat. In most cases it is advisable to apply an intermediate coat of thin block-out white. Also it is good procedure to sand the surface in between each application of paint. Use a fine sandpaper with a light touch and be certain to again brush and use the tack rag after each sanding operation. This results in a smooth finish and is most adaptable to competent lettering.

Always remember that block-out paint is definitely not a primer, but rather an intermediate coat. It is used mainly as a fast drying cover coat so that the finish coat can be applied without excessive delay. Block-out paint also provides the necessary tooth for the finish coat to grab on to and hold.

It is true that on rare occasions block-out paint can be used as a primer. Directions on the label or other literature provided by the paint company will advise you in this regard. Primarily it is an intermediate coat, dependent on the primer beneath it and the finish coat placed over it. You can use it as a finish coat on an exterior sign that is for short term use, such as for a convention, a sale, or a similar purpose. Such jobs are usually "hurry-up" deals and the fast drying characteristic of block-out paint makes it an ideal medium for fast, temporary signs. Although a good quality latex paint will serve just as well for such purposes.

Some signmen follow a different procedure entirely when repainting signs. They tint all the paints to be used with the same color throughout. For example, if the sign is to be light blue, they use a light blue primer, a light blue block-out, followed with the light blue finish coat. Their contention is that should the sign become scratched or peel that such flaws will be less noticeable. This would appear to be an effective procedure.

Chapter 26

The Side Factors of Sign Painting

"A jack-of-all-trades and a master of one!" This continues to be my favorite description of a sign painter. As a sign operator you will at various times require a partial understanding of carpentry, sheetmetal work, electrical wiring, plastic, neon, erection work, etc. Also there is need for immediate knowledge of the proper paints and tools to use on every type of material, including wood, metal, glass, canvas, hardboard, film, cardboard, among others. It is advisable to learn the safe and sensible manipulation of ladders, ladder-jacks, swing-stages, and other rigging. How much you learn depends on how complete a signman you wish to be.

If you plan to specialize in one particular phase of sign work, you need not concern yourself with much of the above. However, one indisputable fact cannot be ignored. Specialist or otherwise, you must master the art of good layout and lettering.

You might be puzzled by the fact that this book does not contain complete instructions in regard to showcard writing, gold leaf application, the alphabets, etc. To thoroughly provide instruction for each separate operation pertinent to the sign profession would be impossible within a single book. This would require a voluminous encyclopedia.

Some of the operations just mentioned are so involved and complex that any complete and intelligent instruction in regard to each such endeavors would require the writing of a separate book. Fortunately such books are available from the publisher of this text.

For example, in regard to gold leaf, there is no finer book available than *Gold Leaf Techniques*, authored by Raymond J. LeBlanc. The various alphabets are excellently presented in the books of J. I. Biegeleisen. Available from the same source are books that effectively cover almost every phase of the sign business. The content of these books is based on actual experience, not upon theory; so each book presents the highest degree of accuracy and professionalism.

The main purpose of this book is to provide the general over-all knowledge needed to serve as a foundation for your immediate development as a sign painter.

ORIGINALITY IN SIGN PAINTING. In no phase of the business is there more opportunity for inventiveness than in layout and lettering. There are, of course, certain jobs where only routine lettering is appropriate. This can be because of the time factor or the economy of the job. An experienced sign painter will realize this and proceed accordingly.

But in all other cases you might ask yourself, "How can I make this job unique? What can I do to bring this job out of the commonplace?" If you immediately develop this policy and adhere to it, you should never have to worry about having sufficient work or be overly concerned in regard to your competitors.

You should also acquire a sort of sixth sense in the understanding of your customers and learn to anticipate their needs. This is not too difficult after you deal with them for some time. Some people are conservative and will be pleased only with conventional lettering. Others are more flamboyant. Getting to know your customers comes almost automatically as time passes, but only if you make an effort to be aware of their individual preferences. Learn their likes and dislikes and work accordingly. Soon they will develop a trust in your ability and, instead of limited specifications, you will hear these comforting words, "Do the job in the manner you think best. We trust your judgment." It is statements such as this that provide you with the necessary freedom for creativeness.

The extent of your inventiveness might apply to an entire sign or, perhaps, to merely one word or phrase. The object is to avoid a monotonous layout. Note how many sign painters will letter an entire truck door with straight block type letters and shade each and every letter. The result is sheer monotony with nothing predominant except the size. Much time is wasted by shading every letter without beneficial result. A computer-type job such as this can be replaced with a good design and accomplished in less time.

The highway bulletin illustrated in Fig. 94 has both good and bad points. The unique quality you should seek is apparent in certain portions of this sign. Note how the graceful sweep of the arrow shape streamlines the entire sign and gracefully fills in the awkward gap on the lower left.

The words "one mile," were applied freehand on the spur of the moment. This casual script is a truly "inventive" lettering since it was not copied from any existent alphabet. It was developed to fill this particular space on this particular sign and to break the obvious monotony of the rest of the lettering.

FIG. 94. Done free-hand and on spur of the moment, the script of "One Mile" and the uniquely shaped arrow bring out the expression of this element of the display more effectively.

Contrast this script and arrow to the conventional letters and arrow that accompany the photograph. This type of script is best accomplished by laying it out as you would a pictorial with quick, confident motions. A casual script should never result in a belabored appearance. It need not adhere to any known letter form, but it should have uniform

FIG. 94A. Unimaginative arrow and black lettering would normally be employed in such a highway display. Visualize this on the display and note the difference.

construction. The over-all formation of the letters should follow-through with regard to uniform stroke widths and slants and the general attitude of the lettering.

When a letter repeats itself, such as the letter E in this case, it should be as similar as possible to its preceding counterpart. This provides stability to the entire word or line of script. Casual lettering should not be haphazard, or the result will be amateurish. The carefree nature can only be achieved through a calculated effort and with a thorough understanding of good design.

Incidentally you might be interested in the color scheme of this bulletin. The main field color is a dark medium gray. "Steinhardt" is white with a heavy red outline. "Cheese" is painted lemon yellow with a black outline and "One Mile" is in plain white. The pictorial panel has a yellow field with a black stein. The heart is red, outlined with white. The frame and posts are white.

Previous reference was made to the fact that this sign has both good and bad points. Top signmen agree that in the quest of perfection that you must be "your own worst critic," and I agree. I recall one sign author mentioning that he could more quickly recognize his errors by turning a finished sign upside down. Then by observing the letters, he could notice any irregularities and improve his future work by adjusting his techniques.

In a similar manner, I can notice my errors by turning my patterns over and examining them from the reverse side. It is beneficial to each of us to occasionally subject our work to a long, hard look.

So let's take a critical look at the highway bulletin illustrated. The letter S in the word "Steinhardt" is too skimpy. Although it is the same height as the other letters it does not appear to be equal. It should have been extended, as customary, a bit above and below the cross guidelines. Both width and height could have been greater in proportion to the other letters. The letter E is too wide with the crossbars over-extended. This letter should have been narrower. There is too much space between the first three letters in comparison to that left between the letters in the rest of the word. The curves of the letters D and R are too choppy and should have a more graceful sweep. The letter C in the word "Cheese" is too small and should have been wider and also a bit higher. The strokes could have been a bit thicker.

The picture of the stein would have presented a better appearance if the handle had been placed on the right, which would be the correct position for the normal right-hand grasp. It is a rigid rule in all forms of advertising layout that the subject of any illustration should face into the rest of the copy—not out! For instance, on an election poster, you will note that a good job printer will always arrange the photograph of the candidate so that it faces into the copy. When you see an occasional poster with the subject facing out, note how your eyes have a tendency to wander away from the copy instead of towards it. This rule also holds true for inanimate objects, such as stoves, refrigerators, automobiles, etc.

In regard to the criticism of this sign, there are several factors that contributed to these flaws. It was the only display done in this size, so there was no sketch. A fold pattern was prepared for the pictorial only. The entire job was done in too much of a rush. The weather was cold and I wanted to letter the entire sign in less than a day. This was to take advantage of the warmest part of the day, and perhaps equivalent to a half-day. With a little more thought, time and effort, these errors could have been avoided.

SIGN DONATIONS FOR PUBLIC SERVICE.

Quite frequently sign painters are approached to produce progress indicators of some type, for fund-raising projects. In most cases, these consist of tall vertical signs with a thermometer painted in vertical position. The bulb at the bottom is painted red when the sign is originally made, and the thermometer level is raised periodically as the fund drive progresses.

Chasing to and from the location every few days to paint this red strip to a higher level can be a nuisance especially if a ladder is needed. It is not a pleasant chore in zero weather. There would be some consolation if you could charge for these trips, but the odds are that the entire job has been donated, including the extra trips.

Therefore long ago I developed the habit of providing those in charge of the fund drive with strips of red film which they can apply as necessary. These films are cut into strips slightly narrower than the inside measurement of the thermometer stem. For material, I use red pressure-sensitive marking or lettering film. All they need to do is cut a section of strip to the desired size, peel off the backing paper and press the film into position (see Fig. 95).

You also can use 6-ply cardboard for this purpose. With this method it is best to use white cardboard and paint both sides of a sheet or two with bulletin color. When the paint is dry, the cardboard can be cut into strips. The people in charge can cut these strips to length and attach to the sign with a staple gun or with red-covered thumbtacks. You might ask, "Why not use red cardboard?" The answer is

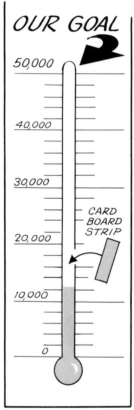

FIG. 95. *Strips of red film or of 6 ply cardboard painted with bulletin color, both sides, can be used by the people handling a fund drive to indicate on a thermometer sign progress toward their goal.*

that you would not have the intense red needed to match the other red on the sign. Most colored cardboards fade rapidly when exposed to the weather. The red bulletin color not only provides the intense matching color, but also waterproofs the cardboard to some extent.

The aspect of donations of this kind can sometimes present a problem. In one experience, I recall donating a job of this nature to a community fund drive. Soon thereafter one of the workers called upon me for the customary cash donation. Although I explained that I had just donated this job, she bluntly remarked, "You surely don't expect that to take the place of your cash donation? do you? Yet this job, without any extra trips, would retail for over $50. By comparison, merchants doing ten times the volume of my business were donating from $5 to $25 on the average. So as all old time sign operators know, it is best to give a regular cash donation based on what others are giving and charge the regular price for the job. This is not always possible, and sometimes circumstances are such that for the sake of public relations you are literally forced into donating such signs.

Seldom do you receive public credit for the job if you donate it. This fact might never be known to anybody other than the chairman of the fund drive. In some cases, he is only too eager to sit back and take full personal credit for all success of the drive. If you donate in cash, you are certain to get listed credit for it and will not be so apt to donate out-of-proportion to what others are giving.

Some years ago, within the period of one year, I was in one way or another "pressured" into donating signs to six various fund drives. The results were as follows: Five of these projects sent people additionally to ask for a cash donation. No public credit was given by newspaper or by any other means for the courtesy work done and only one fund chairman wrote a letter of thanks.

In recent years, when I cannot "wiggle" out of an outright donation of signwork, I have adopted the policy of sending an itemized statement to the fund-drive secretary showing the full retail price. This statement is marked, "Paid by Donation." In this way it becomes a matter of written record.

All of the foregoing does not imply that you should never donate signwork. As a newcomer to the trade, you must learn to judge for yourself when to and when not to do so. Indeed there are a number of non-profit organizations which are worthy of help, especially youth groups. These young folks are usually very appreciative and are only too eager to tell everybody about your generosity. They also might go home to their parents and remark, "Oh, that nice Mr. Doe of the Doe-Re-Me Sign Co. gave us all our signs for the bake sale!"

This not only gives your "community image" a boost, but some of these parents operate their own businesses and will remember you the next time they need signs. A large number of my present-day customers consist of young men for whom I did favors when they were youngsters. They still remember me as the nice guy that furnished all the signs for their Boy Scout Jamboree.

Many of the adult groups also are deeply appreciative of sign donations and when you donate signs they will see to it that you are given full credit in every respect. They will mention it in the newspaper and won't expect a cash donation as well. If you feel that any one job is out of proportion to the general trend of donations being given, then then a proper discount on the bill is the alternative. There also are the group donations where a lumber company will donate the material, a contractor will build the sign, and you will do the lettering. This generally involves a community project, a church group, or a service club.

Speaking of clubs, many examples could be cited to show that there can be a great difference between organizations. Having belonged to various clubs and organizations in several cities, I have at times found it to be an asset to belong and, at other times, it has been a distinct nuisance. In fact I have a slight suspicion that I have been asked to join clubs through the years because those in charge figured that I could be counted on for free signwork.

This type of club is in the minority, since most clubs are operated on a sound business principle and are aware that you cannot donate the work, which is your bread and butter. This type expects you to pay your dues and do your fair share of duties, but will pay for the time and talent of your trade.

Unfortunately there are a few organizations who order work, take it for granted that it is free, and finance it by saying, "Thanks a lot old buddy." Old timers in the trade can practically "smell" an upcoming request for a sign donation of this variety. They evade this with the stock excuses, such as "swamped with work," ". . . a touch of the flue," etc.

You will learn how to avoid unfair requests. Usually this can be done with finesse, but at times you must approach a point of rudeness with a frank "no."

In another city, the pompous official of one club was practically dictating that I donate an expensive two-sided canvas banner to span a street. He mentioned that no money was available in the budget for this item, and "me being a member, etc., etc." I parried by saying, Dr. So 'n So also is a member, but you wouldn't expect him to remove the past president's appendix free of charge, just because there was nothing listed in the budget for this item. That was a far-fetched comparison, perhaps, but the same in principle.

So in regard to public service donations, you must learn to consider all of the factors and then act accordingly. If you need the advertising, there is one way to get a little credit for free work. At the bottom of the sign, in small letters, place the following message: "This sign furnished through the courtesy of . . ."

GOOD METHODS NECESSARY FOR SPEED.

The ability to letter with good speed is essential. This speed must be supplemented with good work habits or you will discover that, by comparison, slower lettering men are producing more and better work.

It takes much time to develop good lettering speed, so you should take advantage of every possible assist. Efficient working methods should be developed along with your lettering techniques. The combined effort will carry over and continue as you become a professional.

While it is advisable to make every effort to adapt to the effective traditional methods, it is not advisable to struggle along with tools and procedures that are not adaptable to your individual performance.

Quite often a slight change of equipment in regard to its construction or placement can contribute to your efficiency. Merely because a process works well for one man does not mean that it is right for you.

For example, some signmen will use a small platform temporarily fitted to the face of the drawing board upon which to set the paint and palette. This places the paint within the shortest reach and it can save time with each successive dip of the brush. Although some signmen make excellent progress with this device, it is of no advantage to my method of working. This does not imply that you should not try to use such a platform. It might be ideal for your individual technique.

My preference is to use a small table immediately to my right (see Fig. 96). Although I must reach farther with each dip of the brush, the time is more than compensated for in other ways. Suppose the requirement is to make five show-cards, measuring 14 x 22 inches. For convenience, I will again describe my procedure: Since I am to use five tempera colors, I arrange these jars on the table next to the palette. There is plenty of room and the jars need not be crowded or moved at any time.

My procedure is to letter all five cards with the first of the colors. The brush is then cleaned and the next color is applied. First I sit down in a comfortable position with the five cards within easy reach. (The cards have previously been layed out from a standing position with all five cards placed in a row on the drawing board.) In a sitting position on a high stool, I apply the lettering with the first color to one card. With this completed, I move the card to my right, and place the second card in lettering position. When this one is lettered, I use it to carefully push the first card farther down the board to make room for the second card. By placing two cards to the right and two to the left, it is possible to letter the first color on all five cards without moving from the stool. A greater number of cards can be handled in the same manner by pushing them farther down the board and resting others in any convenient place within reach. If a tray or platform had been mounted on the drawing board, I could not push any of the cards along the surface. Such a device would be an obstacle to this effort.

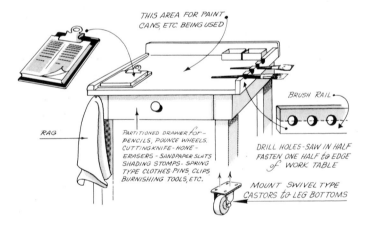

FIG. 96. *Small table on castors can help step up speed and efficiency.*

If I had decided to do this job from a standing position, I would have lined up all five cards in a row, side by side. Then I would have lettered the card on the far left, pushed the table a little to the right, lettered the next card, and so on down the line, pushing the table to the right as I proceeded. The same procedure would apply to banners or any other signs being lettered.

A small worktable such as this is quite handy. The illustration provides a general idea. The top might be 16 by 24 inches. The legs are about 28 inches high and are made of 2 by 4-inch lumber. If lighter material is used, the bottoms of the legs must then be built up to accommodate the casters. High quality casters should be used for ease of movement in any direction. On one end place a brush rail, such as shown, to rest the brushes upon. This rail keeps brushes from rolling off or from touching one another. You might devise any type of rail desired. A spiral-type coiled spring arrangement such as is used for pen holders could be adapted for this purpose. Several small boxes can be placed in the corner of the table top in which to place chalk and charcoal sticks, thumbtacks, razor blades, etc. Attach a good sized absorbent rag to the table as shown.

The palette illustrated consists of a small-paged magazine attached to a clipboard. This provides an excellent palette, especially for pictorial work where there is a need to palette many different colors. Upon each change of color, the top sheet is torn off after use, leaving a clean sheet in readiness. This also applies to lettering. It is never advisable to use the same palette too long. The paint gums up and fouls the brush. You will find that the frequent use of a clean sheet will result in sharper work and less loss of hair from the lettering brushes. A sticky palette is hard on brushes.

A magazine cannot be used for tempera colors because water colors will wrinkle the paper. For this work, you can use the clipboard, but attach small pieces of cardboard within the clip. Another disadvantage of using a magazine is that the pages that contain heavy colored display ads will sometimes "muddy" the colors when the heavy ink deposits dissolve into the paint. Such pages can be removed and discarded. The lightly printed pages can be used for colors that are affected by the printer's ink. All pages can be used for the darker colors such as black, dark blue, etc. Do not use absorbent pulp-type magazines for this since the blotter-like paper will suck too much oil and binder out of the paint. I have used this type of palette arrangement for over 35 years and find it to be most practical, but I use magazines composed of fairly smooth paper and thin cardboard when necessary.

Regardless of what you use within the clip for a palette,

the clipboard is an excellent device. Its weight prevents it from sliding about during the paletting process. It will not blow away in a heavy wind.

The small drawer in the table can be used to contain the frequently used items that are required when working at the bench. The inside of the drawer can be partitioned to suit your needs.

You will discover many uses for a table such as this. It is excellent for projector work. A portable projector can be placed on the top and the table can be rolled back and forth until the picture is adjusted to the desired size.

If you notice that each time you do a job you must prepare a makeshift gadget to successfully do the work, it is time for evaluation. Figure out what you need and try to purchase at least those items that are most frequently required. If you cannot afford such purchase perhaps you can build it in the most efficient manner of which you are capable. Keep all tools and equipment in the same place and handy for use. You will then have it available when the need arises and there will be no need to constantly improvise.

If your goal is to develop the greatest possible speed, you must create the handiest working conditions. Keep your equipment clean and in top condition. Make every move count and be constantly alert for any method that can save time without the sacrifice of efficiency. The elimination of a single movement will not in itself amount to much but over a period of time each improvement, no matter how slight, will add up to a point that will effectively increase your speed.

SPEED WITHOUT METHOD.

Sometimes in an effort to stress the positive results of good procedure, it is genuinely more effective to describe the negative results of poor procedure. The logic of this can be qualified by the following fact. The public in general will long remember an error, a wrongdoing, or a crime. Too quickly does it forget the good. Consider your own mistakes. Isn't it true that your conscience will not too easily allow you to forget an error? Yet it quickly rids itself of correct accomplishments.

The discussion to follow will be based on this logic to impress upon you the negative results of poor procedure as it is applied to the sign trade.

A friend of mine, who is the foreman of a large sign plant, once made this profound statement during our discussion: "You know, Greg, it is not always the fast man with the brush who is the best producer. Some of the slower men have a better production record than the speed merchants, because they are more efficient and make every move count." This remark is not unique; I have frequently heard basically the same statement.

There is no intent here to ridicule speed, because the combination of a fast lettering artist with good method cannot be topped, and such a man is the dream of every shop owner or foreman.

Fortunately most fast men are clean, efficient, and a pleasure to work with. Those to be mentioned here are in positive minority. Perhaps the best method to explain how a very fast lettering artist might nullify his own speed and become a second rate producer would be to use, for an example, a hypothetical workman. This fellow will be a composite of some of the various men I have worked with and, for convenience, let's call him "Speedy," while following his progress through several days work.

As we begin work in the morning, the other men go to their sign kits, select well cared for tools, and go about their work. Meanwhile "Speedy" goes over to his dirty, sticky kit, but he finds that he forgot to clean his brushes and put them in oil the night before. It is impossible for him to use these tools, so he lays them in a pan of lacquer thinner to soften and dissolve the dried paint. This will take a while. The brushes are quite possibly ruined and will never again be suitable for lettering.

Next he sidles over to one of the other men and says, "Hey, Joe, loan me a No. 8 quill 'til I can get some tomorrow." So Joe leaves his work to get old "Speed" a brush, wasting his time in the process. Joe will probably never get the quill back—maybe the handle.

"Speedy" now has the brush and all he needs is the paint. I notice when he attempts to pick a can of paint out of the bottom drawer of his kit, the entire drawer lifts up along with the can. It is stuck to the bottom, because he spilled it over the previous day and did not bother to clean the can or the drawer. Finally he pries it loose, strains it into a clean can, and is now ready to letter.

No, wait! He has no place to set his paint so he wanders around the shop looking for a box or something to use for a worktable. Upon finding this, he then looks about for a palette of some kind. After bumming a cigarette off me and a match, he is finally ready to letter the panel. Now we again realize why he is called "Speedy." His speed is fantastic and the lettering is beautiful. But by now the other slightly slower men are so far ahead that it will take him until noon to catch up, if he can manage to continue working that long.

Most likely he won't, because just about then one of the men, who has been about 10 miles out on a job, returns and wants to know who took the power drill out of its customary place in the truck. The foreman need not look far, because he saw "Speedy" using it several days before.

"Hey, Speedy! You took that drill out of the truck. Go and find it so this guy can get back to work!"

After looking around for about ten minutes, he finally finds it where he left it in a nail keg in the supply room. The other man takes it and returns to his job to join his helper who has been waiting for him ten miles out. The foreman is not in a cheerful mood.

"Speedy" finishes his job by noon and, as usual, is the first one in the washroom to clean up for lunch.

During the lunch break, one of the men speaks up, "Hey, Boss, I found that new screwdriver up on top of that neon I was working on this morning."

Old "Speed" pipes up, "Oh, Yea! Guess I left that up there last week. Lucky it didn't roll off and konk someone on the head." The foreman glances at "Speedy" with an expression that suggests that he might be toying with a little idea along this line.

After lunch the boss tells "Speed" to get ready to go out to finish a ground-level wall job. As usual it takes him some time to get going. He discovers that he has left the shop fitches and cutters standing in a bucket half full of dirty thinner, none of them being cleaned or wrapped. The fitches aren't too bad and he manages to clean these well enough for use. But the cutters are bent up like pancake turners from resting on their own weight. To save time the boss gives him several new brushes and instructs the shop boy to see what he can do with the other ones. In approximately an hour, "Speedy" is finally on his way.

The men left in the shop breathe a sigh of relief as the work returns to normal ("Speedy" provides a constant distraction). Not for long though. Two of the men, who were supposed to go out on a swing-stage job right after lunch, come in the back way yelling for the foreman. "Say, Boss, we're all loaded up and ready to go, but can't find the fall ropes or the stirrups."

"For crying out loud! 'Speedy' used 'em last and they gotta' be around here somewhere. Go look around the north side of the building where he unloaded."

They find the ropes right where the boss suggested—all tangled up in about six inches of grass. The stirrups, which are thrown right alongside, are beginning to rust because the grass has been wet through the nights and early mornings. After an hour of getting this tangled mess straightened out and the blocks lined up, these two men are finally on their way to salvage what they can of the day. They complain to the boss that they do not like the idea of doing high work with ropes and equipment that has been laying around in the wet grass.

Generally a good natured guy, the boss just gives them a dirty look and they say no more about it. For some reason the boss is not happy. In fact the morale of the shop has recently dropped to a low ebb.

The afternoon passes uneventfully and about 15 minutes before closing time "Speedy" returns. He smiles and says he finished his job. He's a likeable guy, even considering his faults. I notice, however, that he again slams the brush bucket down on the floor with none of the brushes cleaned or wrapped.

He gets a break though, because the foreman left early to have a tooth pulled. The lecture "Speedy" has coming about the ropes and stirrups won't be so bad in the morning after the boss cools off.

The next morning "Speedy" is about 20 minutes late. Since it is raining, we all begin work in the shop. It takes the boss ten minutes to say a few polite words to "Speedy", so he does not join the crew immediately. When he does, the boss sends him out to letter an interior valance in a store window. It doesn't take him as long as usual to get ready this morning—only about ten minutes to find the chamois-skin that he left some place around the shop. The dirt is all dried into it from the last job he used it on, so he spends about five minutes softening up the grime and cleaning it, after which he departs.

After lunch when he returns, the foreman asks him to help out in the showcard department. (Oh yes! "Speedy" is an all around man—signs, showcards, pictorials, the works!). Our regular card men are not overjoyed at the prospect, but they are behind on their work.

They bring out a complete set of fresh card colors for him and old "Speed" really turns out the work. But he does not stir the tempera thoroughly, and uses the binder off the top to such an extent that the remainder is apt to cause a chalking problem later when the bottom portion is used. The afternoon over, "Speedy" leaves, and the card men clean up after him.

The jars have been left uncovered and when one of the men begins to replace the covers, he notes with dismay that the light colors look like the batter from a marble cake. "Speedy" has been up to his old tricks, dipping from the blue into the yellow, from the red into the white, etc. The other man is washing out the expensive top grade red sables that were only given a half-hearted rinse by our hero. A toothbrush is used to clean several reservoir pens that are lying on the table caked with dried India ink.

Meanwhile the foreman has received a call from the irate

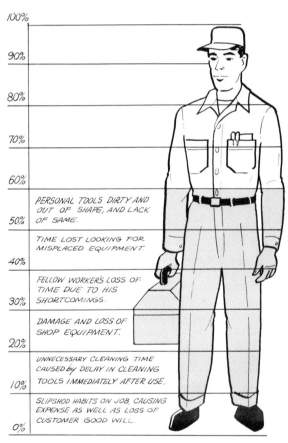

FIG. 97. Figuring a man's working speed at 100 percent, this chart shows how much of his speed is cancelled out by poor work habits. Less than half a man is left to do the work.

store owner where "Speedy" lettered the window. It seems he is quite put out because his name has been incorrectly spelled, and also reports that "Speedy" splattered paint on the dress on a mannequin. He instructs the foreman to have the sign corrected immediately and informs him that the shop must pay for the dress. The foreman does not appreciate this phone call.

So ends two days in the everyday life of "Speedy." All the guys regret that a fellow with this great talent cancels the benefits of such ability, because he never bothered to develop good work habits. We are at the same time thankful that there are not too many like him. "Speedy" got fired the following Saturday. On Monday the morale of the entire shop returned to normal.

Illustrated in Fig. 97 is an approximate percentage breakdown showing to what degree the most expert lettering artist can lose in his effectiveness by using speed without method.

THE LOGIC OF GOOD METHODS.

Much advice is offered to you as a newcomer to the trade, either written or spoken, in regard to what you should do. There is seldom enough emphasis on the things you should not do. Yet it is easier to lose the good will of a customer because of a shortcoming than it is to gain it by doing excellent work. This shortcoming might seem trivial to you, or not even be realized, but it can truly be said that "it is the little things that count". Good public relations can be your most valuable asset.

Doing high class work is not enough. It must be accompanied by other little courtesies that complement the rest of your work, rather than faults that might eliminate the customer's appreciation of a job well done.

For example, consider the following incident, and one that actually happened in a shop where I once worked. A fellow signman, an excellent lettering artist, was sent down to an exclusive dress shop to paint an interior valance-type sign on the top section of the display window.

The display area was cleared out by the owner so everything was in favor of the signman. The floor of the window was covered with expensive, thick-pile carpeting. The weather was nasty with slush and dirt on the sidewalk. Yet this man walked right off this dirty street and into the window area, sadly messing up the beautiful carpeting with his wet shoes. He also set his sign kit right down on the carpeting. The beautiful job that he accomplished on the valance did little to compensate for the thoroughly soiled carpeting.

The store owner was furious when he later called our boss to complain about the mess. The rug was naturally cleaned at the sign shop's expense, but the good will of the customer was lost at the outset.

This is an example of a man who had much experience as a sign painter and knew better. His sign work was neat and professional. In other respects the company had frequent unpleasant experiences due to his sloppy work habits. If this man had been operating his own business, he would have lost more customers than he would have gained, regardless of his outstanding ability.

In this case, he could have avoided all of this trouble with common sense. He could have placed a dropcloth over the carpeting. He could have removed his shoes and entered the window area in his stocking feet. He could have worn rubbers, removed them before entering the window, and slipped a pair of "window-trimmer's" socks over his shoes.

It is good policy to always leave the premises of a job as neat or neater than they were when you arrived. The proprietor appreciates this and can direct his attention to the excellence of your work rather than to the mess you leave behind.

This same principle applies when scraping paint off a window. If it is on the exterior, sweep the scrapings off the sidewalk into the gutter. These paint chips and peelings could be tracked into the place of business and into the neighboring stores. On the interior, do likewise, so the paint scrapings do not get tracked or blown about the premises.

Another way to establish good will is in regard to washing the windows. Since the immediate lettering area must be washed, it requires but little extra effort to wash the entire window. This makes a good impression on the customer, especially the ladies. Many times I have heard the pleasant remark, "Oh, look! He's washing the entire window. Now I won't have to do it!" So their good will is in your favor before you touch a brush.

This extra effort has additional advantages. If you merely wash the working area, and leave the soiled areas around it, the proprietor is apt to get out the brush and squeegee the very next day and scrub the window. In so doing, he might damage the lettering before the paint has had time to thoroughly dry. Also no sign shows up to its best advantage on an area surrounded by dirt. On exceptionally dirty windows it is often advisable to wash both sides of the glass so the sign shows up to its full brilliance.

This same washing principle applies, in some respects, to trucks. If you are lettering truck doors, it is best to wash the entire door from top to bottom. The lettering will present a better appearance and there will not be any grime or heavy road dust to get washed down over the freshly painted sign should it rain before the lettering has properly dried. It is surprising how many signmen just barely wipe off the area to be lettered. A sign isolated on a "spot-washed" area such as this cannot possibly show up to best advantage.

Later when the owner sees the job he is less than charmed by the over-all appearance and might reflect to himself, "The lazy bum didn't even bother to wash the doors." Right at this moment he may form an adverse opinion about you that will perhaps never be supplanted.

It is not implied here that you should wash the windows of an entire store, or even the area of a very large window, if you are only painting a small sign down in one corner. Neither does it mean that you should wash an entire truck when lettering the doors. But you should at least wash an area large enough to compliment the sign work. You must learn to judge the pros and cons of any given job.

At all times you should be concerned with the self-image presented to your customer. I once sent out a man to do an interior window job in a tavern. Shortly after he finished, I received a phone call from the tavern keeper saying, "Stop around here and see what a mess your man left in this place."

I went over and found strips of scrap decals on the floor beneath the window. There were splotches of paint and cigarette ashes all over the window sill. Cigarette butts were stepped out on the linoleum-tiled floor. To top it off, this sign painter had squeezed all of the paper decal backings into wet, soggy wads and stacked them in one corner for someone else to remove.

The proper method of performance on a job such as this is to take along an empty corrugated box and throw all debris from the job into this as you proceed. Use an ash tray for the cigarettes. Wipe up paint drops immediately or use a drop-cloth. When the job is completed, wipe off the window sill with a damp cloth, sweep the floor and place all waste material into the garbage.

With the scarcity of parking space it is thoughtless to park your truck or vehicle in front of the place where you are working. This is sometimes necessary, of course, if you are doing erection work or will need access to the vehicle. But if you expect to be working at a place all day, unload the equipment you will need and, if possible, move the vehicle to an out-of-the-way place. The parking space that you occupy for a day or for several days might cause a considerable loss of business to your customer.

Be as self-sufficient as possible and bring your own rags, towels, water buckets, etc. Try not to annoy your customer by borrowing this and that. Do not block his main entrance, even partially, with ladders, staging, etc., any longer than necessary. Especially, do not set up ladders, blocking part of his entrance while you go down the street for a 30-minute coffee break. That doorway that you block is also the entrance to your customer's cash register.

Another good habit is to try to arrange your work to your customer's best advantage and to your own at the same time. For example, if you have lettering to do on a busy entrance door that is constantly being used, try to do this lettering on an afternoon when the place is closed. At least arrange to perform the work during the least busy time of the day. This might involve working on Saturday afternoon or after hours or even early in the morning. But it is difficult to letter any door when you are interrupted every few minutes by people going in and out. You can letter such a job in much less time when the door is not being used. If the door is situated so that it can be propped open, there is no problem.

Chapter 27

Advantages of An Order Blank System

If each of us had a mind like a computer, we could get along without order blanks. Since we do not have memory banks, it is advisable to develop some form of an order blank system.

The system developed must be geared to the type of business being operated. If a large sign plant is involved, then the order blanks would of necessity be quite detailed. The original preparation of these would require careful forethought to include all the phases of work handled by such a company.

Since few beginners start out by operating large plants, and because this material is being written primarily for the beginner, we shall concentrate on the simple type of order blank.

Assuming that you as a comparative beginner are starting your first shop, chances are that you will not be too "flush" with money. You need not go into an expensive printing job. The forms can be printed on an economical grade of paper. At first you might forego the printing of these entirely and temporarily use plain paper. But, by all means, start out properly by using an order form for your very first job and continue to do so. You will have cause to be thankful that you did as the years go by.

You might ask, "Why have order forms? Wouldn't I be better off spending this time painting signs, instead of wasting it by filling out order blanks?" These and other questions will be answered as we discuss the subject. It is also my hope to convince you that a good order blank system is not just a means of keeping a record.

But more important still, it will cause you to become a more efficient operator, to improve customer relations, and to discover and avoid the continued use of inferior or faulty materials. It will help you surmount difficulties on the job and, in general, assist you in maintaining order in your sign plant operation instead of floundering about in a state of confusion.

You will discover that the benefits derived from filling

out order blanks will more than compensate for the time spent in so doing.

It has been my experience to have worked in several shops that did not use order blanks of any type. A shop such as this is comparable to a three-ring circus. Orders in such shops were often written on the back of old matchbook covers or envelopes. One could not begin a job because there was no coordination. The information on the old envelope would be too sketchy to begin the job or to even find your way to the location. For more complete information, it was necessary to ask the foreman, who might say, "I don't know. Bill, the salesman, sold that job. You'll have to ask him."

Quite politely, I would ask, "Where's Bill?"

The reply to this would most likely be, "How the heck do I know? Maybe he's over at Joe's for coffee."

It would be easy to relate dozens of similar examples, but for brevity, let us concede that the only solution to such a situation would be to inject a dose of order into the confusion.

To begin with, let us discuss the sample of the filled out order blank shown in Fig. 98. Although this is an order blank based on an actual job, it has been revised to contain more detail than normal to better illustrate certain points.

FIG. 98.

This also opens the door for discussion. Usually a typewriter is not used for these, but for the sake of clarity, I have done so in this case. These are normally filled out with pen or pencil. In the upper right hand corner of the sample order blank (Fig. 98), you will note the information in regard to patterns. The word "NONE" would have been sufficient for this particular job, since no patterns were involved.

However, to the right of this main highway bulletin, there is a separate banjo-shaped sign that did not require re-painting at the time. While looking through the order blanks in regard to this job, I found a similar notation. So I thought it advisable to carry this information forward to this updated order blank. This information means exactly what it says. There is a 4-foot pattern for the trademark "Scotty" filed in box number 23. My patterns are divided into categories and stored on end within numbered boxes. In each box there is a yardstick, also standing on end. By knowing the height of the pattern and moving the yardstick around in the box, I can cut my pattern search time to a minimum. Since 4-foot patterns are not as abundant as smaller sizes, it is quite simple to find the longer pattern if one knows the number of the box.

There are many methods of filing patterns. In larger shops where there is ample room, they might be filed in bins alphabetically. The box method works well for me. The important factor is that my order blank informs me that I do have a pattern, where it is filed, and its height. If I had no order blank, it would be difficult to later remember whether a pattern was available, let alone where it was filed. Each shop has its own method of storing patterns.

After the customer's name, you will note the words: "Contact: Clif." This shows who ordered the job and who to contact if a problem develops. The notation, "Last painted: Aug./65" immediately indicates the durability of the previous paint job. Also some customers will complain about a sign with normal deterioration in this way, "You just painted that sign about 2 years ago and it's starting to fade, etc." It is a simple matter then to check the order blank for the correct duration. Also it is easy to put the damper on such a complaint when there are records to prove it. (I must point out that Mr. Grosskopf is not such a man). But the type of customer just mentioned invariably steps up the time period by 2 or 3 years in his own favor.

The order blank as shown is self-descriptive to a major extent and a study of this should provide you with the general idea. After the word "JOB," for example if this were applied to a pick-up truck, you might write: "Cab Doors 71 (Brand name) Truck," etc. The word "SIDES" is generally indicated with either number "1" or "2," indicating whether a sign panel is to be lettered on one or both sides.

After certain words on the order blank you will note the abbreviation, "OPT.", which means "optional." This means that the customer has no preference. This abbreviation is used when the customer says, "Use your own judgment."

Below the itemized lines of general information, approximately 60 per cent of the order form is blank. This space is to be used for remarks in regard to procedure, specifications, etc. The first line reads, "SEE OTHER SIDE: COPY CHANGES." Since this is a repaint with some changes in copy, the rear side of the order blank can be used to list such changes. The second side of this blank can be used for many purposes. In case you do not take a snapshot, you can draw a small sketch showing approximately how you layed out the sign, with color indications pointing to the letter groupings, etc.

If this particular sign had not required copy changes, and had just consisted of repainting the sign without change of layout or copy, I could have changed this first line to read, "Repaint the same as order of Aug./65. Refer to snapshot". This would mean that there was a snapshot attached to the original order blank. Little else would need to be listed on this new order blank unless you would make brief notations of unusual problems encountered, new brands of paint used, etc.

With a snapshot and a detailed order blank of the original job, you can check back on procedure, colors, difficulties encountered, equipment used, and go to the job well prepared. Much time can be saved, because a brief study of the original order blank will enable you to intelligently go about this job with full knowledge of any problems encountered on the original paint job.

This might not be too important on a job a few blocks away where you can run down and take a quick look at the job. But on jobs 10 to 20 miles distant, this type of information can provide you with advance know-how and you can take with you all the proper equipment and material needed.

The top part of the blank area on the order form is generally used to briefly indicate specifications and other conditions that might be helpful in preparing to do the work.

The remaining portion is later used to describe the actual procedure, to keep a time record, etc. It is especially important to indicate any unusual problems encountered. Several years later when a repeat job is required, you can quickly refer to this information and be prepared to cope with such problems.

FIG. 99. This highway sign is the subject of the information on the sample order blank shown in Fig. 98.

Fig. 99 is a photograph of the job described on the sample order blank. Using this and the related order blank as a basis, the step-by-step procedure will now be described. Alternate methods also will be considered.

BULLETIN EQUIPMENT.

The most appropriate equipment to use as staging for a job such as this would be a small light-weight swing-stage. These are sometimes referred to as "baby bulletin-swings." Frequently two separate stages are used side by side to more completely span the area to be painted. Seldom does the new operator own or have access to this equipment. Even the established small operators, who do little of this work, are not apt to own bulletin swing stages. Since this instruction is principally intended for those who are new to the trade, all procedures will be described in such a way that the work can be accomplished with a minimum of equipment.

Those signmen who operate large plants or steadily work for firms that maintain a vast number of highway bulletins would have no need for instruction in this common phase of signwork. These people have the advantage of working with nothing but the best, including power-operated swing stages, well-stocked supply trucks, booms, and other modern equipment. The author is aware that such equipment exists, is familiar with its use, and during a span of 42 years has worked under such ideal circumstances. Many of the large sign plant operators also are well acquainted with the other end of the totem-pole. Having started from scratch with small capital and a beat-up stepladder, they worked long hours and sacrificed much to build up a huge and successful business. One can only have a sincere admiration for men such as this.

They know full well how much fortitude it requires to plan a procedure, develop a layout, and prepare the paint to do a "one-shot" job with a bare minimum of equipment.

PROCEDURE OF THE JOB. This job will be
described as though it were being done at the moment. Since the ground is hard and level and the top of the sign is only 15 feet high, I can safely use heavy-duty A-frame ladders and a plank.

If you do not have this equipment, straight or "running ladders" can be used instead. However, this is not so convenient because the ladder rungs impede the work somewhat at each end of the sign. Also the long ladders must constantly be maneuvered around the light fixtures that extend from the top of the sign. If the terrain in front of a sign is irregular or soft, it is then more practical and safer to use straight ladders and jacks.

Even on level ground an A-ladder set-up might wobble at certain areas. This is usually the fault of a single ladder lsg. A shovel can be used to dig a slight impression in the ground under one or perhaps two legs to correct such a problem. It takes but several minutes to do this and the ladder will rest in solid position. If this type of staging slants at all, the slant should be towards the sign, not in the opposite direction. In this way if the staging should tip it will come to rest against the sign, instead of flopping completely to the ground in the other direction. If a staging is properly placed, there should be no reason for it to tip. The A-frame ladders should only be used on appropriately level surfaces. In connection with a plank, it is also hazardous to use them on soft ground.

The same leveling principle can be used in regard to straight ladders. If the ground is abruptly slanted, it might be necessary to dig a fairly deep hole for one ladder leg so that it rests in a safe, vertical position. A small short-handled railroad shovel is an ideal tool for this and for other purposes. I constantly carry such a tool in both vehicles.

Conditions might be such that you might wish to tie the ladders with ropes or secure them in some manner. With rigging properly placed I have never found this to be necessary. In fact the most serious falls in my experience have been involved with the use of swing-stages, and always because of carelessness. Two of these accidents came about because, in each case, the helper at the time threw a bad hitch into the rope under the stirrup and let go. That end of the swing also decided to go someplace.

With the rigging in position, the work begins. The face of the sign is in good condition, but it must be sanded entirely to remove the usual residue of oxidized paint. This requires a minimum of sanding. The areas near to the horizontal cracks where the sign panels intersect are chipped and peeled to some extent.

The title, "Grosskopf Oil" is my first concern, because these letters will be the first to receive a coat of finish white. Three horizontal cracks intersect this lettering. Therefore I first sand this area, scrape and sand the cracks, and apply a spot coat of fast dry clear flash bond primer only to the bare metal areas. This primer can dry while I sand and clean the remainder of the sign below the dark panel.

After similarly cleaning the bottom area, I apply a coat of clear primer to the bare metal areas as they occur. While this dries, I again move to the top of the sign and spot coat the words, "Grosskopf Oil" with a coat of bulletin color. This is done in a fairly rough fashion with no attempt to follow the letters. My only object is to cover the faces of the letters with the white. The feathered edges that extend beyond the edges of the letters are immaterial. I do not outline these with a ditto or indelible pencil because they will be visible by natural contrast. You will note that I bypassed the usual coat of blocking-out white on this panel. After sanding, this surface retained no gloss and provided tooth enough to accept the finish coats of bulletin color. My final effort on this trip is to apply a roller coat of pale gray block-out paint to the entire area of the sign face below the top panel. It becomes necessary to use a brush to paint along the horizontal joints between the panels. These panels are slightly rounded on the edges and have caused cracks too deep for the roller to penetrate. A long nap roller would do so, but I hesitate to work over the rough finish that would result. The coat of gray covers the old lettering quite well and has neutralized the background.

Upon returning to the job, the next day, my first procedure is to lay out the circular design at the bottom-center. After determining the center for the circle I partially insert a small metal screw at this point. The loop at the end of a chalk line is placed around the protruding screw head and this cord is used as a compass to draw the circular marks. No preliminary measurements are made to indicate the positions. The circular effect is to be determined with the string at the time of marking, because it is my desire to take fullest advantage of the available space. The widths of the borders around the central circle are applied at random in widths that provide the most pleasant optical effect.

No knots are tied in the chalk line for marking. The string around the screw head is pulled tight and is wrapped several times around the wooden portion of a ditto pencil about a half inch above the marking tip. With the string pulled very tight and in marking position, it is held firmly around the tip with my fingers and the mark is drawn for the central circle. The same process is used to indicate the lines for the borders that flank the circle. With the circles indicated, I tighten the metal screw into the surface.

Next I apply a direct layout for the words, "Open 24 Hours." This is first done tentatively with round charcoal sticks. When in accurate position, the lettering is outlined with a ditto pencil and the charcoal marks are removed with a dry cloth.

A coat of white bulletin color is now applied to the inner circular band and to the letters. My application of this white is quite accurate because the flanking colors will be applied before leaving the job.

My next step is to paint the bottom areas to the right and to the left of the circle arrangement with a coat of fast dry background enamel. A light yellow is used for this. This is done with a 4-inch brush because the areas are too small to fool with a roller.

Moving to the top of the sign, I consider the words, "Grosskopf Oil". The lettering is fairly visible, but I decide to quickly indicate the outlines of the letters with pencil for faster lettering.

Since the only difficult peaks are within the letter "K", I use a 1½-inch white-bristle cutter to cut-in around the lettering, and use a larger brush to fill in the open areas.

The top panel is completed, so I move down to work on the circular arrangement. First I use a 1½-inch cutter to paint the two outer circular borders with No. 124 bulletin orange. The cutter is held sidewise and I use the edge to outline these areas and fill in with the same brush held in normal position.

The same brush is to be used with No. 104 bulletin red to paint the central circle, so I rinse out the orange in thinner. For the cut-in work around the letters, "Open 24 Hours" I use a ¾-inch fitch and I use the edge of the 1½-inch cutter to paint the outline of the circle. This brush also is used to fill in the small open areas of the circle.

By now the yellow areas on each side of the circle are dry enough to be lettered. The span is too short and there are too many guidelines needed to successively tape a chalk line into position for snapping. A yardstick is too short to draw these lines with any degree of speed.

When working alone, I use a long, thin wooden slat. This is a smooth lath such as one would normally use for building a trellis. This material can be purchased from any lumber company and is barely ¼-inch thick and about 1½ inches wide. A 7 or 8-foot length is suggested. Usually I purchase these in several lengths, check them for straightness, sand them to greater smoothness, and apply a coat of varnish or other clear finish to the entire strip.

Using such a lath as a straightedge, I use a lead pencil to draw the crosslines for the copy. Past experience has proved this method to be faster on lines of this length than the two-handed snapping method. Next I lay out the lettering, freehand, with white chalk.

This layout is precise enough for the lettering. So using a full No. 20 gray jumbo quill, I apply all of the lettering with No. 156 brilliant blue bulletin color, filling in immediately. The white outlines are applied around the wet lettering with a brush of the same size and type. The outlines are not too precise and are applied a comfortable distance away from the letter edges. I do this freehand with my hand completely up from the surface.

The baked enamel border of the sign is in good condition, but is soiled and has no gloss. Using a single ladder, I use an automotive paste wax to clean and polish this and the bulletin is complete. Before leaving, I replace two burned out light bulbs and adjust the time clock for the lights. With the advent of Fall the days become shorter so there is an earlier need for light.

Comments on the job: In regard to the blue lettering, it is traditional for most signmen to use either regular white fitches or soft fitches for highway bulletins. For many years I did likewise. However, the surfaces of many highway bulletins are as smooth as on commercial signs. Some years ago, I discovered that I could nearly double my speed by using the large quills as described. I still use fitches and cutters exclusively on all rough surfaces, including some metal highway signs. But I see no reason to stubbornly adhere to a slower method merely because tradition says it is the thing to do. Any time that I can increase my speed and work with greater convenience and efficiency, the dictates of tradition become immaterial.

It should be stressed that with a swing-stage and a competent helper, this job could be accomplished from start to finish in less than a day. With precise applications of the white to the letters "Grosskopf Oil", the black could be cut-in around the wet letters immediately. The same would apply to similar areas. It is no problem for an experienced signman to paint around or flush against wet letters. It is sometimes an advantage, because the slight overlap of paint on the letter outlines conveniently provides a slight pull and the fitches and cutters do not tend to slide as they sometimes do on a smooth, dry surface.

It was mentioned that the white outlines on the blue letters need not be too precise. This applies to all sign work designed to be viewed at a distance. In such cases, the layout is the chief concern. If the layout is well designed, the lettering and other designs do not require absolute preciseness. As long as the letters are well-formed, there is no need to peak-off the letters or to correct slightly ragged strokes. To sum up, the entire application can be much rougher than on a commercial sign. The distance of view automatically corrects any flaws that would be apparent upon close-up vision.

A word of caution should be inserted here in regard to all signwork. During your early years you should quite closely follow tested procedures. It will take a few years before you can intelligently effect any major changes. It is advisable to give every professional procedure a fair trial and then if you positively cannot work with this method, you must try to improvise. Just because one man can letter efficiently with a hard fitch on a smooth surface does not mean that you can do likewise.

It is common sense, however, to watch professional sign painters, and try to use the type of tools that these men use. Through long experience these signmen have most likely tried all types and have discovered the tools that will do each job most efficiently.

ORDER BLANKS RESULT IN CONTROLLED OPERATIONS.

You will notice on the sample order blank that the paints and primers used are identified with the brand name. At first this might seem to be of slight significance, so perhaps the best way to illustrate the wisdom of this is to relate the following incident that occurred many years ago.

At the time I had been having problems with the metal primers that I customarily used. So it was not too difficult for a high-pressure salesman to convince me that I should use two different metal primers manufactured by his employer. One was for galvanized metal and the other for black iron. He claimed that these products were infallible, none better, etc. His claim was that the rust inhibitor in the black iron primer was absolutely foolproof. The results?

A customer had four signs already built. Two were faced with galvanized sheetmetal and the other two were faced with black sheet iron. I treated these signs before painting with the utmost care as far as etching, cleaning, etc. Even though the salesman had claimed that his galvanized metal primer required no etching, I used a high quality commercial etching solution, regardless, to be on the safe side. The two black iron signs were thoroughly primed on both sides to prevent rust penetration from the rear. All four of the signs were primed with the salesman's "wonder products".

In less than a year the black iron signs were rusting on both sides and the paint was peeling off the galvanized signs in ribbons. It became necessary for me to clean these signs completely down to the bare metal and repaint them free of charge to hold the goodwill of an exceptionally good customer.

When I contacted the paint distributor who directly sold this paint, he said he would send a company representative to talk to me. I am still waiting for this call. The cost of the paint is not involved in such a situation. This is negligible compared to the time and back-breaking work of refinishing four signs. Luckily I was wise enough to use these primers only on these four signs.

It is salesmen and firms such as these who cause the signman to be cautious about trying out unknown or different products. These people make it difficult for others who do supply dependable products. The reliable companies do not make false claims about their products and the durability they predict is backed up by exhaustive tests of their own.

There are many occasions when one single color will break down on a sign. This can occur on a number of signs. Since it is impossible for any signman to remember the particular brand of paint used on every color on every sign, it is impossible to pinpoint the product at fault. Generally when you notice a one-color failure on a number of signs and you check the order blank to determine the brand name, you will discover that such failure can be traced to definitely one brand of paint.

You might mistakenly think that if you stick to the exclusive use of one brand of paint, produced by a reliable manufacturer, that you will have no problems. This is not true. It is common knowledge among sign painters that even the best paint suppliers will have certain "weak" products. For example, such a company might produce a dozen colors of bulletin paint that provide the ultimate in regard to coverage and durability. Yet two additional colors in the same category might be questionable. This does not always pertain to durability. The sub-quality factor might relate to poor, transparent coverage, excessive drying time, or the paint can be off-color, etc.

In line with this fact, I am using three different brands of bulletin color at the present time, choosing the strongest colors offered by each company.

So you can see why it is advisable to keep an accurate record of the brands used. In this way when there is an occurrence of premature deterioration you can consult the order blank and pinpoint the product.

At the same time you should check the procedure and the probable weather conditions. Paint breakdown is not always the fault of the product. A check of the date on the order blank might indicate cold weather application. All of us have a tendency to thin the paint to an extreme in cold weather. In so doing, we break down the necessary binding vehicle in the paint and this will result in chalking and other deterioration. Available from most paint manufacturers is a "cold weather reducer" that is chemically compatible with their own products. It is best to use this reducer in cold temperatures instead of normal thinners.

In view of this, it would be unfair to condemn a brand of paint until you are certain that neither weather nor improper procedure has been a factor.

After one has been in the sign trade for many years, he will hesitate to try out new brands of paint, even though in actuality, they might be of the highest quality. The average signman will prefer to stick to one of the brands that has proven to be durable. The problem is that it takes such a long time to find out if a paint, a primer, a varnish, or similar product is actually as good as it is represented to be.

If you buy a new shaving cream, you will know at once if it is suitable. You could buy a case without apprehension. It is quite the opposite in regard to paint. After application you must wait for quite a few years to see if it is a superior product and one that you can safely guarantee to a customer. Should you paint a dozen large highway signs with an unproven or unfamiliar brand and all 12 would break down in less than a year, it would be a considerable loss to clean these and repaint them.

After several sad experiences, it is now my practice to try new brands on one or two small signs only. A record of this is maintained on the order blanks and after 3 or 4 years, I can personally determine how the product has endured the test of the elements.

Some signmen conduct their own tests. About 5 years ago I coated one half of a new tin can with an unfamiliar metal primer. When it was dry, I dated it with lettering color over the primed half and threw it into an area at the edge of a raspberry patch. It was here exposed to constant moisture, dirt, sun, etc. The results were excellent. The can was checked at various times, and at the end of 3 years, the side that was primed remained new and shiny, while the bare metal had completely rusted through. Only then did I begin to use this primer exclusively.

In quick defense of conscientious paint suppliers, it is their intent to produce the best possible product. Therefore one should not hesitate to switch to any one of the brands produced by these reliable companies. Normally there would be no apprehension. But because of the small percentage of those who oversell inferior products one would not paint several thousand dollars worth of signs until he had some tangible proof of quality, through reputation, testimonial, tested samples, etc. A signman can hardly be blamed for using a new and unfamiliar product on a small scale at first, before using it on a full scale basis.

Notations on order blanks in regard to your own paint mixes can be an asset. For example, I prefer to mix my own aluminum for lettering. For years I had no problem. Suddenly I was confronted with a number of truck doors where the aluminum had worn off quite rapidly. Memory seemed to tell me that these trucks had been lettered about the same time.

Upon checking back on the order blanks, I found that I had switched to a thinner bonding liquid because it dried faster and flowed smoothly. Immediately this mix was discontinued. I reverted to the use of the heavier liquid that I had used for years, but I used just enough of it to result in a thick mixture. Then I thinned this down to good consistency with the free-flowing liquid. There has since been no trouble; the mix works perfectly and the addition of the heavy binder gives it the toughness needed for durability. The thinner liquid speeds the drying.

The important point to be stressed is that the order

blanks showed me when and why the aluminum began to fail. It was a simple matter to remedy the situation.

An essential indication on the order blank is a listing of the copy or wording used on the job. In regard to large or complicated jobs, this can most simply be done by taking a color snapshot and attaching a print to the order blank. Less complicated jobs such as the doors of a truck seldom require a snapshot. A fast pencil sketch can be drawn on either the back or front side of the blank, showing the form of layout, and a clear listing of the name, address, license, and phone numbers, etc. The rough layout should show whether the title-name was straight, arced or swirled, and both script and printed letters should be indicated as they occurred. Color notations should be made in connection with the letters, shading, etc.

This type of information is especially handy when a truck driver leaves a truck, telling you that the owner wants it painted just like his other vehicles. If you have a pattern from the painting of previous jobs this is no problem. But if a pattern does not exist, you can go ahead with the job by referring to the most recent order blank. There is no need to chase around to obtain the specifications. This copy data can be used for reference to many other jobs besides trucks.

Along the bottom of the sample order blank in Fig. 98 you will note other indications. The date "Promised" and "Completed" entries have been discussed earlier. The information in regard to the date of billing and the date of payment can be most convenient. You can tell at a glance if a customer is "slow-pay" or prompt. The price arrangement in the lower righthand corner lists the basic price, followed by the state tax charged. In this state a customer either pays tax, or if he has an exemption number he must present a slip to verify this fact, and the number is then indicated in this space instead of a tax amount. The actual price of this sign was purposely omitted, because it will require future repaint jobs, so competitive pricing must still be considered an issue. Also to list the actual price here would only cause confusion, because there is a tremendous difference in price ranges from one area to another.

The pricing of signs is a welcome indication on an order blank, because you have it handy in order to do the job. On a repeat job, such as the lettering of a pair of truck doors, instead of rubbing your chin and thinking, "Let's see, what did I charge this guy for his last truck," the information is immediately available.

This ready reference avoids the possibility of charging a customer $20 for a job, and several months later $25 for the same job on another truck. To further complicate things, a few months pass and you letter still another truck for him and charge $22. About this time your customer will realize that you are running your business without a system. Since he has only a few trucks painted, it is likely that he will remember the original charge. Meanwhile you perhaps letter dozens of trucks and cannot accurately remember the prices charged. Most customers expect periodical price raises in line with the economy but will question erratic fluctuation.

It would be possible, without order blanks, to check some of these facts in your regular bookkeeping system, but the entries would be sketchy, showing only the date, name of customer, and the amount and manner of payment. From this you could not know if you had lettered a panel, a pick-up, a tanker, or whether the copy was the same, and if other factors might have caused considerable price variation.

Therefore you will find it a big help to make miscellaneous notations on order forms for certain jobs. Recently I painted an overlaid plywood sign for a customer. When I prepared the billing, the price seemed much too low when I glanced at the total amount on the previous order blank. Upon checking the notations, the memo on the old blank indicated that the material was furnished by the customer. On the present job, I had supplied the material which accounted for the difference in price.

It is not necessary to prepare an order blank for ordinary, one-time jobs, especially when there is small chance for repeat orders.

A few tips for locating order blanks when you need them: My method is to file these in bundles, a month in each bundle. It is often possible to recall the year in which a job was done. By consulting the regular bookkeeping ledger the month can be located quite rapidly. It is then necessary only to look through the bundle for that month to find the blank required.

The order blanks for steady customers, who order work regularly, are kept in separate files. The entire succession of their work can be checked in a matter of minutes. Sometimes I know that I have a pattern on file for certain repeat jobs. Since I also have the name and date of the most previous job marked directly on the pattern roll, the order blank can be located quickly.

It is understandable that a large sign plant would require a better filing system than this. Such plants would naturally require order blanks of broader form. Some firms use large, detailed blanks for complicated jobs, and smaller, more simplified forms for ordinary work.

The format of the sample order blank is quite simple. You can plan the basic layout for your blanks to suit your individual operation. These can be revised and broadened as your business grows.

Chapter 28

Miscellaneous

SHAVING LETTERS ON GLASS. The razor blade illustration (Fig. 100) shows an age-old method for squaring up strokes when working on glass. Merely extend the strokes over the guidelines wherever convenient. When dry, trim the strokes with a new blade. Do not try this with used blades. As soon as a new blade fails to provide a sharp letter edge, switch to another new blade.

FIG. 100. Age-old method of squaring up strokes when working on glass.

SQUARING LETTERS WITH CELLOPHANE TAPE.
The use of cellophane tape to square up the strokes of lettering is illustrated in Figs. 101 and 102. Strip the tape across the guidelines as shown.

Run the thumbnail firmly over the edges next to the lettering to insure perfect adhesion. When lettering, extend the
strokes over the tape and guidelines. Carefully pull off the
tape and the strokes will be neat and square. When applying the tape, fold the right ends over slightly, pinching the
adhesive together to form a small tab. This eases removal of
the tape. Masking tape is too thick for this purpose and
usually results in a ragged edge.

FIG. 101. and FIG. 102. Use of tape to square up ends of strokes
of letters.

Avoid placing the tape over the curved letters or the
graceful sweep of the curve might be distorted by a flat
section as shown in the illustration of the single letter R.
Some suggest that the tape should run all the way across
and that the curved letters can be touched up later. This
results in a patched-up appearance due to a paint "pile-up."
Note that the top strip of tape on the example word "Pri-
vate" does not extend over the letters P and R.

Each of these methods has advantages over the other.
The razor blade method allows for trimming stroke-endings

298

in between letters. There would seldom be room, nor would it be practical, to apply tiny pieces of tape at these points. Also in) words containing curved letters in alternate sequence such as, "Cheeseburgers", the razor blade method is more practical. This method is especially useful when lettering a large number of doors in a new building. Continue with the lettering and as the letters dry, go back and trim the strokes. Do this progressively as you proceed with the work throughout the entire building.

The tape method has two distinct advantages; it can be used on just about any smooth surface and the tape can immediately be removed. The other method can only be used on glass and trimming cannot be done until the lettering is dry. Do not try this razor blade method on plastic signs.

INTERIOR WINDOW VALANCES. A window
valance is a sign painted across the top of the window with a solid field color for a background. A similar sign at the bottom of a window is an "apron." Both are generally painted on the interior of the glass, so the lettering must be done in reverse or backwards.

There are several layout methods for painting an interior valance. You can apply a direct chalk layout to the exterior of the window. Or the pattern can be drawn with heavy pencil lines on white paper. This can be taped to the exterior of the window. These layout lines are clearly visible when lettering on the interior. Also you can prepare a pattern perforated with a pounce wheel and transfer the layout to either side of the glass. The most accurate method is to apply this to the interior of the window and work directly around the pattern lines.

The following procedure is to be used for dark letters on a light background color: With the pattern in position, you proceed with the lettering as usual except that it is done in reverse. A small pocket-sized mirror can be used to occasionally check the lettering for good formation. This saves the time required to run outside to see how the letters will appear when viewed from a normal position.

If this is a two-trip job you can use bulletin colors for the lettering and the background can be applied on the second trip when the lettering is dry.

To complete the job in one day, you will need fast-dry lettering colors. For this you can use paste japan colors available in either tubes or cans. An approximate mix for this is to place the equivalent of a heaping tablespoon of paste into a small can. Add to this a level teaspoon of fast dry gold size or clear varnish. Turpentine should be used if further thinning is necessary. These amounts can vary according to the thickness of the brand of paint being used. Especially with black, you will need to experiment with the mixture. The black should be mixed to just that point where the color becomes opaque and is no longer transparent. If too much paste color is used without enough sizing or varnish, the lettering can possibly dissolve or work-up into the background color when it is applied. These colors dry very rapidly.

When the lettering is completed, the next step is to draw a line across the predetermined bottom of the valance. Beneath, and along the line, place a strip of cellophane tape the full width of the window. Rub your thumbnail along the upper or contact edge of the tape for perfect adhesion. Masking tape can be used for this, but it might leave a sawtoothed edge.

As soon as the lettering is dry, wipe off the surfaces with a damp chamois skin. This removes any oily film that sometimes curdles the background paint.

This background paint can now be applied with a large brush, and immediately stippled (see Fig. 123). An illustration of a stipple pad and instructions for making such a pad also are contained in a section on plastics in this book.

Bulletin colors form a tack too quickly to allow for stippling. They can be used on smaller areas, however, if a small amount of linseed oil is added. My preference is to use a high quality, oil-based house paint for valance backgrounds. This paint tacks slowly and allows sufficient time to tap the stipple pad on the surface to remove the brush marks, overlaps, etc. With proper stippling, the finished field color should be as clean and uniform as frosted glass.

Either white bulletin or house paint can be tinted to any pastel color desired by adding the necessary positive color.

DARK BACKGROUND VALANCE.

On valances with dark colored backgrounds, you cut-in the paint around the pattern outlines. The letters remain as clear glass. When dry the colors are applied to the letters and stippled for uniform transparency. If various colors are used on the lettering, then each letter is individually painted and stippled. This results in a mottled, unsightly appearance around the letters as seen from the interior. The best way to remedy this is to later apply a coat of white to the back of the entire valance.

If the letters consist entirely of one color, you can use

the same paint to immediately cover both the letters and provide the finished background.

Due to the variance of contraction and expansion, a painted valance quite frequently causes a window to break. This can be expected especially on dark backgrounds and on large expanses of paint. It is advisable to allow at least a half-inch margin of bare glass around the entire painted area. Never paint directly up to the edges of the window casings. This can only be done when using white or very light colors, but then only when the painted area covers 20 per cent, or less, of the window space.

Insurance policies often have clauses in regard to window signs and glass breakage. Advise your customer to check his policy and mention the possibility of such breakage. In all cases make it clear before-hand that you cannot assume responsibility for glass breakage.

It should be mentioned that some sign painters prefer to apply the background color to window valances with a roller. Your best procedure would be to experiment with both methods and choose the one you find to be most efficient. Also some signmen apply a full coat of a clear protective finish over the entire valance area. My practice is to apply a one-stroke line of clear automotive enamel along the bottom edge of the sign. The clear finish is extended about a quarter of an inch below the bottom edge of the valance. The edges of any window signs are the most likely places to expect the occurrence of paint breakdown. This is usually due to the abuse of the rubber squeegee used in window cleaning.

TAPING PATTERNS IN POSITION. A useful

method of taping patterns in position is shown in Fig. 103. This works especially well when you must tape a pattern in position for a window valance, where the top of the pattern must fit flush against the top of the window frame. While the pattern is still on the drawing board, cut a series of holes, as shown, along the top of the pattern. On the job, all you need do is shove the pattern snugly against the top of the window frame and place strips of masking tape over the holes. The bottom edge of the paper can be taped to the window as usual, so no holes are required.

This method is especially adaptable wherever a pattern must fit within a frame or an area where there is no place to lap the tape across the edge. Additionally I find it to be a time-saver on certain flat signs where the tape could be lapped over the edges.

For example, let us suppose I were to letter six flat, unframed signs about 2 feet square. I would first cut an oblong hole in each corner of the pattern. Next I would place all six of the signs in a row along the drawing board, and fasten the pattern to the first sign with a strip of tape over each hole. After pouncing the pattern, I would lift the entire pattern, tape intact, move it to the next sign and press it into position at the tape points. I would pounce this and move from sign to sign with little effort.

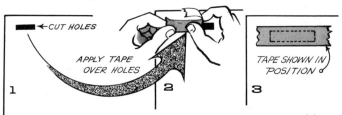

FIG. 103. Useful method for taping patterns into position.

The pattern can be rolled up and filed away without removing the tape. Thus it can be used again. The roll of paper will not stick together enough to cause any problem. This is a much faster method than lapping strips of tape across the paper and over the sign edges and peeling the tape free each time the pattern is moved. The strips might have to be removed and changed after prolonged use. Tape with adhesive on both sides also can be used without cutting holes, but these patterns, when rolled, will have a greater tendency to stick together.

PATTERNS FOR IRREGULARLY SHAPED TRUCK DOORS.

When lettering trucks with odd shaped doors it is helpful to make two patterns. For example, the fender wells on "snub-nosed" trucks will cut into the lettering area of the door. The lower area will have a quarter-round contour. On one side of the vehicle, the fender well will be to the left and to the right on the other. The pattern for one door will not fit the other.

If only one truck is involved, then a direct layout is advisable. But this information applies to duplication of design on several trucks with identically shaped doors. In the making of patterns for irregular doors of any kind, it is not always necessary to perforate each pattern separately. Cut one piece of paper to its full square or oblong shape, as wide as the maximum width of the door at the top and to its vertical height. Securely tape this piece of paper to the truck at the top edge. Press one hand against the paper holding it flat against the face of the door. Run the thumbnail of your other hand along the paper in the groove formed where the excess corner of the paper overlaps the fender well. The resultant crease depicts the contour of the truck door. Indicate the approximate positions of the door handle, locks, etc.

Using this paper as a guide, lay it on the drawing board over a second piece of paper of equal size. Cut through both pieces at once along the crease. By reversing one piece of paper, you will have a section to fit each side of the truck.

Lay out the pattern on one piece of paper, allowing for the door handles, etc., since these must be reckoned with later.

When the layout is completed, the time saving procedure begins. Place the blank piece of paper, in reverse position, on the drawing board and fasten with tape. Lay the paper containing the pattern over this and, with careful manipulation, you can adjust the top piece so that each copy grouping will rest in proper position on the paper underneath. Perforate with the pounce wheel through both sheets of paper in one operation. You must shift the top piece as necessary to its proper position since the contour of each piece of paper is in the reverse of the other.

Always keep the top edges of the paper in alignment and the copy will fit on both doors.

This method is better than an attempt to squeeze one pattern into position on the reverse shaped door while out on the job. This would be impractical when lettering a fleet of trucks.

LOOSE METAL KNOCKS OFF PAINT.

When building metal signs, especially highway bulletins, fasten the metal tightly. Do not skimp on back-bracing. If a fairly large area of metal spans too great a space without a brace, this portion of the metal will snap back and forth in the wind. This constant snapping action will actually loosen and snap off the paint, or at least contribute to paint breakdown. Through the years, I have noticed that my paint failures occurred on signs in those sections where the metal was loose and flapping back and forth in the wind. The paint on the tight metal was still in excellent condition. After setting an extra piece of wood in the rear framework and tightening the metal, the problem was apparently solved, because this did not again occur in these specific areas.

CORRECTING ERRORS.
Each of us is apt to make a mistake in the lettering process. The first tendency of the beginner is to dip a rag in turpentine, gasoline, or other solvent and remove the unwanted letter or smudge. This is not advisable, especially on a high shine or freshly painted surface. The turpentine or solvent might flatten the paint and cause a bad appearance on the area where a letter, for instance, has been removed.

In cases such as this, it is better to use a soft, clean rag dipped into linseed oil to make the correction. This must be done with care, using a minimum of oil, so that excessive oil will not run into the adjacent lettering. When the error has been removed, all traces of the oily residue must be thoroughly wiped off with a clean, dry rag. If an oil film remains on this area, you will have trouble relettering. The paint will "feather out" and prevent the application of a sharp-edged letter.

The use of oil will not hurt the gloss of the field color. It would be poor policy to present a sign job on a new truck with "flattened" areas. These areas are most apparent when the surface is viewed obliquely with the light reflecting the over-all gloss of the surrounding area.

The practical way to remove a letter is to wrap a rag around your thumb or finger, dip it lightly into the oil, and then, starting at the outer edges of the letter, wipe the excess paint into the letter—not away from it. Continue this process, by shifting your finger to a clean spot on the rag dipping it again into oil, until all of the unwanted paint is removed. I have often removed errors by dipping into the lard or olive oil within the small container in the top of my sign kit, which I normally use for a brush preservative. With this method, paint can be removed after it has dried for quite some time and still not ruin the gloss of the surface.

Chapter 29

Pictorials and Sign Work

The ability to do at least simple pictorial work can add much to your effectiveness as an all-around commercial sign painter. Those who have no particular artistic ability should not be discouraged by this statement, because there will be a constant demand for people whose ability is limited to lettering. So concentrate on becoming the best possible lettering artist and the rewards will be gratifying.

Most people who choose the sign trade do have an artistic flair or they would not have become interested in the profession. It is to this majority that the following is directed.

The ability to reproduce or originate pictures or trademarks might be the factor that causes a customer to consult you instead of a competitor.

This type of work need not be as complicated as you might assume. Signmen paint for laymen, not for art critics. Much of this work is viewed from a distance, such as on highway bulletins, etc. Usually the illustration is incidental and the lettering is the first point of interest. Consequently your pictorial efforts do not necessarily require perfection.

As an aid to this type of work, it is advisable to purchase an economical opaque projector. For the benefit of those who are unfamiliar with this item, let me explain: When you place a small copy of a picture or trademark within the projector you can cast an image upon pattern paper fastened to a wall. You can enlarge the design to the size desired with all color separations visible. A serviceable projector can be purchased for a reasonable amount, although more expensive and diversified models are available. This is a wise investment, because enough time can be saved in a short period of use to more than recover the cost, not to mention the accuracy that results in the work.

A few jobs have been chosen for illustration that are not too complicated. You might not be able to accomplish such work immediately, but this will provide a goal for you to strive for as you develop your ability.

This is not to be a lesson in fine artwork. The methods

and materials will be at variance with those used in art schools. This is necessarily so because sign painters must work in competition with the clock to show a profit. Our colors must stand up in bad weather and are subject to repeated washings and other abrasive abuse. So soft paste-type oil colors are impractical for our purposes, unless they were mixed with bonding agents to toughen the finish.

For convenience, we shall adhere to the use of bulletin colors even though their fast drying qualities will interfere with blending. Fortunately, on most pictorial sign work, the blending process is at a minimum as compared to finer art, which is usually viewed close-up. Because visibility is usually our chief concern, our colors are bolder and vivid. The color separations are also sharper and more pronounced.

The first discussion will involve the "Krueger Campsite" panel (Fig. 104). Follow my step-by-step procedure: The sign is to be painted on two sides, and the material consists of a 4 by 8-foot panel of medium-density overlaid plywood, ½ inch thick. A strip of paper, 4 feet wide is folded in the center to draw a fold-pattern for the fancy cut at the top of the panel. (This procedure was previously described.)

The pattern is pounced on the top of the panel and is cut out with a saber saw. All edges are then thoroughly sanded. The panel is brushed and a tack rag is used to remove the remaining dust. Next, using a "throwaway" roller, I apply a coat of good grade white primer to both sides and edges. This is set aside to dry.

On a piece of brown kraft paper cut to fit the panel, I

FIG. 104. Step-by-Step detail of the procedure in painting the "Country Campsites" pictorial is presented by Gregory. Photo lower center shows fish of sign pictured upper center, before lettering was applied. Same fish pattern was used on pictorial on window of Sportsman's bar.

lightly rough out a pattern with chalk. In doing this, I first draw the skyline separating sky and grass in a position that will accommodate the copy. Sufficient space must be allowed at the bottom for the detailed portion of the pictorial, but the lettering on top is the primary concern. I rough in the grass area, the tent, and bare space in front around the campfire. My object is to determine how much of the lettering can be worked into the picture itself to allow as much room as possible for the sky. By adjusting the grass line a bit, I can insert the words, "trout pond" as shown and a good-sized "welcome" at the bottom.

Using the words "trout pond" as a suggestive size, I snap lines for "playground, showers, toilets," which leaves ample room above for the principal lettering, which I then lay out in detail.

The entire pattern is now accurately layed out and perforated. The trees are not on the pattern. These can be drawn later directly on the surface as room permits. Actually all that is needed on the pattern for the bottom part of the picture is a detailed drawing of the tent, the campfire, and three crosslines, one for the skyline and the two lines that separate the grass from the ground area in front of the tent.

Because the primer that I use leaves a flat, toothy surface, there is no need for an intermediate coat of blocking-out paint. Some signmen might prefer to apply such a coat. I do apply a coat of blocking-out white to the edges only to retard further suction.

The panel is set into vertical position and I apply the pattern. At this point of progress only the pictorial is pounced in completion. The bottom guidelines for "camp-sites" and "playground" with its final letter d also are indicated with the pounce bag, because these represent the limits for the trees.

For the actual painting, I prepare just about every shade of paint in the shop, placing a small quantity of each into small 6-ounce juice cans. Bigger cans are used for the white and light blue only to accommodate a bigger brush. For this painting, I shall need one 3-inch brush to lay on the white and blue of the sky, several 1½-inch cutters, a couple of ¾-inch fitches, and perhaps two ½-inch fitches.

To insure layout retention, the pounce lines of the picture should be pencilled before the painting begins.

The paint is arranged on the worktable so the lighter colors are on the far side of the grouping, and the darker colors on the near side. Colors should always be arranged in this way. This reduces the chance that drops of the darker colors will accidentally be dripped into the lighter colors. Next to the jars, I set a can containing a small amount of linseed oil with a bit of turpentine added to it. This is sparingly used, when necessary, to facilitate blending.

With the 3-inch brush, I lay on the entire sky area. This is done by alternately applying white and light blue and blending it together. The white in the can will be discolored, but this can later be used to mix into light blues. The panel is turned and the sky area is applied to the other side. This is the only time the 3-inch brush will be used. The sky area is painted in a matter of minutes and no attempt is made to form precise clouds. The lettering will cover a big part of this background. The blue should be on the light side, and not too dark, to later provide good contrast for the lettering.

Just above the grass at the skyline, I use a fitch to work in a little orange, yellow, purple, and red, fading it gradually up into the blue to suggest sunset. It is sometimes advisable to use a bit of white in this process to sort of "juice up" the colors and to accent the vividness of color.

Next I paint the grass areas using emerald-green and yellow near the skyline, gradually darkening this toward the bottom until it is a very dark green and black. This is blended to some extent as I proceed toward the bottom. However, the final touch-up blending is done a bit more carefully by blending the *lighter* colors into the dark, adding the necessary amount of light color sparingly.

The ground area is then painted around the campfire, mixing as I proceed with white, yellow, red, black, and green to get the pleasant bright ground color, not too dull or dark. The tent and campfire are left blank at this point, painting roughly around same.

The trees are spotted in next, where space permits. This is done in a somewhat "dry-brush" technique. I dip a ¾-inch fitch into medium green and fan most of the paint out of the brush on to the palette. No attempt is made to make actual limbs or needles on the trees. I just put small, individual brush marks in the approximate positions where the green of a pine tree would naturally occur. This is done to form the general shape of a tree. The same brush is dipped into yellow and I stomp a few brush marks on the left sides and the tops of the trees where the fading rays of the sun might in actuality strike them. Then on the right sides, I brush on a few patches of very dark green, blending all of this over slightly into the earlier applied medium green.

308

All that is necessary on trees such as this is to use a fairly dry brush and carefully maneuver the brush marks about until a passable shape of a tree results. It might help you to mentally assume that the remaining sunlight is coming from a position along the skyline, a bit to the left of center. Envision the general position where such light would strike, and all lighter colors are applied at such points. The darker colors would naturally occur on the opposite sides of these lighter applications. Finally the tree trunks are indicated with light brown running at intervals and vertically down the centers of the trees. You can use a small fitch for this, painting with the tip.

The opposite side of the panel is then painted up to the same point in the same way and is left to dry. When I resume work, the pattern is again applied. The pouncing is done with white talcum powder on the dark fields and powdered charcoal on the light areas. The lettering is done first as far down as "playground." "Krueger's" is No. 104 bright red, "Country Campsites" is in black and the rest is in red. (The top three lines are later shaded primrose yellow, one-stroke, using a large quill.)

The tent is painted in shades of khaki with quills first and immediately blended with a small fitch. The interior is black. Tent stakes and seams are dark brown. Logs on the campfire are in shades of brown with grayish-cream log ends. Rocks about the fire are in several shades of gray.

The words: "Trout Pond" and "Welcome" are in one-stroke white. The final touch is the smoke spiral. This is indicated by using the tip of a fitch, dipped in white and almost dry, followed immediately by application of a faint line of gray fanned down the center and just touching the white at intervals.

The entire sign is given a coat of clear enamel when dry since intermixed colors have a tendency to fade. This protective coat is optional.

The pictorials shown in Fig. 104 were done in much the same manner. Note that the same pattern was used for the fish in all instances. The pattern was reversed for the change of position. The corner close-up of the fish shows detail before the "Sporting Goods" copy was applied.

The compensating factor in this background type of pictorial work is that most of it is covered or "camouflaged" with lettering so the artwork need not be perfect. However, the result is an attractive and colorful sign.

You will note that the "Sportsman's Bar" window presents a fishing scene to depict summer and the deer inset suggests winter—or year-around sports. This was not painted on the glass. A hardboard panel arrangement was used to fit into the window on the interior. This was fitted in such a way that it could be removed for window cleaning.

SIMPLIFICATION OF PICTORIALS.

A reverse approach was purposely used in the first part of this instruction in regard to pictorials. By first presenting a slightly more difficult type of pictorial work, the logic is that the discussion to follow should, because of its simplicity, be comparatively easy for you to understand and to accomplish. It is hoped that the three phases now to be presented will provide you with a greater degree of confidence.

One of the most essential requirements in the operation of any shop should be to maintain an extensive picture file. Such a file is referred to by professionals as a "morgue of clippings." You should begin to develop this from the very first day of practice.

At first you do not require an expensive filing cabinet. A suitable box can be quickly constructed. Sometimes a drawer will suffice. The first step is to buy from an office supply store a couple dozen of heavy manila file folders. These are described as "23-cut," "5-cut," etc. This means that the identification tabs at the top are in variant positions. The object is to alternate these folders within a file so one tab does not hide the other. All tabs should be visible for quick reference. If you cannot afford to buy a filing cabinet, you can build a box of a size that will accommodate the folders. This container should have a lid to keep the contents clean.

Into this file you should place clippings of every conceivable type of picture, trademark, lettering, etc., that you might some day need for reference in connection with sign work.

Each of the folders should be plainly labeled, describing the contents and alphabetically filed. Your first folder might be labeled "Animals", and into this you should place pictures of every animal that you come across, both comic and serious. You might have another folder labeled "Costumes" to contain pictures of drum majorettes, bellhops, Uncle Sam, auctioneers, chefs, etc. Other folders might be designated as "Alphabets," "Birds," "Fish," "Mechanized Equipment," "Sign Ideas," "Trademarks," to name a few. The broader the breakdown, the easier the reference.

The trademark file will generally be the thickest and most frequently used file in the container. Clip every trade mark you might need out of newspapers, and magazines, especially those common to your area. In all cases watch the trend of the times. For example, at present there is a special interest in anything connected with space, such as rockets, etc. Also when checking your file for a particular item, if you discover an obsolete trademark, discard it. Do this with any material that will no longer be of use. This prevents the file from becoming too bulky and you can avoid paging through useless pictures, designs, etc.

In line with any copy work, it is advisable to be familiar with the copyright laws. You cannot make an exact copy of registered material, unless it is for the owner, without risk of legal complications. However, most pictures used in a different context, and with a few changes as to color, shape, etc., can sometimes be used without violating the law. Since I am not a legal authority, it is best to personally check the laws because they vary from state to state.

The discussions to follow are based on the assumption that you will be using a projector, but you also can enlarge or reduce designs by using the "square method." But for your own benefit, make every effort to buy a projector. You will never regret it.

The best approach for the novice to pictorial work is to simplify the illustrations as much as possible. The simplest form of pictorial, of course, is the silhouette (see Fig. 105). Frequently a customer will settle for a neat silhouette in lieu of a more complicated picture that you are unable to execute.

FIG. 105. Start with silhouettes.

A young friend of mine in the sign business once contacted me about a horse trailer. His customer wanted a trailer to be lettered and also required the painting of several pictures of a horse's head in full color. The young man was not yet capable of doing this advanced pictorial work. Upon my advice, he suggested to his customer instead, the use of simple silhouette drawings similar to the horse as illustrated. The client agreed and was well pleased with the finished job. Through simplification, he managed to do the job and retained a customer.

The silhouette is not always used for simplification, but for economy as well. A customer might want a full-color picture, but cannot afford the price of same. Or he might feel that the condition of the trailer or vehicle does not warrant such expenditure. This was the case with one of my customers. His horse trailer was light blue, so a horse design was painted on each side and on the front. The silhouettes were painted with brilliant blue and each was outlined with white. The result was attractive and the price was in line with the customer's circumstances.

Incidentally this particular horse design can be an excellent decoration for the gable end of a barn. For example, if it is enlarged, cut out of overlaid plywood and painted white, it looks sharp when attached to the end of a bright red barn. The color of the horse can be adapted to the color of the barn.

A silhouette-form is not necessary in order to prepare a copy. Let us assume that you must design a silhouette of a bird dog to be used as a decoration on a garage door. All you need to do is find any clear picture of such a dog, in side view, and place it in the projector. Cast the image on the pattern paper and just draw a pencil outline around the figure. Omit the details. For example, do not place an eye in any silhouette, because you will then have to follow through and indicate other details. You would no longer have a simple silhouette.

Study the picture of the bird in Fig. 106. This simple cartoon-style has many advantages. Cartoons provide the greatest flexibility. They need not be authentic and seldom is there any attempt to do this in cartoon work. For example, the colors used in the illustration suggest a robin, but the same bird could be changed to represent a bluebird by substituting blue in the gray areas. Such procedure would be ridiculous if applied to serious pictorial work.

This type of art is ideal for showcards, sale banners, etc. If I should use this bird in robin colors on a number of paper banners for a spring sale, the procedure would be as follows: First I would prepare a pattern and transfer the design to each banner. Then I would outline the designs in pencil. For a suggestive background color around the pictorial area, I would use an aerosol can to spray light blue around the bird. I would concentrate the color close-up to the outlines and gradually fade the spray effect away from the bird into the surrounding blank area to cause a sort of halo effect. Next I would paint the bird in the colors indicated.

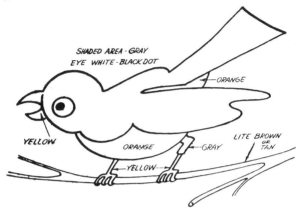

FIG. 106. Simple Cartoon Pictorial.

Although cartoons are usually outlined, I would not, in this case, apply a complete outline around the illustration. The outlining would be confined to the open beak and perhaps the legs. The outlines would be black. If I did not plan to outline the legs, I would paint them a deeper color than yellow such as a rusty orange to provide color contrast.

Those who are a bit more advanced or proficient could easily dry-brush a few applications of lavender, offset on one side with a touch of purple to the branch endings. This could suggest lilacs. In this process the branches would not be "stumpy" as shown, but would be dwindled to points.

Now we approach a more difficult pictorial in the discussion of the fish (Fig. 107). A professional sign artist would not use this method for painting this particular picture. He would blend the colors and perhaps apply a slight suggestion of water, skyline, trees, etc.

But this is one method by which you can, with the aid of your projector, produce a passable pictorial. Especially on a highway bulletin, an illustration such as this need not be perfect. If the over-all shape is authentic and the color scheme is somewhat true to life, the result can be effective.

For the benefit of the beginner, the colors shown on the fish have definite divisions. The black areas are painted black on a full color copy of this fish and the reeds should be painted with various shades of green.

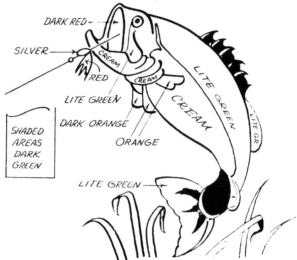

FIG. 107. *More Complicated Pictorial.*

According to your talent, you might choose to improve the color scheme. You might deepen the red in the mouth gradually toward the throat, blending a bit of dark blue to provide depth. Perhaps the cream around the gills also could be blended into a deeper tan on the underside with just a hint of fire-red at the gill divisions. The orange fins also could be blended with slight additions of red or rusty orange. The amount of blending depends entirely upon your ability. Use fitches for such blending efforts.

To prepare a picture with color divisions, select the figure you plan to copy and place it in your projector. When the picture has been projected, carefully outline the image with pencil. Then use a pencil to draw the major color divisions. In blended pictures there is usually a center point where one color merges into another. Draw these separation lines through the approximate centers of such blends. You must use a little imagination to decide where to bring a color to an abrupt end or to continue it and break it at a more strategic point. The knack for this will develop with experience.

Later when painting the design or picture, use the original as a guide to proper color placement.

To supplement this instruction, it is suggested that you secure several books on pictorial art. Also note that many public schools offer adult night classes in art for a small fee. These classes seldom teach art as it is applied to sign work, but the basic fundamentals learned in this way can be adapted to your requirements.

INTEGRATING PICTORIAL AND LETTERING.

People who come to you for signs will frequently mention that they would like "something just a little different" Sometimes this can be done by merely using a line or two of stunt lettering, by the placement of an odd-shaped panel within the layout, or by cutting the sign into an odd shape or design. But there will always be the customer who will insist on a pictorial. If the pictorial is complicated, you might have to refer this person to another shop. Fortunately such people are usually satisfied with a simple pictorial effect and you can manage to do the work.

The real puzzler is the customer who demands that a pictorial be worked into a sign, but because of the copy involved and the size of the sign, you know that there is not enough room for a pictorial. Regardless of explanation to this effect, he will insist on a pictorial. It is at this point where you must use your creative ability to offer him an alternative.

There are several methods of doing this. The "Eat in your Car" illustration in Fig. 108 shows how the entire sign can be converted into the pictorial, providing ample room for the copy. This sign is an exceptionally good example to use because there were several involvements. Similar situations might confront you from time to time.

Originally this sign had the word "Hamburgers" and included a price figure. The customer had a problem. Due to the lack of room and legal restrictions, he could not erect any more individual sign units in front of his restaurant. His principal sign consists of a larger, electrical, plastic-faced sign mounted on two metal posts. On these posts, and below the main sign, he already had a number of auxiliary signs mounted, so we had to adjust these to provide room for the two "Hamburger" units to be attached to each side.

After some time, he decided to stress the fact that people could eat in their cars. The problem was that there simply was no room left for additional signs on the posts. Furthermore he did not want to sacrifice the hamburger signs, since he judged these to be of equal importance. Since the price of hamburger was going up and would no longer be a selling point, I suggest that the signs be repainted as hamburger pictorials and replace the existing copy with the words, "Eat in your Car".

FIG. 108. Pictorial cut-out informs that hamburgers are available, and lettering tells that they can be eaten in the car.

In this way, we were able to get across the new message and still retain the "hamburger image" to emphasize this specialty. The picture speaks for itself and projects the hamburger message without words. This demonstrates the effectiveness of a sign cut and painted to its own image. For instance, a cut-out ice cream cone can advise the public that cones are available. The copy space on the cone can be used for copy completely impertinent to the ice cream. This principle can be used for many products.

When working with cut-out signs of irregular shape, it is essential to consider one important factor. If two such signs are mounted back to back, and if both are sawed into identical shapes, one of the signs must be flipped before painting. You cannot paint two such panels with the identical sides facing towards you, because when they are later mounted on opposite sides, the contours will not match. The matching contour would be to the left on one side of the mount and to the right on the other.

Also in a case such as these hamburger panels, where

5 or 6-inch posts separate the panels, it is advisable to paint
the back sides in sharp contrast to the face sides In this
case, black was used. If the backs were to be painted the
same "crust" color of the hamburger bun on the reverse sides
there would be a distortion of shape on one end as the
motorist viewed the sign from the angle of his approach.
The background of that portion which protrudes on the
opposite side must provide a sharp contrast to clearly define
the sawed outline of the side being viewed from whatever
angle.

The "Grunewald" sign shows how a pictorial effect can
be incorporated within the lettering (see Fig. 109). This
company has a slogan, "We Move the Earth" and generally
on all equipment we use a simple pictorial of the world
globe. This is usually painted as a separate entity. On this
sign, however, there was not room to paint both copy and
globe in separate positions unless the size of the lettering
was severely diminished. So the globe was arranged to fit
within the confines of the letter G. This resulted in a novel
arrangement and provided the necessary room for the
pictorial without sacrificing much lettering space.

FIG. 109. Pictorial map is incorporated in first letter of copy,
not only solving problem of lack of space for pictorial, but also
utilizing pictorial and lettering expression.

The lighter area of the globe is painted a pale green with
dark green land areas. The lettering in the name "Curtis
Grunewald" is painted with black and has a cream-colored
shade. The two bottom lines are dark green and were

lettered in one-stroke fashion with a No. 20 jumbo quill. The field color of the sign is white.

The customer liked this sign so well that he is considering using the big G with the globe as a trademark for his business. This will provide additional work in regard to the pen and ink drawings necessary for the printing of letterheads, etc.

A design such as this letter G and the globe is not too complicated. This can be accomplished for the most part with a compass and a straight-edge. You can easily determine the land areas with a projector.

SIGN PAINTING WITH DEPTH AND SHADOW.

As experience increases, most sign painters put forth a greater effort to put depth into the work or to achieve a third-dimensional effect.

You might not realize this, but when you apply the shading to your first letter, you are striving to impart depth to the work. Simple shading is indeed one of the most elementary forms of third-dimension. The intent is to cause certain words and phrases to stand out from the commonplace copy and to "grab" the eye of the reader. Your basic function as a sign painter is to do more than identify. More correctly, it is to arrest the attention of the viewer by providing enough impact to hold his interest long enough for him to get the message. Most frequently your sign must compete with other signs nearby or surrounding it. If your sign does not effectively accomplish this, you have failed your customer to some degree.

There are various methods of drawing attention to signs, such as, animation, light, reflective materials, sheer size, uniqueness and others.

There are various mechanical ways in which to provide true depth. These would include items such as sculptured or molded figures attached to a sign or cut-out objects and letters mounted to the sign in such manner that they extend away from the sign face as separate entities. These methods depend upon additional material objects, rather than upon actual painting for the third-dimensional effect.

In the early stages of your development, it is essential for you to acquire a good understanding of light and shadow and at least some of the most basic fundamentals of perspective. The following subject matter will principally be concerned with light and shadow and the ability to create the illusion of depth through the process of painting only.

The primary interest will not be directed to the pictorials alone.

Study the photo of "The Skillet" in Fig. 110. This job was done for another sign company. Note the maximum depth that was created. This sign is a two-sided neon drum, built in the customary manner, perhaps 0 to 12 inches thick. The faces are absolutely flat. At first glance, it will appear that the letters in the word "Skillet" are actually extending away from the sign face. The letters in the word "The" appear to be, as they are, flat against the surface.

FIG. 110. Letters at top appear to be flat with rim of skillet, while the others give the illusion of actually standing away from the sign face.

This effect can be created with little extra effort. In this case, the frying pan was painted first in various shades of white, gray, and black. The surface-lettering was applied with two coats of white and outlined with bright red. The depth factor on this sign is the placement of the word "Skillet." The frying pan is painted in perspective, so there is one area that appears closer to the view of the reader. The rest of the picture apparently fades into the distance. The point nearest the viewer is the front edge or rim of the frying pan. To create the "floating" illusion, the lettering must be layed out so that it bridges the nearest edge with a portion of the letters extending above the edge and a portion of them placed below. This procedure will always result in a similar effect.

The background can be a box or any object that provides a suitable perspective. This can be effective on cylindrical shapes. Let us assume that you have painted a pictorial of a long gasoline storage tank. If the picture was painted with the tank in full side view, and you curved the letters to fit the contour of the tank, you could not expect this effect. However, if you painted the same letters in absolute vertical position across the center of the tank at the closest point of perspective, the letters would then appear to be extending away from the tank surface.

Therefore letter placement is the main factor in this treatment. For example, if the word "Skillet" had been moved up to rest completely within the solid black area of the pan, this effect would have been lost.

In addition to lettering, placement can become an important issue in the painting of any object. In my home I have a full-color, life-size picture of Robin Hood with bow and arrow. He has the bow string pulled to full length with the arrow in position. The aim is directly forward and the tip of the arrow is painted in prismatic form. This is a conversation piece because no matter where the viewer stands, regardless of angle, he cannot escape the direct aim of the arrow. The viewer is the target. This is the result of one single factor. When I painted the picture, I purposely fixed the eyes to look directly at me. Therefore even if I walk upstairs and look down at the picture from the upper landing, he continues to aim directly at me. If his eyes had been painted to look slightly to the left or right he would be aiming at an imaginary object. People can never understand why Robin Hood maintains a steady "bead" on them regardless of position.

The answer is in the indisputable law of placement. If a person looks directly into the camera when being photographed, the result will be the same. No matter from what angle you view such a photograph, the person will continue to look directly at you. This is common knowledge to artists, photographers, etc.

Next let us consider the photograph of the cow unit as shown in Fig. 111. Such units form the main part of the background for cattle sales. Other signs and displays flank these units on each side at the sale location. Each unit is built by using three 4 x 8-foot panels joined together. These are constructed to be bolted together from the rear for quick assembly at the point-of-sale and to later be taken apart for ease of transporting.

Upon ordering these units, the customer wanted to convey the impression that a cow had crashed its head through the center of the backdrop. A different breed of cow might be sold each day which accounts for the Guernsey cow pictured in Fig. 112.

FIG. 111. Holstein cow appears to be thrusting head through background of this sign, which is used as "backdrop" for stage employed by auctioneers and other auction officials.

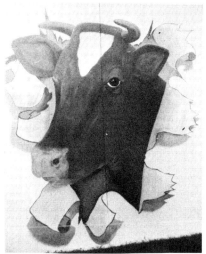

FIG. 112. Guernsey cow replaces the holstein of Fig. 111 on days when only Guernseys are presented.

The most difficult part of this approach was to form the original layout so the head of the cow actually appeared to be some distance away from the sign face. Since the space on each side of the cow's head was limited, the crash effect had to be confined to allow enough space for the lettering.

On the first rough sketch, I made the crashed-paper effect bigger all around than the cow's head. No parts of the paper flanges were placed behind the cow. This was no good and I felt ridiculous. The cow appeared to merely be standing behind a ragged hole looking through, and contemplating me with a stupid look. At this point I deserved such observance.

Finally it dawned on me that if I expected the animal's head to appear to be sticking out some distance from the hole, I would need to provide shaded effects behind some portions of the cow's head. So I arranged for certain parts of the ragged edges to rest behind the head, back of the ears, and particularly behind the nose. By placing a gray shadow under the nose during the actual painting process, it seemed to push the cow's head right out where it belonged.

The backgrounds of these signs are white. The jagged pieces of the crash portion are all in varied shades of light grays with shadows behind the jagged edges to cause these to stand out. The effect of distance is accentuated by suggesting a field and the sky to the rear of the cow. The upper half just behind the cow's head and within the torn edges is painted light blue and the bottom half is painted green. These small color indications gave the impression that the animal was standing in a pasture behind the jagged opening. These colors also provided the necessary color needed to "snap-up" this otherwise drab color area.

SIMPLE CUT-OUT ADDS TO DEPTH.

The photo in Fig. 113 showing the "Pair-O-Dice" sign depicts a simple treatment. The paint only procedure was abandoned in this case to the extent that the dice were cut out of ½-inch overlaid plywood in one solid piece. Since this was a double-faced sign, two units were cut, and again one set had to be reversed when painting so the contours would match when mounted on opposite sides. One pair of dice would hide the back side of the other.

Although this is an uncomplicated sign, it is an excellent example of what the beginner must consider in the study of light and its resultant shadow. Since the letters are shaded on the left and bottom, we must assume that the light is striking the sign from above and somewhat to the right. The dice must be painted accordingly. Note that the dice are painted a darker gray on the bottom, lighter gray on the sides, and remain completely white on the face sides. Technically speaking, there would be no basis for shade at all on the right side of the cube on the left. Considering

FIG. 113. Shades of script and letters add to dimensional effect of the pictorial of the dice. While no shadow would be cast on right face of cube at left, the use of shade completes the cube shape of the dice.

the imaginary light source, this side would be directly in this light and therefore remain white. This was necessary in order to pronounce the cube shape. Such liberties must sometimes be taken to provide the required form. Only another tradesman or artist would notice this.

DEVELOPING SIGN IDEAS.

As a sign painter you are expected to be a good idea man. A customer will nearly always appreciate a masterful piece of work. But there is no better way to gain his complete confidence than to have the additional ability to conceive a good idea, present it to him for approval, and carry it through to completion.

Today's businessman is harassed by other problems and has little spare time. Therefore he likes nothing better than to dump the entire thing in your lap and say, "You take it from here." Even the advertising men of larger firms, although trained to develop ideas, have such a constant drain on their reservoir of ideas that they appreciate dealing with a signman capable of coming up with a few suggestions.

Where do we get ideas? This is a good question. A fertile mind is required, of course, and indeed the biggest share of our ideas will be picked out of our own imagination. However, there are days when even the mind of a genius will draw blanks. Therefore we must supplement our imagination with the ideas of others.

Avoid copying the work of others directly, but try instead to use another's idea as a nucleus and build on it. Insert your own originality and use your own technique. This will help develop your own creative ability.

An excellent example of this is the photograph "See Us First" (Fig. 114). An automobile dealer had consulted me about developing several highway bulletins but wanted something unique. He requested no idea proposals or sketches, but told me to use my own judgment and go ahead with the signs.

FIG. 114. *This was taken from the suggestion of an illustration in SIGNS of the Times, Sept. 1965, issue, page 72.*

On this day my imagination was coming up with zeros, so I began paging through an older issue of *SIGNS of the*

Times magazine (September, 1965). When I came to page 72, I noticed a group picture of several outdoor bulletins, featuring in each a series of eyes. The use of multiple eyes is not a new device, but it can be effective. Years ago a company featured a display, seen mostly in restaurants and bars, depicting a cartoon character with several eyes and eyebrows which resulted in a "shimmering" effect.

So although it was not a new idea, it did stimulate my imagination, which resulted in the comic character with three sets of eyes as illustrated in the photo. The character is in full natural color against a pale blue field. The main part of the bulletin is pale yellow. The man's tie is red, and rests on a black field. The tie is outlined with white and the letters beneath are white, cut-in with black.

The important factor here is that I did not directly copy from the idea source, but used a completely different approach and my own technique. This sign resulted in much favorable comment. Identical units were painted without change. So three distinct benefits resulted—public interest, customer satisfaction, and additional work.

The sign jobs to follow in this discussion are not of a world-shaking variety, but instead are examples of the type of work that will be part of your activity as a sign plant operator.

The "Wisconsin Cheese" bulletin (Fig. 115) illustrates how a plain sign can be improved with the use of a shadow box border. Although this is one of their smaller bulletins, the sponsors of these signs favor the third-dimensional effect provided by this type of frame and specify this on all signs, large or small.

The construction of such a frame is simple. Use 2 x 6-inch lengths of lumber placed edgewise against the face of

FIG. 115. Shadow box border enhances the appearance of a relatively small sign.

the sign all around the extreme outer edges and nail them to the plywood facing from the rear. The faceboards of the border are then nailed to the edges of the 2 by 6s as illustrated. These boards are 1 x 8 inches, but wider boards can be used for larger signs.

For your interest, the color set-up of this sign is as follows: The field is light yellow. "Enjoy Wonderful" is lettered in black. "Wisconsin Cheese" is red with white outlines. The wheel of cheese is painted with off-orange shades, or the natural color of American Cheese, resting on a background of brilliant blue, slightly lightened with white.

The lettering across the bottom board also is blue, but right here this procedure should be severely criticized. It is not good design to apply lettering to the frame boards of any sign. In this case it would have been more advisable to attach a separate board underneath. This board could have extended about a foot longer on each end and cut on a slant or rounded on the ends. (An example of this is shown in Fig. 114). The actual frame boards of a sign should remain plain to set off the sign. Note how the lettering, in this case, crowds the sign and causes a chopped off appearance at the bottom. This was done against my advise.

CARICATURES OF CUSTOMERS. There is the rare customer who requests the use of comic pictures or caricatures of himself on his signs and on other advertising. It is understandable that at the moment, you might not be able to do this, or many of the other things now being discussed. However, it is advisable to consider all procedures that will eventually become a necessity. You can gradually develop your talent and increase your ability accordingly.

Fig. 116 is an example of caricaturization. This should not be confused with the serious type of portrait picture that might be used on election bulletins. Comics are prepared in a simple manner with a minimum of detail.

You might wonder why this type of work qualifies to be included in a discussion about sign ideas. Suppose you have a customer who desires a unique quality within his advertising. If he is a congenial fellow, with a face that would be easy to draw or paint in comic style, then you might suggest the use of his likeness. In my experience, customers have ordered twice as much work than originally planned because the novelty of the idea stimulated their interest in advertising.

Such was the case with the customer involved in Fig. 113. In line with a big promotion, the client was groping

FIG. 116. Pick out odd features to emphasize in caricature work.

for a novel advertising approach. His most basic need at this time was for unique newspaper ads. Five comic pen and ink drawings were prepared. These were full figure cartoons of the man in various positions with basically the same head on each. The expressions were changed to suit the position. He was well pleased with these drawings, has used them frequently, and has extended such use to sale banners, outdoor advertising, etc.

A few basic rules apply to this work. Caricatures are most easily accomplished when the subject has certain irregularities of features. It is much more difficult to do a comic picture of a handsome person with regular, well-defined features. But, if the subject has a big nose, large ears, a bald head, fuzzy hair, wears horn-rimmed eyeglasses, etc., it is simple to catch a resemblance. The odd features are exaggerated. In newspaper cartoons this is done to a gross extreme. But when dealing with a customer you are limited to his personal vanity and must use care in exaggeration or you might offend him.

In line with pronouncing the odd features, a large nose and small eyes and beat up hat would immediately suggest Jimmy Durante. The convenient way to gain this knowledge is to follow the newspaper editorial cartoons and pay attention to what the artists do to political personalities.

It is not advisable to suggest caricature work to a customer who has regular features or, for that matter, to an introvert with a "no-nonsense" attitude.

MISCELLANEOUS IDEAS. The illustration in Fig. 117 shows how a problem was handled for a customer some years ago. This firm owned highway bulletins located along the four main approaches to the city. The desire was for some sort of message during those periods when a sale was in progress. The signs were 8 x 12 feet. It was suggested that a 1 x 16-foot board be attached below each sign. Both sides would be painted white, and the commonly used side would contain the lettering, "Featuring Name Brand Merchandise." The copy on the reverse side would read, "Store Wide Sale Now in Progress." These were attached as shown on illustration.

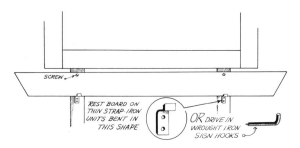

FIG. 117. Arrangement for changeable slats for highway signs to permit display of timely messages.

When the sale began, an employee of the store would be sent to the locations to turn the boards around. The boards were later reversed to teh original position when the sale ended. This solved the problem without blotting out any part of the main sign; the method was effective and convenient. This attachment could be planned to eliminate the need for screws. The logic of using screws was that if the board could be removed too easily, it might be used by a "thrifty" kid to help sheet up the side of a tree house or for some other youthful endeavor.

The picture in Fig. 118 shows how you might put a little zip into the lettering of a stock car or similar vehicle. This is in full color. The picture is self-explanatory.

Your quest for ideas should never cease. Be prepared for those days when your "idea factory" shuts down. The folder in your file labeled, "Sign Ideas" should be well used. Take advantage of the high priced talent that develops ideas for national advertising. Clip all such material and place it

FIG. 118. A bit of comic indication of speed for a stock car or similar vehicle.

on file. Pay special attention to trucks passing through town, highway signs when traveling, commercial signs in other cities; to matchbooks, labels, packaging, etc. Keep a camera handy or prepare quick sketches. This idea file should be replenished constantly. It can be the best "friend" you ever had when you are hard up for an idea.

THE SLACK PERIOD BEFORE
CHRISTMAS. To some sign operators the season preceding the holidays is a busy and profitable period. Others find it to be a slack time of the year. Experienced operators are aware of ways in which to stimulate business and to turn it to their advantage. Newcomers should not accept this as a slack period, but should instead promote it to its full potential.

The biggest problem is to secure the work far enough in advance. One consolation, especially in smaller cities, is that the customers who do wait until the last minute and consequently have to be turned down, will usually be the first to contact you the following year with orders in hand.

There is a variety of work to be done before Christmas time and if you need work, you should advertise the fact that you offer this service. People will be interested in displays to be placed in front of their homes or places of business. Greeting signs, either on the windows or for the interior, are required. Cut-out figures for lawn displays are in demand.

Generally if you complete one striking display or sign for a citizen or merchant, somebody down the block will soon contact you to do similar work. Customers do play "follow the leader," and good work advertises itself.

These displays need not always be complicated. Fig. 118 provides an example of simplicity. No cut-out work is involved. At this time you might not be able to do this pictorial in blended form as shown. This illustration is used merely to suggest an idea. You can simplify this picture to a great degree and retain effectiveness.

FIG. 119. *Simpler than some of the more elaborate Nativity displays that are popular, a display like 119 can have effectiveness, as well as economy, in its simplicity. Such pictorial treatment can be simplified ever further.*

You might use this idea of an open Christmas card, but select a less complicated design and lettering style. Some hardboard manufacturers furnish free brochures with detailed patterns for cut-outs, complete with instructions regarding construction, color, etc. Your projector can make it possible for you to do work that might otherwise be beyond the realm of your talent.

Many ideas can be developed by saving all greeting cards that might one day be adaptable to Christmas display work. Holiday issues of newspapers are loaded with ideas and many of the greeting ads contain illustrations of simple composition. Children's coloring books also provide an excellent source of material.

Because such units are used only once a year, and then temporarily, less expensive materials can be used for construction.

If cut-out figures are involved, there is a factor in regard to the saw cuts. When using a saber saw the cut will usually splinter or "rough up" the cut more on one side of the material. The rough cut can occur on either side, dependent upon the blade. Unfortunately it is usually on the good side facing up. In this case, you should reverse the pattern and saw the figure from the reverse side. The smooth edge will then result on the side to be painted. Try a sample cut in a piece of scrap to determine the action of the blade.

Erection can be a problem in cold sections of the country, especially when there is deep frost penetration. For small units, thin metal rods can be driven into the ground, and the units can be fastened to these on the rear side with metal pipe or conduit straps. These are the half-round straps with a flange on each end, commonly used by plumbers and electricians.

For larger units, metal posts can be used somewhat like those used in the erection of municipal stop signs. I use snow fence posts, purchased from a farm equipment dealer. These usually contain a series of pre-drilled holes along the upper length of the posts.

An effective method for driving these into the ground instead of using a post maul is as follows: Secure a piece of iron water pipe that will comfortably fit over the top of the post. This can be about 30 inches long or longer. Attach a heavy dead-end cap on one end of this with a pipe wrench. To pound the post into the ground, slip this pipe over the post, and place the post in position. Next take hold of the pipe with both hands, raise it up as high as possible without its slipping off the post, and bring the pipe down on to the top of the post with strong, solid whacks. Of course, you must start the post into the ground at first by holding the post in one hand, and manipulating the pipe with the other hand, with less enthusiastic whacks. The pipe itself can be used to push the post into vertical position during the initial phase of the driving process.

Metal posts penetrate the ground quickly with this method. If the frost is too intense to permit the use of posts, then a free-standing rack or device must be improvised to hold the units in vertical positions.

There are attractive possibilities for the shadow box effect in displays. You might paint a solid back panel in deep blue with star effects to suggest the night sky. About 4 to 6 inches in front of this, dependent on the depth available, you can place a panel consisting of cut-out camels, shepherds, etc. Subdued, indirect lighting can be arranged in between the panels so a pleasant glow is cast onto both figures and background at night.

So fill those slack days with work. Do not overlook the window banners, signs painted directly to glass store windows, etc. It is absolutely essential to advertise the fact that you do this type of work.

COMMENTARY. In regard to this entire discussion on pictorial work, perhaps you will never become an expert in this field. But with the aid of a projector and simplification, you can broaden the scope of your work.

Beginning with the most simple forms and gradually expanding your attempts, you might be able to accomplish more than you now expect. So do not be too discouraged with your early efforts.

This does not imply that you should attempt to do artwork that is "over your head," or too difficult. If any given job is beyond your capability, it is much wiser to refer the customer to someone with more experience than to "botch" it up and displease your customer. He will respect you more if you are truthful in regard to your ability.

We often hear the statement, "You're born with that!" This statement disgusts me. Each time I hear it, I think, "Boy, if you only knew how many back-breaking hours were spent in order to learn a trade, you wouldn't talk so stupid!" You are born with nothing except the ability to yell for more milk! It is true that some are born with the natural ability to grasp a certain subject or to more rapidly develop a talent. Einstein could not count up to ten until he learned how to do so. Even latent talent must be developed. What it boils down to is that everything must ultimately be learned.

Chapter 30

Introduction of Plastics

Perhaps no one product has done more to revolutionize the sign industry than plastic. The advent of acrylic plastics and similar products provided the sign trade with practically an unlimited potential.

Many believe that the use of plastic signs began quite recently. Although invented earlier, it was not until about the mid 1940s that plastic was used to any great extent for signs. A short period of trial and error followed before the tremendous impact of this great medium was felt by the sign industry. Here at last was a medium that provided the industry with the opportunity for maximum creativeness; a medium that afforded a full measure of effectiveness for both day and night sign advertising.

As it is with many new products, some of us were at first skeptical about the material. This was mainly due to ignorance regarding the product. General know-how was in its infancy.

With their usual strong code of ethics and reliability, the manufacturers soon supplied us with the necessary instructions and specifications to speed the intelligent use of their products. They have continued to do this through the years and have kept us abreast of all the new developments in the field of plastics. It is mainly through this splendid cooperation that the sign industry has progressed so rapidly in this fascinating medium.

The foregoing has been related to you as a beginner because the ability to work with plastics will be of vital importance to your development as a sign painter.

There is an ever-increasing demand for plastic signs. Constant improvement by both manufacturer and sign designer makes possible today what was perhaps not possible a year ago. New techniques and more adaptable auxiliary products continue to nourish this progressive trend.

The major purpose of this book is to get you "off on the right foot" as we approach each phase of sign painting. It would be impractical within the pages of a general instruction book to even touch upon the many facets necessary to complete a major plastic installation. Indeed this would require a separate book, involving contributions from a number of men, each being a specialist in his own field.

Few men, if any, could carry through a diverse project such as this from inception to completion without contributive knowledge and manual help.

The various types of plastics have certain characteristics not found in usual sign materials. Write to the manufacturers for literature. These people best understand their product, so study their instruction brochures, etc., thoroughly. This material can enable you to avoid much trial and error.

With several exceptions, practice work on plastic is basically the same as described for glass. You cannot "shave" or trim the letter ends of the strokes with a razor blade as you can on glass. You can use the cellophane tape method of stripping.

Although most plastic work is done with the spray mask method, there remains a need for hand lettering. This would include lettering dealer's names on courtesy panels, etc.

Since most freehand lettering is done on acrylic plastic, it would be advisable to use this for practice. Although this is available in clear, a sheet of opaque white is suggested for practice. This can be purchased from any plastic dealer.

Layout marks show up plainly on the sheet. The constant removal of the practice strokes for further work will help to acquaint you with the problems encountered in plastic work.

Your first difficulty will be the electrostatic charge common to plastics. Never wipe the surface with a dry rag. the static build-up caused by vigorous wiping with a dry rag will be sufficient to magnetically attract half of the dust in the shop.

Should you attempt to letter on this surface, the paint might literally spurt from the brush onto the sign. It is impossible to letter on such a surface (see Fig. 120).

Excellent plastic cleaners are available from sign suppliers. Some contain a component to remove static. Static removers also are available in spray cans. For general wiping, such as removal of layout lines, use a clean, damp chamois skin.

Practice procedure follows: Place the panel on the work bench. If it is clear acrylic, position the panel over a piece of white paper for optimum visibility. Clean off excess dirt with damp chamois skin. Remove static with either antistatic liquid or spray can.

FIG. 120. *"Boy, this sign's got more pull around here than I have."*

Layout marking is done with a soft, graphite black pencil. (This pencil is available as a separate item in most supply catalogs, described: "will mark on any surface.") A 2½-inch stroke is suggested for letter height in practice.

The brush work can be done with a quill or flat as preferred. On a properly prepared surface, you will find that bulletin colors work very well.

When the practice panel is full of strokes, remove the paint immediately with rags saturated with white gas or turpentine. Clean the resultant film right away with soap and water, rinse, and when dry the practice procedure can be repeated.

Ideally it is best to adhere to the procedures recommended by the plastic manufacturer. There are times when this is not convenient for various reasons. There is no intent here to dispute the manufacturer's instructions, but among the things we do learn through long experience is to improvise. Regarding the turpentine for removal, I have used this hundreds of times with no adverse results. Also over a thousand plastic panels have been lettered in my shop with bulletin colors, lettering enamels, etc. All have stood the test of time as well as any normal surface. Some have been exposed for 10 years with excellent durability.

Caution! Before using any solvent, whether mild or strong, always *test it first* on the flange or extreme edge of the panel. Do this with every panel even though it appears to be from the same batch. Never apply a solvent to the actual face of a plastic panel until this test is made. Some plastics will withstand the attack of solvents. Other forms of plastic might dissolve or "craze."

Before continuing actual practice work on plastics, it might clarify things a bit to dispel a few of the misconceptions regarding the field of plastics in general.

In conversations with other signmen, I was surprised to discover how many avoid doing plastic signwork. Their excuses were typical, such as, "too much fooling around," "too many different kinds of paints and materials involved," "the surface is too tricky," "not enough profit for all the grief," etc. Adverse attitudes such as this are prompted by lack of know-how and are a roadblock to progress.

The very fact that I am not a big operator, nor a specialist in plastics, places me in a better position to void the above remarks. If I can manage to cause my work with plastics to be pleasant and profitable, any other average signman can do likewise.

Combine a normal understanding of the product, workable procedure, the ability to improvise, and you have all the necessary ingredients.

It is hoped that as we now continue with practice work, you might cope with each difficulty as it occurs. Up to this point you have learned how to eliminate static and how to practice. Continue this practice until a good degree of skill is acquired and until you develop a sort of "feel" for the surface.

Do not admire the big, beautiful plastic spectaculars and expect to jump directly from the practice bench up to that level of perfection.

Major plastic signs are handled with the spray mask method, screen printing, etc. Hand lettering is confined mainly to incidental work such as lettering dealer names on privilege panels.

Parent companies furnish their dealers with volume produced signs. The major portion of a single sign such as this contains the permanent message of the parent firm or distributor. Usually at the bottom there is a much smaller blank space reserved for the dealer's copy. These are referred to as courtesy or privilege panels.

Sometimes these panels are separate units that slide into self-contained slots at the bottom of the main sign. Panels such as this can be removed and replaced without touching the main sign within the basic part of the unit.

In other cases, the courtesy panel is merely a blank space on the main panel so the entire sign surface must be handled. Your first attempts at doing salable lettering on plastic should be limited to this elementary type of work.

Assuming that you have practiced diligently upon a variety of surfaces, in both comfortable and awkward positions, it should be possible for you to do some of this work right on the location. It is often more convenient to make small copy changes in this way than it would be to remove and replace very large panels.

You were previously advised to confine your early attempts at actual signwork to simple jobs, such as small real estate signs, etc. There is no reason why plastic courtesy panels cannot be placed in this category.

This type of sign is usually installed with the bottom at least 20 feet off the ground and is seldom exposed to close scrutiny. Therefore slight flaws in the lettering are scarcely noticeable.

Most courtesy panels are surface-lettered by hand. The firm that supplies the original sign usually pays for this work and has economy in mind and with good reason.

The beer brewing industry, for example, has more basis for economy of dealer identifications than any other. These people are familiar with the fickleness of the retailer, especially the tavern keeper. It is not uncommon for a beer company to erect a large plastic sign only to have it removed in less than a month and replaced with another sign from a competitive company.

In my experience I changed the tavern name on the same sign as often as three times in less than 2 months. In some cases, the lettering paint was still in the elastic stage at the time of removal.

This is the reason why the spray mask methods recommended by the manufacturers of the plastics are seldom used for courtesy panels. These unreasonable and frequent change-overs demand the fastest and most economical methods possible.

The illustration in Fig. 121 is an example of a short word on a long panel. A bold, extended letter is used to gain length and to provide maximum impact for the word "Eat."

Fig. 122 embodies most of the errors common to the inept sign painter. The word "Eat" has been congested in the center. The center stroke of the letter is too high and stubby. The cross stroke of the letter A is too low.

The most obnoxious error is the placement of the clumsy

EAT

FIG. 121. The right way to present a short word in a long panel, a problem that will be frequently encountered in lettering dealer names on plastic privilege signs. Extra-expanded letter fills space nicely and is easy to read.

FIG. 122. Congested lettering and clumsy scrollwork is the wrong way to solve the short-words-long-panel problem. Center stroke of the E is too high and too shabby, and cross-stroke of the A is too low. Dot after T is an out-of-place effect also.

scrolls on each end and the heavy dot under the letter T. This is a common fault of some signmen. They cannot tolerate empty space on any sign, but fill it up with embellishments. This type of gingerbread merely distracts from the message. Scrollwork should certainly never be used in any circumstance until it can be done gracefully.

Unless specifications demand otherwise, try to letter your first courtesy panels with opaque black. If color is used, avoid conflict with the colors on the main sign. Do not "flash-up" the privilege panel to such an extent that it will detract from, or overshadow, the well-designed message of the supplier. A privilege panel should be lettered in a simple, neat manner.

When working with plastic signs and auxiliary products, it is advisable to adhere to the specifications and procedures provided by the manufacturer. Such information will be printed either directly upon the product or on the brochures that accompany the purchase.

To follow the manufacturer's recommendations insures best results. However for reasons of economy, lack of immediate supply, etc., there will be occasions when you will have cause to improvise.

We just discussed the frequent copy changes required on certain courtesy panels. Quite often, the reverse is true. Many merchants and dealers have plastic signs installed that are quite certain to be permanent and without a fore-seeable need for change of copy. At times such as this, correct procedures should be used. If the courtesy panels are to be lettered with opaque black, then it is satisfactory to use the freehand lettering method.

Should colored lettering be required, it is then advisable to use one of the several masking methods. Many of the parent firms supply units upon which as much as half of the sign face is available for the personal use of the dealer. Therefore the dealer is most apt to desire a neat, colorful lettering job on this portion. This might involve a duplication of his own symbol or trademark. Since this instruction is confined to the basics, no attempt will be made to describe the involvements of such intricate design.

It does seem advisable to at least introduce you to the proper procedure for the application of color to plastic sign surfaces. Almost all signs of this type are furnished with the field or background color applied. The explanations to follow will therefore be concentrated on surface applications.

The end result of any application of color to a plastic sign should be a smooth, even color distribution without mottled areas or brush marks much like frosted glass. Although there are other methods to achieve this result, the masking process is most common. All supplies needed are available from local sign supply firms or through mail order catalogs.

First let us consider the liquid film method. The masking medium employed is usually a water soluble coating that can be sprayed or brushed upon the surface. Apply a thin uniform coat to the entire area to be worked upon. Complete coverage is essential with no allowance for bare areas.

For layout it is best to prepare a perforated pounce pattern. When the masking film is dry, place the pattern on the sign face and tap a charcoal powder pounce bag over the perforations to transfer the patterns directly to the surface of the film. This pattern can be applied directly to the bare plastic surface prior to application of the film, providing the film is to be sprayed. But many beginners, lacking spray equipment, might be forced to brush coat the masking film. In so doing, the pounce pattern dots would be obliterated. In either case a special graphite pencil (No. 8008), can be used to draw the letters directly upon the plastic panels. There is still some chance of losing part of the layout with the brush-on method. On a two-sided sign, it is best to prepare a pounce pattern regardless.

When the pattern has been transferred to the surface, use a sharp pointed No. 11 knife to cut around the outlines of the letters. Very little pressure is required on the knife (see Fig. 123).

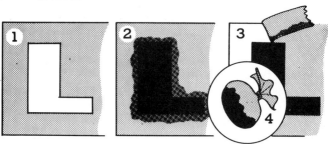

FIG. 123. Film is in position in (1), letter has been cut and the film peeled away, leaving the area ready for the application of color. In (2) paint is applied to the exposed letter with spray, brush or roller. Stipple pad is then used, as shown in inset (4), to even out color, if brushed. The solid black and dark surrounding area depict contact area. In (3) the excess masking film is stripped off after the paint has dried.

Next remove those portions of the film from the areas that are to be painted. Leave the remaining film intact. The desired acrylic colors can now be sprayed on the exposed areas or applied with a brush or small roller. If a brush is used, the paint should be stippled.

To prepare a "stippling pad," wrap a square section of fine mesh cheese cloth or window curtain material around a wad of cotton batting. The size of this is determined by the size of the area to be stippled. In this process, apply the paint to the exposed letters with a brush. Do not paint too far ahead before stippling. For example on a 6-inch letter, paint about two letters at a time and immediately tap the stippling pad over the paint until all brush marks and mottled areas are evened out. It is a good idea to apply a bit of paint to the face of the stipple pad before using or you might lift too much paint from the first several letters. You need do this only once at the very start of the stippling process.

Bulletin colors can be used with the stipple method instead of acrylic paint. Technically the spray method provides the best results throughout this process. When the paint is dry the remaining film can be peeled off the sign, resulting in a neat, transparent design.

The second masking method involves the use of the ready-to-use films available in roll form. There are several varieties. One is a laminated two-layer material, consisting of an adhesive sheet of film with a heavy backing paper. Another is available in transparent single-layer form. Once these films are applied to the plastic, the procedure is essentially the same as that used for the liquid film application.

COMPROMISE PROCEDURES. An attempt will now be made to acquaint you with compromise procedures which can be used successfully with a bare minimum of equipment and material.

You must zero-in on the following fact: The manufacturers understand their products and best results are obtained by following their specifications.

But it is impossible to describe compromise procedures —and these must be recognized as such—without sometimes being at odds with the manufacturers. These are not one or two-shot experiments. I have used these procedures hundreds of times with success. The results have withstood time span tests ranging from 5 to 10 years.

Later on as you become more competent and affluent, you can decide which procedures are practical to continue and which to discard in favor of those specified by suppliers, which employ highly trained technical personnel to develop their products and to help you with information on contact.

The best way to describe several compromise methods is to present a typical job that can be done with the equipment and materials one usually has on hand.

The signwork: A restaurant has changed ownership. Along the structure's roof ledge is a series of plastic signs previously installed by a soft drink company. The beverage firm's personal advertising consists of separate units. Adjacent to these units are two individual courtesy panels consisting of opaque white plastic. The panels are 2 feet high and 8 feet long. The previous owner's name is lettered with solid black paint upon the surfaces of these panels.

The new owner's requirements are that you remove this lettering and replace it with the new name. He wants the word "Lou's" on one panel and the word "Cafe" on the other. He desires red letters instead of black. Because the procedure to be used does require that the letters be outlined, you must at this point explain that the red letters will be outlined with black. There is seldom an objection.

The instructions: Remove the panels from the frames

and take these to the shop. Place them across a table or on the floor with the face sides up. Lacquer thinner will be used for removing the old lettering. It is a very strong solvent and it will cause some types of plastic to dissolve or craze. Although mentioned before, it is extremely important to first test the reaction of the lacquer thinner on each and every piece of plastic. Conduct this test along the extreme edge or flange of each panel. If the plastic remains clear, glossy, and stable in this area after a thorough test, it is then safe to apply to the face of the sign. If adverse results occur, then a patented remover for plastics must be used.

To remove old lettering: Saturate a rag and generously apply the lacquer thinner to all of the letters on the panel. Generally the paint dissolves rapidly. If the paint is very old and brittle, it might be stubborn. In such cases, sprinkle non-scratch cleansing powder, such as the old-fashioned type of Bon Ami®, directly over the lettering. With rags constantly saturated, continue the rubbing action. Meanwhile keep the rest of the lettering wet at all times to allow for continuous dissolving action. Change rags frequently and wipe off the excess paint residue as you progress.

When the paint is completely removed and the sign face is clean, saturate a clean lint-free rag with lacquer thinner and apply a coat of this to the entire sign face. Do not wipe off this final coat. Allow it to dry and this will help eliminate the electrostatic charge common to plastics.

Avoid sliding motion across the plastic from this point on. Do not wipe with a dry rag. Excessive sliding of pattern papers, brisk rubbing with the pounce bag, or the constant sliding of the knuckles in one area might cause a new static build-up. Some of the patented static-eliminators will retard repeat build-up for a longer period of time.

The lettering—without the use of masking film is accomplished as follows: Let us assume the finished letters in "Lou's" are to be 20 inches high. The letters are to be of the thick-and-thin variety, with the thick strokes 6 inches wide and the thin strokes 4 inches wide. Prepare a perforated pattern or layout directly to the sign face with a sharply pointed mark-on-anything pencil as previously described. Allowing for the outline of approximately $\frac{1}{2}$ inch, prepare the layout with the letters 19 inches high, the wide strokes of the letters 5 inches, and the thin strokes 3 inches.

Apply the outline with a lettering quill or flat brush using either opaque black bulletin color or lettering enamel (see Fig. 124). Paint around the outer edges of the letters.

344

When the outlines are dry, the red is applied with regular bulletin color. Before application of paint, prepare a stipple pad. The red can be applied within the confines of the black outlines with a small cutter, or you might prefer to use a lettering brush around the inner edges of the outlines and fill in the larger areas with a cutter.

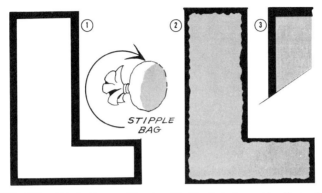

FIG. 124. (1) Letter outlined with black before stippling. (2) Appearance of letter following the stippling process. (3) Finished letter after second outline application.

After the red paint is applied to each letter, immediately stipple the letter before the paint "tacks." Tap the stipple pad up and down against the red area. Work out the brush marks and maneuver the pad on the wet surface until the paint appears to have a sprayed-on appearance. Before any stippling begins, don't forget to apply a bit of paint to the face of the pad. When stippling the red be careful not to stipple over the outer edges of the black outlines. The primary reason for the outline is to serve as a stop-line for the stippling process.

The stippling process can be done most effectively by backlighting the panel. Either place the panel on a pair of skids in front of a window, or light it from the rear with floodlights.

Following the stipple work there will be an irregular overlap of red paint on the black outline as shown in letter (2) in Fig. 121. When the red paint is dry, all that remains is to again outline the letters with black. This can be done quite rapidly because the outer edges and peaks of the original outlines remain. You can stay a slight bit to the inside of these outlines and confine the precision to the inner edges of the black outlines where they join the red centers. The second black outlines are applied only to cover the red overlaps. The completed sign should favorably compare to a spray mask job.

Throughout the country sign plants handle plastic signs in various ways. Many of the large firms fabricate plastic signs from start to finish within their own facilities. Others purchase the sign blanks or panels in the necessary size and form and do their own painting, wiring, and erection. Some sign plants find it more convenient to merely prepare a precise pattern with color indications and turn this over to a plastic company for complete fabrication.

There is an ever-increasing trend toward this last method by both large and small sign firms. This might be due to a shortage of competent help, an overload of general signwork, lack of equipment, or for other reasons. The plastic firms that specialize in this type of work and do so every day are qualified in both skill and equipment to provide the ultimate in efficiency and excellence of result.

A constant overload of both sign and commercial artwork places my personal operation in the latter category. Fortunately there is an excellent plastic company located about 7 miles east of our city. On large or complicated jobs, it is beneficial to me to take advantage of their skill and equipment by preparing patterns and presenting this work to them for completion. Meanwhile my time is free to continue with other work.

As a new operator, you might not have ready access to a nearby plastic firm or perhaps have not yet established such a suitable connection. This is not sufficient reason for you to avoid plastic work entirely. Regardless of how small your operation might be, a respectable amount of plastic sign work can be done within your shop, using materials commonly on hand, and with a minimum of equipment.

In addition to the signs turned over to the plastic firm, I still complete hundreds of courtesy panels and do not bother this firm with small or less complicated signs.

Shortly before preparing this instruction, I was contacted to repaint a small double-faced plastic sign. To validate previously mentioned procedures, I *purposely* did this entire job by improvising on every step of the job. This was done, even though all the specified materials were at hand, to prove to you that it is possible to improvise. But this was certainly not done to imply that this is correct procedure.

This was therefore painted with contrived improvisations

to provide a basis for this instruction. There now follows a step-by-step description of the procedure.

The double-faced sign consisted of two plastic panels, measuring 24 x 36 inches in size. Screen printed on the inner side of each panel was the original multi-colored message of a nationally advertised product. The customer wanted this paint removed and repainted with his own copy, "Sunrise Natural Foods." Also he mentioned a "sunrise design" in casual style that might be used as a permanent trademark. Design, layout, and color were left to my discretion.

To remove the existent paint, I placed both panels face down on a work table. Next I tested lacquer thinner along the extreme outer flange of each panel. The result of the test was favorable. After testing, I poured a generous portion into each of the saucer-shaped panels and spread it about. The paint dissolved rapidly and after the panels were spotlessly cleaned, I applied a coat of patented static remover to both sides of each panel. This application was the one compromise to correct procedure, because these panels would be subjected to considerable handling.

The panels were to be surface lettered so the inner sides were sprayed white. To do this I placed each panel upright against a window for backlighting. Using an ordinary pressure spray can of good quality white enamel, I applied a thin "fan coat" to each panel. This process was repeated at 10-minute intervals until five or six coats of paint were applied. This resulted in a good body of paint and still provided effective transparency. In the spraying process the spray can should be held at complete right angles to the surface. The arm must be moved steadily back and forth. Never should the spray unit be held at center and the wrist twisted to spray off to each side at variant angles.

The time in between spray applications was used to prepare a perforated pounce pattern for the entire sign (see Figs. 123 and 124).

There was no time limit to this job, so I applied the sun design first. For masking purposes, I cut two rectangular pieces of white pressure-sensitive marking film with a controlled adhesive. This material is normally used for lettering, etc. These pieces were cut large enough to accommodate the sun design. The design was transferred to these films from the perforated pattern with a pounce bag containing black charcoal powder. The outlines of the design (Fig. 125) were penciled and then cut out with a No. 11 knife. The cutting was done before application to the sign faces.

This is optional. The solid rectangles of film could have first been applied to the faces and then cut.

The pattern was then taped to each sign face and the layout transferred as usual. Removing the backing paper

FIG. 125. Production procedure of "Sunrise" sign is illustrated in Fig. 126.

from films Nos. 1 and 3, these were placed in position. Film No. 2 was set aside for future use on this job. The area of the sun ray was left bare. The edges of the film surrounding the ray (No. 2) were rubbed firmly along all edges for adhesion. A coat of lemon yellow bulletin color was brushed to this area with a No. 20 gray quill and immediately tapped upon with a stipple pad for uniform transparency. I carefully removed the two pieces of film and replaced these on the original backing sheets which had been set aside for this purpose. The wet yellow paint was wiped from the edges of the face sides of the film before it was applied to the second panel. At this point, all that existed on the panels were the two yellow sun rays. The lettering was then applied with opaque black bulletin color.

The following day, film No. 2 was placed exactly over the yellow on the first panel. The outer edges of this film had no functional part in this phase of the work. The only concern was to position this to serve as a mask for the central half-circle. The edge of this film was "thumbnailed" for seep-proof adhesion. A length of cellophane tape was stripped across the bottom as shown in Fig. 126. The exposed half-circle was then painted with No. 124 orange bulletin color and stippled. The film and tape were then removed.

In the illustration you will note a thin horizontal line running across the bottom of the sun design and extending on each end. This was painted into position with No. 102

bulletin color, using a thin striping quill with a mahlstick for a guide. The beginner might prefer to allow the orange to dry and mask the area for this stripe with cellophane tape, if he is not yet adept at striping.

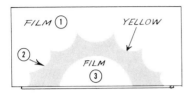 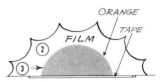

FIG. 126. Production procedure of "Sunrise" sign shown in Fig. 125. On the left, films Nos. 1 and 3 are in position. Area No. 2 is exposed and ready for yellow color application. Note cellophane tape along bottom. On the right, Film No. 2 is in position, tape at bottom and Area No. 3 is exposed and ready for orange color application.

Although conventional methods were purposely bypassed in this procedure, the results were comparable to a job done in the specified manner. Because of past experience with the same paints, good durability can be expected.

SPECIALIZATION. We are living in the age of progress. From an inventive standpoint, there has been more development within the past 20 years than during the 100 years preceding this period.

One can scarcely become familar with new processes, equipment, and materials before others hit the market. This applies to all fields of endeavor. There is an ever-increasing need for specialization. This will soon be a fact of life. No one person can hope to sufficiently expand his knowledge and ability to keep abreast of such rapid development. Also this would be financially impractical, if not impossible.

Within the sign industry, the need for specialization has had its greatest impact within the bigger cities and upon the larger sign plants. To a lesser degree, this fact must be considered by the smaller operators.

It is doubtful if the need for either the one-man or the small city sign shop will ever be eliminated. But such operators must prepare to flex according to contemporary demands.

A good example of this would be the small operator and his work in regard to plastic signs, the electrical wiring of same, and the erection.

There is an effective trend developing in small cities. Customarily the general electrical contractors confine their work to the normal demands of their trade. Occasionally they are contacted by local businessmen to repair electrical signs. Calls for this type of service increase to such extent that it becomes advisable to purchase a boom truck, because in addition to sign repairs, the electrical contractor has other work that can be eased with the use of a crane.

The acquisition of the boom truck soon results in calls from small sign operators within the surrounding area for erection work. This first contact often develops into a long and profitable relationship between the owner of the crane and the local sign shop.

The electrical contractor through his sign repair work, plus the sign erection, is soon contacted by other firms in regard to completely new plastic sign installations. Since he has no desire to enter the field of general sign painting, he now contacts the local sign operator. So we now have two specialists working together.

At this point the third contractor enters the picture. Within a reasonable driving distance of most cities, there is a plant that fabricates and wholesales plastic signs. Because most of his customers furnish their own patterns, he does not find it expedient to hire a steady sign painter or designer.

This situation now develops as follows: The businessman desires a plastic sign installation. The electrical contractor is willing to supply this need, but must first contact the sign painter. Together they discuss the requirements of the sign with the client.

With the specifications in hand, the sign painter then contacts the plastic plant to get a rough estimate of cost. Thus the sign painter makes his second contact in this hypothetical chain of events.

After receiving the estimate, the signman adds his own expected charge and presents this total bill to the electrical contractor. He, in turn, figures the total cost and finalizes the arrangements.

When all details are settled, the signman prepares a detailed pattern for the plastic wholesaler, who then fabricates the sign. The electrical contractor then installs the unit to complete the job.

So here we have three contractors working together, each being essential to the other. If the small shop operator hopes to exist and compete with the larger plants, this is the sort of working relationship that must be developed. It is the only way in which the small operator can cope with the necessity for specialization (see Fig. 127).

FIG. 127. "Hey, Gertie! How about another tranquilizer?"

The success factor here is that each member of this "team" should be skilled in his trade. A conscientious tradesman has little respect for a slip-shod workman. The end result can only be as good as the weakest link in this chain. Cooperation, honesty, and respect are necessary for a combination of talent such as this to succeed.

This combined effort also stimulates the sales volume of each of the three companies involved. As the sign painter in this combine, you will soon discover the benefits.

The electrical contractor will frequently need your services in the manner just discussed. He is certain to call upon you to prepare patterns. His needs might involve secondhand plastic signs. In these cases you possibly can handle the entire repaint jobs on such units without contacting the plastic firm.

Also he is equipped to handle your erection work until you can enlarge and purchase a crane.

Since the plastic firm does not employ a sign painter,

it is natural that he will contact you whenever he has need of patterns or hand lettering.

Because of their connection with sign work, both the electrical contractor and the plastic wholesaler are often approached in regard to general sign work. If your working relationship and the quality of your work is good, they will refer these contacts to you.

Likewise you are in a position to reciprocate by sending to them a considerable amount of work.

Specialization also can be extended to those sign firms that specialize only in electrical units. These operators occasionally require general sign painting, but their most frequent need will be for patterns. To intelligently supply this need, you should be aware of certain problems and how to avoid or surmount them.

Plastic sign panels are manufactured in various shapes. Figure 128 shows the most commonly used forms. These are in addition to the plain flat panels, which are not pictured.

Frequently there will be some confusion in regard to size. When contact is made for the patterns, the client will generally list the outside measurements of the panel. Such dimensions are useless unless you are familiar with the shape of the panel to be used or can personally measure the lettering area.

FIG. 128: When the pattern for the plastic sign is completed, color instructions can be placed on the face of the pattern.

If contact is made by phone or in person, this confusion can be cleared up immediately. But if the specifications are mailed to you or dropped off at the shop during your absence, measurements such as 4 by 6 feet or 4 by 8 feet are meaningless.

Round-figure dimensions such as this, almost always,

are the outside measurements. It would be impractical to proceed with such vague information.

As the designer of the sign, you must know the actual size of the sign face before you can determine the space available for the copy. The shape of the panel also is a factor. Therefore you must contact the client for more accurate specifics.

The full face example in Fig. 129A shows a 4 by 6-foot panel. Note how greatly the copy area diminishes. The protruding face of this panel drops away from the **outer** flange at an angle. The drop of this angle, plus the width of the flange and the necessary margin, reduces the copy area to a maximum of 38 by 63 inches. You will notice that the side margins are 4½ inches, compared to 5 inches at top and bottom. Whenever the maximum area is used in layout, the side margins need not be as great as those at top and bottom.

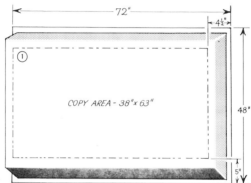

FIG. 129A. A 4 by 6 foot panel after it has been formed.

No. 129B on the illustration shows the end views of three panels of variant shape. The first example is the angle-shape just discussed. This form allows more freedom of margin on the actual sign face. The angle itself provides some margin around the entire sign face. The margins on this type can, when necessary, be reduced accordingly.

The square form does not provide this extra allowance of margin, so the layout is designed the same as it would be upon a flat panel. The margins as shown on the two top drawings is the suggested minimum. Especially on a square panel, wider margins would be preferable.

The round panel is rather old fashioned and is no longer used as much as it was some years ago. You will encounter this shape most frequently in repaint work or second-hand signs. Note the reduction of available copy space in comparison to the other two panels. This type of sign face is not only saucer-shaped on all edges, but the four corners of such a panel also are round. This further diminishes the space. The suggested margins, as shown, are ideal. However, letter-size requirements, etc., often force the sign painter to extend the letters or designs partially over the curved edges.

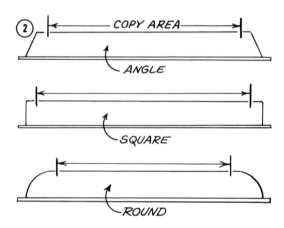

FIG. 129B. *The end views of three formed panels of various shapes.*

Briefly this demonstrates why the outside measurements of a panel are of small value. It is essential to know the size of the sign face, and helpful to be familiar with the shape.

Being new to the trade, you might assume that this confusion of size, etc., would be eliminated after the first several dealings with the same client. This is not the case. After five to fifteen years of working in connection with other electrical sign firms, I still have clients who call on the phone and say, "Four by Eight." Like a broken record, I patiently say, "Gimme the size of the face!"

The size factor can often be a source of disappointment to the ultimate owner of the sign. At the time of sale, the businessman might have been informed that he was getting a 4 by 6-foot sign. In regard to outside measurement, this would be true. At the time of erection he is sometimes astonished to find that the "big sign" he had expected has taken on such small proportions. Since he knows nothing about extrusions, flanges, and angles, this is understandable. The extreme result is that some of these people mistakenly feel that things were misrepresented to them at the time of sale.

As the pattern maker, this does not reflect upon you. But whenever you personally sell or contract for such a sign, it is ethical to explain the facts. The customer will then know exactly what to expect and, because of this, he might order a larger sign.

PATTERN PREPARATION. To intelligently prepare a pattern, you should be familiar with the customary working procedure of the plastic company that will eventually produce the sign panels. You will soon know the preferences of the plastic plant that fabricates your personal signwork.

When preparing patterns for an electrical sign firm, it also is advisable to be familiar with the requirements of the plastic company to which this firm takes its work. Only with such knowledge can you prepare the patterns to be compatible with the method of production used by each plastic plant.

Some sign companies paint a full-color reproduction of the sign on white poster paper and present this to the plastic plant to be used as a pattern. This method is especially suitable when color or design is complicated, involving trademarks, pictorials, etc.

If the pattern consists of larger letters only, these are layed out in the usual manner and accurately outlined with heavy pencil lines. Either brown or white paper can be used.

Quite often the sign will contain both large and small lettering. My procedure in this case is to outline the larger letters with pencil and to paint the smaller letters just as I would on a paper banner. This brush lettering would apply to letters 6 inches high or less and would depend somewhat on the letter style.

You might prefer to draw all the letters with precise pencil outlines. However, experienced signmen can generally do the smaller letters faster and more accurately with a brush. These can be lettered with any color or type of paint you choose. This color is changed as specified for the sign during production.

Unless the plastic company specifies certain colors, it is usually your job to plot the color scheme. It is then advisable to ask these people whether the sign is to be flashy or conservative. You should at least have some idea of color preference. When the pattern is completed, you can place either color indications or instructions directly on the face of the pattern. Any other information that might be helpful in production should likewise be indicated.

These patterns need not be perforated unless so specified by the plastic company. Most of these people who do the intricate work using your patterns are highly skilled. Never underestimate their ability. From constant application of designs, lettering, etc., they develop an acute understanding of layout. Also their needs might vary. If they request white paper, don't try to substitute brown. Their procedures require certain specifications.

COMMENTARY. This brings to an end our little "peek" into the field of plastics. The sole purpose of this brief instruction was planned to introduce you to this fascinating medium. The hope is that you might become interested and eventually intensify your effort. The use of plastics rates a top position in the sign industry. The possibilities are practically limitless. How far you choose to go in this field is your decision. It is suggested that you begin now to learn all that you can. Plastics are here to stay!

Chapter 31

Artwork for Reproduction

With all of the materials now available, it is possible to do artwork for reproduction by using completely mechanical procedures. The variety of work that can be done in this way is limited, but it is sufficient to make it well worth your while to study the instructions to follow. Do not skip this discussion because you lack confidence or feel that you do not possess enough talent to do this type of work. It might surprise you to discover how simply much of this work can be accomplished once you have the necessary know-how.

All of this will be explained later as we progress. To begin the discussion, it should be interesting to learn how sign painting can automatically lead the signman into doing such artwork.

Occasionally you will be approached by a customer to design and develop a trademark. This type of request usually comes from new companies, but old established firms also might need the same service if they are introducing a new product or an additional service. Others might desire a complete change of trademark because their prevalent design is not in keeping with the modern trend.

While this activity might not constitute a major part of your business, it can be a highly profitable endeavor. At no time has there been a bigger demand for such service. Years ago it was customary for the average firm to use the same trademark year after year. At present both large and small firms are constantly searching for a new look and some change their designs, at least partially, quite often.

Considering the ever increasing stress being placed on advertising, it is advisable for the signman to have some idea of how to develop a trademark.

If you are not too skilled in lettering or artwork, your first thought might be, "Why not simply advise my customer to contact a regular commercial art studio to have the original trademark designed?" Your logic could be that you will be content to have the subsequent signwork involved.

This line of thinking has several flaws:

First: You might not *get* the subsequent signwork, because the minute you tell your client to go to the art studio you might be surrendering his business. Art studios frequently include sign painting within their services or have a working arrangement with another sign firm. Or your customer might lose confidence in your ability and go elsewhere for any follow-up work.

Second: Some large firms prefer to have their advertising done by one company and avoid chasing from one firm to another.

Third: The budget of a small company can be limited and insufficient to hire a top-notch, big city art studio to do this work. The primary reason for contacting you could be because such firm is willing to accept a less elaborate design, one that is within the bounds of your talent.

Fourth: When you originate a trademark for a customer, he will invariably feel that since you developed the idea that you are the only person who can properly execute any future work. Although this is a misconception, it is a safe bet that you will get all the follow-up work involving the trademark.

Perhaps the foregoing will qualify the constant stress on the point that you should not let the work get out of your hands!

If you qualify to develop the trademark yourself, there is no problem. Should you be able to do so, then consult with your client and accurately determine his needs. Then personally contact an art studio to do the original artwork. Again your customer's financial status must be considered. But even if you only break even on this phase, the subsequent sign work should more than compensate you.

For this discussion, a job was chosen that involves most of the procedures used in the development of a trademark and the resultant signwork.

This customer has been in business for many years and we handled their work for 15 years. When contacted to design a completely new name and trademark we were swamped with work. The owner was in a big rush for the trademark, etc., so I suggested that to expedite things, he should contact another company. In doing this I broke one of the cardinal rules that you have been advised against—sending a client elsewhere. Fortunately the situation worked out in our favor.

The company requirements were to have the new name, "Scotty," designed upon a shield to form an emblem. To supplement this the officials wanted a picture of a Scotsman, or a dual trademark, wherein each could be used separately or in conjunction with the other. They were not satisfied with the design submitted by the other company, which was understandable. The word "Scotty" was merely printed with a "garden-variety" of broken italics in all caps. This alphabet is so common in use that it could hardly provide the unique quality required for an individual trademark.

The picture of Scotty consisted of a full figure, a very old and feeble appearing Scotsman holding a gnarled cane, tottering legs, seamed face with bags beneath the eyes. The drawing was complicated with much intricate and unnecessary detail. This would be costly to reproduce on any future signwork.

There are key considerations in the development of any trademark. The designer should try to develop a type of lettering that is unique. After long exposure to the public, this lettering should be individual enough to be recognized at a glance without actually reading it. A standard alphabet cannot provide this "one-and-only" status.

In this case, what must we consider when planning a suitable pictorial? What should the picture convey? What must gasoline retailers strive to promote? Power! Get up and go! Eonomy! Service! Traditionally any reference to the Scotch indicates thrift, regardless of design, although I have known some very generous Scotsmen. But does this old and feeble specimen, who would fall over without his cane indicate "Get up and go?" In his obvious physical condition would he be able to provide service? Certainly not!

It is essential to adapt any picture to complement the product it represents. In this case the figure should be well designed, because in a sense, he must eventually become a little "public relations man" for his product. The product or business to be advertised must always be carefully considered. The design should be in keeping with the same. A speedy letter for speed, heavy treatment for power, a dignified approach where dignity is significant.

We will now discuss the actual logic and mechanics used in preparing the "Scotty" material. Our first decision is to do away with the full figure. Unless a very large sign is involved, the head of a full figure is too small to effectively convey much expression.

In discussion we agreed that it was essential to put some "snap" into the picture. My first step in the designing process was to junk the old-man idea. Instead I decided to use a youngster with a pixie expression. With a sparkle in the eyes and vivid colors, he would suggest friendly service and the other "zip" needed in the advertising of gasoline.

The public should immediately feel a spontaneous friendliness toward a comic pictorial. Since the Scottish theme was being used to indicate thrift, my concern was to design the picture cute enough to avoid resentment by those of Scottish descent. The wrong implication in regard to any race of people can often cause a reverse reaction.

My additional hope was that the finished design would appeal to the children. It is surprising how much influence the kids have upon their parents' buying habits, merely by saying, "Oh Daddy, let's stop here!"

These details might seem to be of small consequence, but advertising experts agree that there is much downright psychology needed in advertising. It is likely that many of the products sold in today's supermarkets are purchased because the kids like the package. The contents are secondary.

In the case of "Scotty," I did not at once prepare the pen and ink drawing. A rough sketch was drawn with pencil. Then a 20 x 30-foot bulletin was erected on the edge of the east ramp of the main station and painted. A full-color pictorial of Scotty was painted in the upper righthand corner, as shown in Fig. 130. (This photo is a bit distorted, since it was taken from an upward angle).

FIG. 130. Use of head, only, enables more effective presentation of local expression.

The color set-up was as follows: His tam was painted emerald-green with white stripes. The green was darkened in the area just beneath the tassel. The tassel was bright with two shades of red; bright on the front section and a red, the band was black and the dollar sign was black on a lemon yellow disc. The ribbons on the right were painted near-maroon on the rear section. The face was in flesh tones with pink cheeks and nose. White highlights were blended into the face to suggest light. His hair was in blended colors of orange and brick color.

THE FINAL DESIGN OF THE TRADEMARK.

To maintain an intelligent sequence in the development of a trademark, it is necessary to now continue with a discussion of the pen and ink work as it pertains to this particular job. The illustration as shown in Fig. 127 was largely done freehand with small dependence on mechanical helps. It is not expected that you will be able to do such work at this point of progress. You can later refer back to this description as occasion demands.

Normally this technique would be described in the final pages of this instruction on artwork. However, immediately following this, you will be provided with step-by-step instruction for doing reproductive artwork in simple form and almost entirely with mechanical applications.

We shall now consider the final pen and ink drawing for this trademark, including the word "Scotty" applied to the face of the emblem. The one absolute specification for this job was that the customer desired this particular shape of emblem and also the horizontal "dart" immediately below the lettering. So I was obliged to adapt the lettering to this definite size and shape. My main concern was to design a letter style that was quite unique. One of the better ways of doing this is to begin by "roughing out" quick pencil sketches of possible adaptations of the word. In the process, one must mentally consider the limitations of the prescribed space and ignore standard alphabets.

After drawing about a dozen random arrangements of the word "Scotty," I finally decided to use the one shown. It was then trued up and adapted to fit within the confines of the emblem.

It is advisable to mention at this point that too many talented sign painters shy away from doing artwork for reproduction. Some have remarked that they have difficulty in doing small work. If this is your problem, you will be relieved to know that it is not necessary to prepare the original in small size. The printers can reduce a large illustration to a great extent. A certain amount of reduction actually improves artwork. For example, if a line contains a slight crook or wave, this will nearly correct itself when reduced. If your pen and ink talent is limited, it is possible to make the drawing larger. You can then use brushes to execute much of the work, perhaps all of it.

The amount of reduction is entirely up to the artist. Many artists maintain that the best method is to prepare the original twice the size of its intended use. Some prefer to draw to exact size, although this requires maximum skill. Others will commonly prepare the original as wide as 18 to 20 inches to be reduced to letterhead size. Large reductions require the workman to use great care. The letter openings and spacing must be large enough to prevent them from closing up when greatly reduced. A line that is too fine on a large drawing could virtually disappear in such process.

A step-by-step description will now follow in the preparation of the Scotty illustration in Fig. 131. The original drawing is to be 9 inches high. On a sheet of paper, I draw a vertical center line and measure and indicate the space within which the emblem must fit. Next I lightly draw the left half of the emblem only. Due to the irregular shape, this must be done freehand. These lines are adjusted and readjusted until they present the required form. The design is then accurately pencilled with a soft lead pencil.

The paper is then folded through the vertical center with the pencil marks to the inside. I place the paper on the drawing board with the reverse side facing up. With my thumbnail, I firmly rub all over the back of the section just pencilled. This process transfers the marks from the left side to the right side of the center fold. When opened up, the entire outlines of the emblem are visible. The fainter lines on the right half are now gone over with a pencil. The word "Scotty" and the dart below are lightly pencilled within the outlines and when in accurate form are precisely drawn with heavier lines.

The comic head is then drawn with pencil to fit within the 9-inch vertical limit. This finished pencil drawing is then presented to the customer for approval.

The more accomplished artist might avoid this preliminary work and draw directly on the cardboard to be used for the finished artwork. However, we are proceeding with the assumption that we are not extremely accomplished and must use cruder methods. On simple work it is frequently possible to draw directly on the cardboard. I have found it to be convenient to draw complicated illustrations on paper and later transfer the design to the bristol board. In this way, all corrections, erasures, etc., are made on the

FIG. 131. Step-by-step procedure in creation of this trademark is related by Gregory.

paper and not on the finished drawing. The less erasing one does on bristol board, the better surface one has upon which to work. Even the best bristol boards suffer somewhat from too much abrasion. A neater job results, and if the finished artwork is ruined, the original paper drawing is available. These paper roughs can be filed for possible future use.

For the finished drawing, I will use high surface, 3 ply, 100 per cent cotton fiber bristol board, referred to by some as pure rag. Two surfaces are popular in this material. The smoother type is sometimes called "high" or "plate" and is intended for fine pen and ink work. The other is referred to as "medium" or "kid-finish" and has an egg shell surface. The latter has advantages in regard to shading procedures. When shading pencil is rubbed over this surface, it hits the high spots and results in a pebbly appearance.

One hundred per cent rag bristol is recognizable. All you need do is hold it up to the light and it will be transparent, much like a lamp shade. This material is white all the way through and withstands considerable abuse. Ink can be erased from this surface and it remains white and workable. The cheaper cardboards have a gray straw-board filler and the slightest erasure can ruin a drawing. It is foolish to use cheap boards for illustrations.

Using a No. 2 pencil, I scribble over the back side of the paper covering the entire area of the design on the opposite side. This is used in the manner of a carbon paper. Next I fasten this to the bristol board in proper position with small pieces of masking tape and accurately draw over the lines with a sharp No. 4H drawing pencil. Why not use carbon paper instead of the "self-carbon"? Carbon paper is messy and defies neat erasing.

The illustration will now be drawn with pen and ink. My policy is to first do the most difficult portion of any drawing. This is where a serious error is most apt to occur. In this way a new drawing can be started with at least a minimum of time invested.

It is apparent that the extreme outer line of the emblem will be the most complicated. Using a D-2 reservoir pen, I draw this freehand. Irregularities of line are common when drawing a continuous curve such as this, even if it is possible to use french curves. These can be corrected when the ink is dry with white tempera color, poster color, latex, etc., using a small brush suitable to the paint. You would use the same technique employed when cutting-in around letters. A word of caution—ink cannot successfully be applied over showcard color. If an entire letter must be replaced, it should be erased and reapplied with pen and ink. A good quality, fresh black India ink should be used. If some brands of ink once freeze and thaw out they become useless. Such ink will no longer withstand erasing.

The cartoon of "Scotty" is drawn next, using a C-3, flexible nib reservoir pen, alternately reducing and increasing pressure for line variance.

The black area is painted around the "Scotty" copy with a red sable and black showcard color. The dart-like peak can first be applied with pen and ink and a straight-edge, either rule or triangle. Black poster color also can be used instead of the card color. Some artists will prefer to use pen and ink to cut-in around the entire design and fill in the large areas with a brush. India ink is not too effective on large areas since it does not cover well enough in one coat to provide the jet black necessary for reproduction.

Artwork for reproduction is not confined to the use of pen and ink. Pencils and other techniques can be used, but in all cases it is essential to check the intended printing process. Limited equipment or lack of knowledge can sometimes prevent a printer from reproducing certain forms of artwork.

When the drawing is completed, an aerosol spray can is used to apply a coat of fixative. This can be either matte finish or clear.

It should be mentioned that most trademarks with irregular shapes have within them a "key" for proper placement. The customer should be advised of this so he can properly advise the printer and others who reproduce the design. In this case, the top line of the dart beneath the word should at all times be in absolute horizontal position. The drawing will then be in correct position.

Much follow-up work has resulted from this design through the years. First I made additional separate drawings of the emblem so each could be used individually. The word "Scotty" is often used without the emblem, especially on highway bulletins. Small patterns were made for emblems to be used on attendants' uniforms, bowling shirts, etc. Quite frequently a body has been added to Scotty to illustrate certain points on signs, in newspaper ads, brochures, etc. For example, he might be riding on top of a rocket, holding up pennants, placing out a "welcome mat," holding up a bank savings book, etc. Other work, such as decals for the gas pumps throughout the area, was involved in addition to plastic signs. This was what I meant when I previously advised a flexible trademark. It creates repeat business year after year and provides the signman with a foundation upon which to base many new ideas for interesting signwork.

MECHANICAL ARTWORK FOR REPRODUCTION.

It is possible for the average sign painter to do a substantial amount of artwork for reproduction. This can be done with mechanical applications. The one absolute personal requirement is an understanding of correct layout and spacing.

Do not quickly brush this aside with a defeatist attitude by saying, "I can't do it." You *can* do it! All it takes is perseverance and knowledge of the process. The addition of this service is one way to supplement your sign work to fill in those slack periods caused by cold weather, rain, or lack of regular sign work.

The instruction to follow will be an effort to teach the basic fundamentals. The extent to which you confine or extend this work is up to you. If you develop an interest and decide to advance, then you will necessarily have to provide yourself with further instruction.

It is suggested that you first learn to do the forms of artwork that are in constant demand. This would include the design of letterheads, business cards, headings for newspaper and magazine ads, matchbook covers, etc. There also is a need for this work in line with brochures, house organs, annual reports, and host of other items.

In recent years printing equipment has been condensed in size and simplified to a point whereby many firms have their own printing departments. No longer is it necessary to send artwork to engraving firms to secure plates. Often, the printing can be completely done on a local level through offset methods.

Years ago this type of artwork had to be done by hand in a complicated, laborious fashion. Few signmen had sufficient training or the right kind of talent to do this work. Some sign painters, however, also are accomplished technical artists and adept at pen and ink work. Just a few years ago, I was still doing television lettering, etc., by hand because I had not yet realized the value of the materials now available.

Today within most any sign and art supply catalogs you can find everything you will need to do a professional job. My reference now is to transfer lettering or alphabet sheets, shading screens, texture, and symbol sheets, etc.

The lettering sheets are available in two basic varieties. These categories are divided still further into sheets that have certain characteristics suitable for the intended purpose of use. One variety consists of lettering mounted on clear acetate sheets. These are described as "adhesive lettering sheets." When using this product, you must cut out the entire square of clear acetate to which the letter is affixed and mount this upon the artwork. This will look much like a piece of cellophane tape with a letter attached to it. Some brands have a shiny finish, others a matte finish.

This variety is the most durable because when application is completed the acetate sheet remains over the letter, providing a natural protective coating. However upon presentation to your customer, it is plainly evident that it is a "paste-up" job and not original work. To the intelligent customer this should cause no concern because his main objective is a neat piece of artwork.

The second variety is the transfer style. You need only to remove the backing sheet, place the alphabet sheet over the artwork, with the desired letter in proper position. You then rub over the letter or burnish it, and when you lift the sheet, the letter only will adhere to the artwork.

This variety has no covering and appears to be original pen and ink work. It is much faster and easier to apply. It is suitable for lettering personalized diplomas or certificates, using Old English, scripts, or other suitable alphabets.

When the artwork is complete and all smudges and guidelines have been removed, it is wise to apply a protective coat of spray fixative. This comes in aerosol cans which are available at most art and sign supply outlets. It is advisable to test the spray fix on a sample application of the product being used *before* applying to the actual artwork. This avoids the possibility of ruining the illustration should the fixative cause curling or "lifting" of the lettering. When this does occur, it is difficult to trace the cause. You should never assume that because a certain brand of lettering withstood the application of a certain spray fix at one time that it will do likewise 6 months later. This assumption can be made if you are using the same sheet of lettering and the same can of spray fix. But it is advisable to test each new sheet and each new can of spray. Either manufacturer might have changed the formula and therefore the original test would no longer be valid.

Be careful and apply a very thin fan coat. This dries rapidly and it is better to apply several thin coats. The highest quality spray fix can ruin the artwork if you load on a heavy coat in one application. Artwork that might receive much handling, such as diplomas, should be given five or six thin spray coats. A good matte-finish (flat) can be worked over in any medium after application. The shiny type of permanent spray fixes are generally only applied after the illustration is complete and requires no additional work.

All the catalogs from which you will be ordering pressure sheets include complete descriptions and instructions for proper application.

Your first step would be to consult your supply catalogs and order all the free catalogs offered concerning pressure sheets. Each catalog presents alphabets in many sizes, also sheets containing arrows, scrolls, numbers, rules, etc. It is advisable to have a variety of catalogs, because the alphabets and patterns not available from one firm might be offered by another.

The standard type faces found in most print shops are generally available in most catalogs. Additionally each firm offers a number of "hand lettered" alphabets. One supplier specializes in hand lettered selections.

It is good procedure to alternate the hand lettered varieties to a big extent with the standard type faces. This provides the personal touch or freehand flair desired by your customer.

Illustrated in Fig. 132 is the principal part of a letterhead design. This was a two-color job requiring two drawings. My procedure would be as follows:

FIG. 132. This 2-color job required two drawings.

On a thin piece of paper I trace an outline of the three counties and route of the Wolf River by placing a paper over a road map. This is the master drawing, so the map must be in the correct position on the paper. Turning this paper over, I pencil over the drawing area on the reversed side to make a "self carbon."

Next I cut two pieces of No. 73 plate bristol board, 100 per cent rag in content. These are cut the same size as the tracing paper or master. All sheets are exactly 8½ x 11 inches. The master carbon is then placed over each of these pieces and with a sharp pencil I go over the lines, transferring the map and river outline to each.

This is to be a two-color print job, so a separate drawing must be prepared for each color. I now have two pieces of bristol with this map outline in exactly the same position on each. One of the drawings will consist of the lettering, the arrow, and the river only. The other will contain only the map. One piece of the bristol is placed on the drawing board and I accurately draw over the lines with a pale blue pencil. The original pencil lines are lightly erased. The blue lines endure light erasing and remain. The blue pencil is used because pale blue lines do not reproduce. However, recently some printing firms have been using highly sensitive reproduction equipment that picks up the slightest mark. So the blue lines must be extremely light.

Guidelines are drawn and the pressure lettering is applied as illustrated. Care is taken to arrange the lettering to rest between the county line divisions. The lettering is intentionally placed off-center to achieve a casual, yet well balanced layout. In application these script letters can be connected throughout the sentence, but the broken script effect as shown is intenitonal. Spray fix is applied at this point. The arrow and river line are now drawn freehand with india ink. This completes the first drawing.

Next I place the second piece of bristol over this drawing and place it on a light table. (this can be done against a convenient window). 100 per cent rag is transparent and the positions of the lettering show through. Tiny dots are placed at all points where the lettering will intersect and the lines must be broken. The lettering would be confused if the outlines of the map ran across in continuous line.

The map outlines are now applied with a ruling pen and the shading screens are applied (see your catalog for instructions). Not that the top and bottom screens are the same density. The center screen is lighter for definite contrast. Spray fix is not applied to this second drawing.

When the letterheads are printed, the map area is printed first in bright blue. On the second run through the press, the first drawing is printed over the map area with black. The color registration possible to the printer can only be as accurate as the original drawings. His job is easier if the two drawings are placed in exact position on two cards of identical size.

A one-color job would obviously require only one drawing. To further simplify procedure, the pen and ink lines could be eliminated with the exception of the river. The shading screens would be sufficient, providing that enough contrast existed between the screens. Also a suitable arrow could be used from a pressure sheet consisting of many miscellaneous arrows. If lettering is to run across screens, it is sometimes better to prepare a separate set-up for the screens. For various reasons, lettering over a screen on a single drawing will take on a fuzzy appearance and not be as sharp as the lettering that is printed on the open areas.

So actually the only freehand work on this drawing would be narrowed down to the outline of the river and the cutting of the screens. In regard to screening, some artists prefer to use the needle method for cutting as suggested by most manufacturers. I prefer to use a No. 11 cutting blade.

POINTERS ON REDUCTION.
It was previously mentioned that artwork is often prepared in larger form and reduced as required in the reproduction process. Round figure measurements can be mentally calculated at once. If the printed artwork is to be 3 x 6 inches and you plan on a one-third reduction, you know immediately that the original drawing must be 4½ by 9 inches. But when both dimensions are fractional, this figuring can be complicated.

Figure 133 shows a simple method to enlarge or reduce a drawing and retain the same proportions. You need only draw an exact outline of the specified dimensions, extending the bottom line to the left. Then draw a diagonal line as shown, extending far past the upper righthand corner. In this case, the original artwork will be 6½ inches wide. So at this point on the bottom line, you would draw a vertical line extending upwards. The point at which this line intersects the diagonal line (No. 1) determines the height.

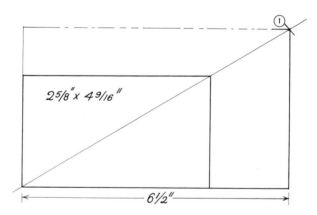

FIG. 133. Simple method to enlarge or reduce a drawing and retain the same proportions.

Regardless of the width, the correct point of height occurs wherever the vertical line intersects the diagonal line. If you decide to make the drawing 18 inches wide, the height would correctly revert to 2⅝ inches upon reduction if all lines were accurate.

On irregular shapes you would still draw a regular

squared outline of the area. The outermost pen and ink marks, both vertical and horizontal, would be the starting points for such an outline.

Reductions also must be considered in the use of shading screens. For example, if your drawing was twice size and you desired a 60-line screen effect on the reduction, you would use a 30-line screen on the original. These reductions are usually illustrated in the screen catalogs.

When preparing illustrations for reduction it is advisable to check these occasionally with a "reducing glass." In this way you can predetermine the finished appearance.

INSTRUCTION FOR MECHANICAL APPLICATIONS.

Through experience you will become familiar with the individual characteristics of the various brands of pressure and adhesive-type lettering and related products. Your skill will increase, and you will discover that there is no end to the creative effects possible. The versatility of these materials will become increasingly more apparent.

Theory is a fine thing, but it takes performance to achieve actuality. So do not be discouraged if your initial attempts at this mechanical type of artwork are a bit on the clumsy side.

Regarding pressure lettering, shading screens, etc., there are short cuts and professionalisms that normally would be learned only through experience.

The shelf life of pressure sheets is unpredictable. There is no way to determine how long the supplier had the sheets in stock before your purchase. When any of these application sheets, regardless of type or design, become too old their effectiveness is questionable. The letters and designs might become brittle and do not transfer properly. Parts of a letter might adhere to the artwork and the rest will cling to the backing sheet. The adhesive-type sheets from which the letters, screens, etc., are cut, will dry out and the adhesive will not adhere to the artwork.

If part of a letter breaks off when transferring by pressure, it might be possible to patch this with pen and ink. If not, it is advisable to apply another letter. You might be able to erase the faulty letter. If there is sufficient space between the adjoining letters, you might press a small piece of cellophane tape over the broken letter, burnish this, and lift it off. Also the letter can be carefully scraped off with a small, sharp cutting knife. The adhesive-sheet type can be removed by lifting one corner of the transparent material with the tip of a knife or cutting-needle and stripping it off just as you would a small piece of cellophane tape. This is why it is best to use a good 100 per cent rag, plate-finish bristol, because it will withstand erasures and other corrections.

Since shelf life must be considered, it is not wise to overstock. Do not store the sheets in a hot, dry place. Do not stack too many sheets on top of one another in flat boxes. The continuous weight of the top sheets can ruin the letters or other designs on the bottom sheets by pressing them too tightly to their own individual backing sheets. Experienced users who do stock a wide variety and a large number of these sheets, try to keep them separated in a filing cabinet, on edge, so there is no weight upon any of the sheets. Also, the sheets can be stored in a cabinet with shallow drawers.

The signman who does this work to a lesser extent, should use the sheets as soon as possible. This requires planning, because you will have a number of broken alphabet sheets from which certain letters have been completely used with many of the other letters still remaining. There are numerous trick ways to use these left overs. Such methods will be described later. For the present we shall consider one of the more conformative methods which is especially useful on donation or near donation jobs.

The three-stage illustration in Fig. 134 (1, 2, & 3) is an example of a booklet cover in which an unusual number of various alphabets have been used. This was planned to utilize nearly depleted alphabet sheets. Normally one would not use this many variations of alphabets on a well designed cover. This was done with as much tact as possible without sacrifice of too much quality.

Assume that you were to do this cover design. You would proceed as follows: The artwork is to be prepared to actual size, 8½ x 11 inches, with no reduction. It is to be printed in blue and red, so two drawings will be required. The blue area will contain the map and most of the copy, so this should be done first. This drawing also provides the key for the placement of the red application to follow:

Find a picture of a map near to the size desired. Trace this directly on the bristol board in proper position also indicating the outline of the county area. Place a sheet of the shading screen over the map area and lightly rub your fingers over the general area of the map. With a No. 11 knife (or needle) cut around the design, staying about a ¼-inch away from the outer edges of the map. Carefully lift the screening sheet from around the map and set it aside.

The next step is to cut around the actual outline of the map and lift the scrap screen from around the edges and discard. Also cut out the county area and lift the screen to expose the white bristol board. Lay a piece of clean paper over the screened area and thoroughly burnish it, beginning at the center and rubbing the burnishing instrument toward the edges. Good adhesion is essential.

The lettering is then applied as shown in drawing No. 1. Follow the instructions in the catalog. Some brands vary the instructions for application to suit their own product.

FIG. 134. (1) Art for dark blue printing. Lettering and screen are pressure sensitive. The 40/8 emblem was cut out and mounted as a unit. All of this is in black for sharp photography and then printing in dark blue.

This particular job is simple because of the margins. When applying the letters in the four top copy lines, begin at the right margin and successively apply the letters toward the left. With this type of layout it does not matter much where the uneven or ragged margins occur as long as they remain within the width limit of the artwork.

The extreme bottom line requires centering. This lettering might be applied to a separate strip of thin cardboard at random. Again it must not exceed the width limits. The strip of cardboard can then be cut down to comfortable size and easily attached to the artwork at center. Any design to be cut out can be entirely covered on the rear side with double-coated masking tape. In this way you can cut through the design and the tape at the same time. After cutting, this enables you to peel the backing from the other side of the tape to expose the adhesive and press the unit in place without fooling around with glue. If you prefer you can use liquid or paste glue, spray adhesive or mounting cement.

The placement of the word "Shawano" is not too difficult. One easy way to position it properly is to lightly indicate the width of the word in the desired position. Place the letter W at center of this span. Then apply the three letters on each side.

The 40 et 8 triangle is furnished to you printed in black on a thin white material, commonly called a "glossy." You must cut out this design with a small cutting knife and mount it as a unit over the screen. This completes the first drawing.

To prepare the second drawing, cut a piece of bristol to the identical size of the first illustration. Place this over the card containing the map and backlight it. With a light blue pencil, draw a faint line to indicate the position of the left side of the map. This line need only be long enough to show the righthand limits for the dates and the year. Also indicate with a small dot the location of the small star in the county area depicting the city.

The left margin for the month and dates also is flush, so these letters and numbers are applied from left to right as shown. The star also is applied. The only consideration here is to arrange for an attractive placement, allowing comfortable margins on the left edge and between the letter endings and the edge of the map outline (see drawing No. 2). This drawing, although black on the artwork, will be printed in red.

This job could be drawn completely on one illustration, and the printer could make his own color separations. Two drawings were specified on this job. Also the top lettering could have been applied first and the map applied over that.

Outside of cutting out the map and the triangle, there is no hand artwork here at all. Your best approach to this type of work would be to consider it to be a small display card and do the layout work with this thought in mind.

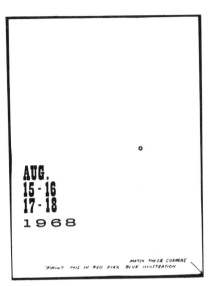

AUG.
15 - 16
17 - 18
1968

MATCH THESE CORNERS
PRINT THIS IN RED OVER BLUE ILLUSTRATION

Fig. 134 (2) Art for red printing. Since only the date headline and the disc surrounding the star are to be printed in red, these are in black for photographing for the plate. The map and county area outline and instructions at bottom are in light blue and will not photograph, being only guides to the printer.

FIG. 134. (3) Printed cover combines the red and dark blue.

There are tricks in every trade. This phrase might be overworked, but will never become obsolete.

Perhaps the major difference between the veteran and the less experienced workman is the old-timer's ability to improvise. This certainly applies to the use of "ready-to-apply" lettering sheets.

One of the common problems is that of using all the letters of one character. For example, I do much work for one firm that has a very unusual number of letter Fs in the company trade name. This results in alphabet sheets lacking all capital Fs. The trick in this case is to substitute the letter E when necessary, carefully scraping away the bottom cross stroke and converting it to an F.

You too will soon learn how to improvise as you become more familiar with this process. It seems odd that the manufacturers do not produce separate sheets containing one letter only, or at least generous groupings of the most frequently used letters. My F problem could then be remedied by purchasing a sheet containing only that letter. For example, suppose you are personalizing diplomas with Old English. One firm only has one solitary capital C on a sheet. Therefore on a name such as Charles C. Corcoran, you would require three sheets for one name with all the rest of the letters remaining. This is one case where it is not possible to improvise, except to hand letter.

Before proceeding with a unit of artwork, check the alphabet sheets to be certain that you have available all the required letters. This is especially essential to small town operators, since there seldom is a local supply source. If it is a rush job, you cannot wait for mail order replenishment. When deadline work is involved, the small town operator must "make do" with the materials on hand.

There are numerous methods of "stretching" an alphabet. Should you find lacking a certain capital letter within an alphabet, you might look through the lower case letters of other larger alphabets and adapt one of these. This would apply to letters such as C, I, O, S, V, W, X and Z.

The entire heading as shown in Fig. 135 was purposely designed to demonstrate methods of improvisation. The word "Improvise" is an excellent example of its own definition. The letter M is actually the letter W applied upside down. The letter P is a letter R with the oblique down stroke carefully scraped away. This process could be reversed. If you lacked the letter R you could add a down stroke to the letter P to form the R. The letter V was formed by inverting a letter A and carefully scraping away the small cross bar. This type of scraping is best done with a No. 11 blade with a thinly tapered, very sharp point.

Finally the letter E was originally a letter F. A small cross stroke was added to the bottom to convert it into a letter E. Pen and ink can be used for adding such strokes, but this is seldom necessary. In this case, the bottom cross stroke of the letter E was formed by applying the vertical stroke of a lower case i from the same alphabet. The excess was cut away at the right end of the stroke. It is not difficult to find a stroke of the same width for attachment or patching a letter.

IMPROVISE
for VaRiEty

FIG. 135. This heading was designed to demonstrate methods of improvisation.

Certain stroke applications can be accomplished by using this same principle. For example to change the letter P to a letter R, you might take a letter I from the same alphabet and apply this in proper position below the loop of the P. This stroke can be trimmed to shape at the bottom and either scraped or cut away.

A simple method of exploring the possibilities of improvising is to study the alphabet sheets both upside down and sideways. This also applies to symbol sheets and so on. Merely because a scroll or symbol is vertical on the sheet as purchased does not mean that you must use it in that position. It might suit your purpose to apply it sideways, upside down, or in other fashion. The material is as flexible as your ingenuity.

Some of the remaining letters from partly depleted sheets can be used for trick headings. These might consist of a "hodge-podge" of letters from completely different alphabets to form words such as "Variety," also shown in Fig. 122. This demonstrates an extreme selection of type faces grouped together. This type of thing should be confined to frivolous words or phrases, such as "Krazy-Days Sale" or "Fun Festival," etc.

There also is the trick of joining two letter Vs together to form the letter W. As a stand-in for the letter A, the letter V can be inverted and a cross stroke added. The letter Z is easily turned into the numeral 7 by scraping away the bottom cross stroke. Numerals such as 6 or 9 can be turned upside down to replace each other.

Naturally these procedures do not apply to all alphabets. But a certain amount of flexibility is possible with most.

THE PROFESSIONAL TOUCH
IN ARTWORK.
Technique is important to both sign painting and pictorial work. The illustrations in Fig. 136 and 137 were prepared to qualify this statement. This comic bull was originated many years ago for a cattle breeding

FIG. 136. Wrong! Note that the lines in this drawing are of uniform width with no "snap" or suggestion of depth.

organization. This trademark has since been replaced with a modern, symbolic design. The art was used in full color on trucks, signs, etc. On both signs and on pen and ink work, the animal was posed in many activities and wearing costumes of every description. When used for the company, the long firm name was lettered on the front of the sweater. The address, city, etc., were lettered on the service kit he carries. Because of this copy, both figure and service kit had to be a bit distorted to accommodate the necessary lettering. Otherwise a more correct form would have been possible.

Upon first glance, you will perhaps think that the two pictures are identical, since they are almost exact drawings of the same figure. It is the difference in technique that is important.

FIG. 137. Right! Study this drawing and note the variance of widths of the lines. Note how the simple application of shading screens provides a more finished appearance.

The drawing in Fig. 136 is incorrect because of a common fault in procedure. The lines have no variance of width and are monotonous. They appear to have been made with a stick and lack character. Therefore the illustration lacks the "snap" and depth of line that is all important. A 5-5 reservoir pen point was used for this drawing, which is the wrong type of pen to use for this particular kind of work.

Now study the illustration in Fig. 137. Note how the lines begin with a fine stroke, graduate to a much heavier stroke and diminish in width as the line is completed. This technique provides depth to an illustration. For example, note how the line becomes very fine as it crosses the right knee of the figure. This suggests that the trousers are stretched tightly at this point. The horizontal lines or "speed marks" leading away from the left foot are tapered to emphasize the zip. Compare the tapered "dust marks" just below the service kit with the same marks on the other drawing and note how the variance of stroke and boldness of line accentuates the speed and snaps up the illustration. Nothing can more definitely stamp a cartoon as the work of an amateur than gray scratchy pen and ink lines. This can result in poor reproduction. The lines should not have an uncertain appearance, but should be bold and confident.

For outlining this drawing a C-5 and C-3 style of reservoir were used alternately, and the solid black areas were filled in with a small brush and tempera black.

You will soon discover upon practice that the choice of pen is most important in lettering and illustrating. A flat nibbed pen, such as the C-5 or similar pen can provide an extremely diversified selection of strokes. The interesting line variances are achieved in several ways. By holding the pen in fixed position and not turning it as the stroke is made, you will find that the horizontal portion of the stroke will be fine. When you make the curve and start coming down with the vertical stroke, the line will gradually become bolder. By decreasing and increasing pressure on the pen, the width of the strokes can be controlled and varied from light to bold at will.

Taking care of the pen points and keeping them cleaned for prolonged use provides a great advantage. After long use, the nibs become more flexible. New pens are stiff at first and each has its own "personality." My process is to break in new pens on less particular work and use ones that have been broken in for finer work. In this way you always have suitable nibs that you are familiar with for tricky work.

Note how even the limited application of shading screen provides the finished appearince not to be found in Fig. 136. Some beginners will try to get this gray effect with gray paint. The fact is that gray will not reproduce on an average line drawing. If you examine a close-packed screen that appears to be gray with a magnifying glass, you will discover that it consists of tiny black dots.

When burnishing screens for adherence, it is advisable to place a piece of clean typing paper over the screen and rub over it. This is preferable to rubbing directly over the bare screen. With paper over the screen, you do not run the risk of smudging the drawing with a soiled burnishing tool and there is less chance of breaking down the edges of the screen applications or letters.

There are times when a brush will work better than a pen to provide the stroke desired. Some artists use a brush for the entire drawing, while others alternately use brush and pen. Several very small crow quill pens should be available for very fine lines, cross-hatching, etc. These require special pen holders to accommodate the insertion of the tubular shank common to such pens.

Transparent triangles serve as excellent straight edges for pen and ink. Some of these have a beveled edge to allow for this, but many artists find this still does not raise the triangle off the surface enough to avoid smearing the ink. It is common for sketch men to tape three pennies to the flat surface of the triangle, one on each corner, and about $\frac{1}{2}$ inch away from the edges. My preference is to attach small pieces of double-coated, foam tape at intervals along the edges of the triangle about $\frac{1}{4}$ inch away from the working edges. The fiber backing on the sides of the tape that come in contact with the drawing surface is left in place. These are applied to only one side of the triangle. Either method raises the triangle to a workable degree. French curves can be "gimmicked" in the same manner.

In regard to line variance such as illustrated, there is no better way to learn this than to study the work of the leading comic artists. (This, of course, cannot take the place of a prescribed course of study in a reputable art or design school.)

This line variance principle also applies to all pictorials applied to signs with few exceptions. It also is essential to use line variance to do attractive scripts, Old English and other lettering as well as scrolls. Once mastered, this type of stroke is faster than the uniform strokes used on block letters, although such strokes are essential for their purpose.

Conclusion

CONCLUSION. Welcome to the sign trade and thank you for reading this book. It is hoped that the contents will help you to reach your ultimate goal.

The sign industry has much to offer. It can provide you with security. Even during bad times, competent sign painters are seldom out of work, unless by choice. There is practically no limit to the opportunity for advancement. The pay is comparatively excellent.

But even as the sign trade has much to give, you must give something of yourself.

The expert professionals—the old-timers—are retiring or passing from the scene at a much faster rate than they can be replaced, yes, but do these new people bring with them an equal amount of skill and versatility?

At a time when advertising is at its peak with the great demand for new talent, the supply of truly efficient sign painters is at a low ebb.

To put it simply—the sign industry *needs* you!

Index

Also Available from ST Publications

The ABC of Lettering
J.I. Biegeleisen

Atkinson Sign Painting
Frank H. Atkinson

Book of 100 Type Face Alphabets
J.I. Biegeleisen

Book of 60 Hand-Lettered Alphabets
J.I. Biegeleisen

Gold Leaf Techniques, Third Edition
*Raymond LeBlanc, Arthur Sarti, and
Kent H. Smith*

Mastering Layout
Mike Stevens

Modern Ornament and Design
J.N. Halsted

1000 Practical Showcard Layouts
H.C. Martin

Practical Sign Shop Operation
Bob Fitzgerald

Strong's Book of Designs
Charles J. Strong and L.S. Strong

The Theory and Practice of Poster Art
Duke Wellington